HOW TO BEAT
THE SYSTEM

About the authors

Annie Ashworth and Meg Sanders are an acclaimed writing partnership, whose collaborations include *Trade Secrets* (2001), *Trade Secrets: Christmas*, books for *The Good Web Guide* and *Fat Club* for ITV1. They both live in Warwickshire.

HOW TO BEAT THE SYSTEM

Annie Ashworth
and Meg Sanders

ORION

Copyright © Maverick TV Ltd 2002

All rights reserved

Maverick TV has asserted its moral right to be
identified as the Proprietor of this work.

First published in Great Britain in 2002 by
Orion
An imprint of Orion Books Ltd
Orion House, 5 Upper St Martin's Lane,
London WC2H 9EA
Second impression published in June 2002

A CIP catalogue record for this book is
available from the British Library

ISBN 0 75281 845 7

Typeset in Palatino by
Selwood Systems,
Midsomer Norton

Printed and bound by
Butler & Tanner Ltd,
Frome and London

To system beaters everywhere

'Nam et ipsa scientia potestas est.'
Knowledge itself is power.
FRANCIS BACON (1561–1626)

'When I asked my accountant if anything could get me out of the mess I am in now, he thought for a long time. "Yes," he said, "death would help."'
ROBERT MORLEY CBE, actor, (1908–92)

Contents

HEALTH   57

HOUSING   80

LAW 112

LEISURE 133

MOTORING 166

Acknowledgements

We have badgered anybody and everybody in our search for tricks and scams for this book. We would like to thank all those we have accosted for giving away the secrets of their trade so generously. The following deserve special thanks (in most cases we have omitted their professional details for obvious reasons!):

Katherine Lapworth, Sarah Von Holstein, Sarah Kilby, Susanna Emerson, Nicky Kenward, Elaine Townshend, Graham Beach, Rupert Symons, Jeremy Wakeling, Phil Boardman, Derek Moulding, Tom Rochford, William Pusey, Helen Gunton, Simon Harries, The Law Society, Priscilla Chase, Kevin Duck, Stephen Bruce, Nick James, Phil Burne, Marie Rendall, Linda Blackwood, John Crocker, Lee Waterhouse, Bryn Curwood, Mike Harrison, Chris Rees, George Marshall-Thornhill, Roger Freeman, Mike Billsborough, David Taylor, Mike Bates, Wayne Jones, Steve Pitts, Warwick Preparatory School and Warwickshire County Council Education Department.

A few words of caution:

'Tax avoidance is legal, but tax evasion is illegal.' It is important, therefore, that readers make use only of the legal loopholes recommended and thus avoid the system, rather than evade it and become liable to criminal sanctions. We have tried to point out in the text where particular care should be taken to ensure that you stay on the right side of the law. So take care and be sensible!

Foreword

From the minute we are born, we are keyed into the system. We're branded with a national insurance number and become a statistic on a computer. No sooner are we out of our nappies than we are squeezed into the education system, and then tortured by exams and job interviews. Even when we're finally earning our way, we're taxed on our hard-earned cash and bombarded with bills. Suddenly we have to open a bank account to pay a mortgage, tax our car, insure our house, our health and even our lives, and borrow money to achieve it all.

Now the system is beating us; we've become a name on the electoral roll and a credit card number. We're categorised by our postcode, credit-rated by our spending habits, spied on by CCTV and hunted down by our car number plate. Even our Internet use is monitored. We flounder under an avalanche of form-filling and junk mail. And even when we shuffle off our mortal coil, we pass the red tape on to our loved ones, who are expected to register our departure.

Under all this pressure, it is easy to be cowed by authority, and simply go along with the system because we don't know any different. Life can cost us even more, because ignorance is expensive.

But where there is a system, there is a way to break it, or at least exploit it. This book has delved into all areas of our everyday life, from birth to funerals, school to the workplace, our health to our leisure, to find out the way things work, and figure out how to make them work for us.

We have been relentless in our quest to track down the people on the inside, who really understand the system because they are responsible for it. Lawyers, accountants, police officers, teachers, civil servants, doctors, bank managers, travel agents – we've badgered and coerced them all into divulging their secrets. For the first time, they reveal here what we have to do to jump the queue, find loopholes, duck red tape and dodge the proverbial 'no entry' sign. In other words, how we can get the most return for the least money or effort.

Our detective work has unearthed the fact that we make life far too hard for ourselves. With a bit of canny thought, and armed with the information you'll find on the following pages, you'll be able to storm ahead confidently through life. After all, faint heart never won fair treatment.

May this book become invaluable to you and help you to realise that in the motorway of life, there is always an alternative route. Good luck and good dodging!

Annie Ashworth and Meg Sanders

Education

'There was a time when we expected nothing of children but obedience, as opposed to the present, when we expect everything of them but obedience.' *Anatole Broyard*

The Parent's Charter gives parents the right to:
- say what school they want their child to attend and appeal if they don't get their first choice
- see basic performance information on schools and colleges
- get a summary of the most recent inspection of their child's school
- get a full written report on their child's progress at least once a year.

If potential parents had any idea of the problems that can arise when it comes to educating children, the population would probably fall even further than it already has. Britain does have an excellent, though over-stretched, state education system (though some would disagree strongly here), and its teachers are given far less credit than they deserve for their skills and forbearance.

However, much of a child's educational success is due to the effort invested by parents. And it is an effort. It is not just putting your child's name down for a chosen school and then plain sailing. The right education is dictated by the area you live in, the intelligence of your child, the depth of your pocket and your career. Ensuring your child has the education he or she needs and deserves involves parental involvement right along the line, and an insider's knowledge of how to get into, exploit and beat the system.

STATE PRIMARY SCHOOLS

There is no person more frightening to behold than a parent determined to get their child into the right nursery. Though children don't have to go to school until the term following their fifth birthday, we Britons have our children pounding playdough and learning their Letterland words from the minute they can sit up.

Free pre-school places are now offered to every four-year-old, for a maximum of five two-and-a-half-hour sessions per week, for 33 weeks of the year (or three terms of up to 11 weeks). This facility means that primary schools, especially good ones, are in heavy demand, and getting your child into a good one is a real challenge.

When looking for a house potential parents should ignore the location, the size of the garden, the pollution, and all those other things we consider when buying a home and buy within the **first priority area** of a good primary school. The first priority area is usually the first few streets around the school, especially in cities like London, and can often be measured in metres from the school gate. It is children from this area that have precedence when it comes to school places. Once your child has been accepted into the school, **wait a few months and then move to the house you really want to live in**. He or she can still stay at the school.

Research the options pre-conception by **speaking to estate agents** in the area who should be clued up on the local nurseries. Though life is easier for the parent outside of London and major cities, if you have children to educate make 'Which is the best school?' the first question you ask an estate agent.

There is very little democracy when it comes to pupil selection for popular inner-city primary schools. So even before your child is at the right age (better still, even before you give birth), **support school events** like bring-and-buy sales or fêtes. Bake cakes, offer to help out, make yourself a familiar face. It never does you any harm and can only ease the way when you come to apply.

You won't be the first person to be tempted to **lie about your address** (examples include people who rent property in the first priority area but live elsewhere, or use the address of family or friends). However, it must be remembered that this is fraud and schools and local authorities take it very seriously, but not half as seriously as other parents who have been denied a place or have lost at appeal. Hell hath no fury like a spurned parent.

Elaine, a teacher, has a two-year-old son and is in the process of choosing a state primary school for him:

'There doesn't seem to be a consistent admissions procedure between the schools in our London borough – they all seem to have their own system for entry, and even visiting a school can be difficult. They positively put you off. We couldn't even get to look round the school where my husband is a governor! It is the secretaries who put you off, but it is your right to look round. Collect an application form from each school and send lots of them off to as many schools as you want. You are put on the waiting list, and when you get offered a place, you can then say yes or no. Even if you go to a nursery which is part of a larger school, it is no guarantee of a place. You have to go through the whole admissions procedure again. It's ghastly.'

PRIVATE PRIMARY SCHOOLS

If you think state primaries are choosy, private primary schools turn selection into an art form. In the opinion of most, your child is, in fact, a secondary consideration. It is actually *you* who is being selected. Even being wealthy does not guarantee you a place.

Many private primaries visit you at home (to check out the furnishings?) and insist on two- and three-year-olds taking **'aptitude tests'**. You can floor the opposition by making sure you have a wonderfully stimulated child who has an interest in books, can speak articulately and has an encyclopaedic knowledge of Thomas and all his fellow engines.

Pushy parents can demand **special coaching from tutors**. Most will refuse, but needs must when the devil drives.

The secret of getting your child into a popular private primary is to **put down their name at birth** – and even that might not be soon enough.

Clever conceptions

If you have missed the boat with getting your older child into the school of your choice, you can try putting down a younger, even an unborn sibling, for the school. Harriet couldn't find a place for her daughter at her preferred school when they first moved to Fulham. Pregnant with her second child, she had a scan, discovered it was a boy, and put his name down. She was told by the (slightly surprised) school that they would accept the baby and the older sibling.

Failing everything, if you are a teacher, **get a job in the school** you want your child to go to, and you will have a good(ish) chance of success. Schools also need an army of administrative staff and voluntary helpers. You might even be eligible for a discount on the fees.

STATE SECONDARY SCHOOLS

If your child attends a state school, you must be keen to get the best from the system or you wouldn't be reading this. State education, like the NHS, is a subject that raises passions. For the most part, this is because of the discrepancy in the quality of state schools which vary depending on the area, the quality of the head and the budget of the local authority. Ensuring you have picked a good school depends entirely on where you have chosen to live.

If you've got your eye on a particularly good secondary school, **work backwards** and find out the primary school that will give you the best chance of entry. (See page 2 for the importance of where you live in getting acceptance into the school of your choice.)

Once you've found a school that you like, **the challenge is to get your child accepted**. Your first choice will probably be everyone else's number one. Give yourself the advantage. Write charming, witty letters of application to the school. It's not unlike applying for a job: the more appealing your application, the better chance you have of a school giving you one of their limited places.

Make sure you **mark your first choice on your application form** and send it in before the deadline. Different authorities have different deadlines, so check the dates carefully. You won't be put at the top of the list just because you get your application in first. Admission authorities have to give precedence to parents who have stated a preference. If you don't, your child will be allocated a place at a school that is within a reasonable travelling distance.

> **FACT:** As many as 660 children can be after as few as 90 places at popular schools.

Increase your chances by involving your child in **extra-curricular events** like sports, dance and languages. The National Curriculum is now so demanding there is little time or room left for anything else, and outside school activities are important throughout a state school career.

Schools find it hard to refuse if you can **offer work or goods in kind**. There have been cases of publicans offering to supply booze for PTA (Parent-Teacher Association) functions and builders offering repair work for nothing. It's an unfair advantage but it's dog eat dog out there.

The Local Education Authorities, rather than individual schools, make the rules with regards to schools' admissions. **If your child has been rejected entry** into the school of your choice, you can appeal to the LEA. But it's no good berating the school and its head teacher – you need him or her on your side in order to stand a chance of winning your appeal.

When visiting a potential school (and this applies in the private sector too) ask to see some of the **pupils' work books**. Are they all copied notes or are they freely composed? Has the work been marked? A tick doesn't necessarily mean anything. Look for corrections and see what the child has been asked to do about them. If something is wrong, have they been told why? Have they got to make the corrections themselves so they understand where they went wrong? Marking the work and pointing out the errors and how to improve are all signs of quality teaching. Bear in mind that you will no doubt be shown the work of the most able children!

As a parent you can be empowered by having lots of information about a school. For an independent view, all **Ofsted** (Office for Standards in Education) reports are available to anyone. The school should send a summary of the Ofsted report to all parents, and full copies should be sent to the media and to local libraries. State school reports can be found on the Internet at www.ofsted.gov.uk/reports/index.htm. They will tell you the weaknesses and strengths of a school and give suggestions on how it can be improved. All state schools in England are regularly inspected. The aim is to improve standards of education and achievements in schools, giving independent advice if necessary.

Ask to see **exam results** and SATs results and find out where the leavers go on to. This should give you a good idea of how the school caters for the high achievers and the slow learners. It's no good for a school to boast that they once got someone into some fabulous secondary school or university if it happened years ago. Be interested in the last two years' results. School performance tables for all LEAs can also be obtained from the Internet: www.open.gov.uk/dfee/perform.htm.

The way to have an influence is to **be involved**. Make sure you are elected on to the PTA, be a presence at school events and, let's be frank here, ensure that your child gives good presents to his or her teacher.

To make sure you are in the right place to make a difference and be responsible for creating the system, **have yourself elected as a school governor**. This is no picnic, and involves a great deal of work and a close relationship with the school, but it is an effective way to be a power for change. And it's not as difficult to get elected as it sounds. Most parents don't want the responsibility – so if you ask to be nominated, be prepared to take on the role. You may well get it.

The pupils who suffer the most in the state system are the brighter ones (who get held back in large classes) and the slower ones (who get left behind). You can **beat the imbalance by helping at home**. You will need to be involved; oversee homework and make sure everything they are doing is good – this is especially true if you plan to move them into the private sector at secondary stage (see page 6). You can **keep abreast of the National Curriculum** via websites such as www.ace-ed.org.uk, www.learn.co.uk or the National Grid for Learning at www.ngfl.gov.uk.

Get the most from your child's class teacher. You will have more time with them if you **skip parents' evening** (plead other commitments), and make an appointment to see them after school. Your time is less likely to be so short, and you may have a chance to see some of your child's school books (and compare them to those of his or her classmates).

(For **homework** see under Further Education on page 18.)

Time out

It is within your rights to **take your child out of school** (state or independent) during term time for up to 10 days in any one school year. Beware though, it may seem only a few days to you, but catching up on missed work and taking in the new information can take a child weeks; sometimes half a term can go by before they realise that they've missed a significant development in any subject.

Church schools

All is not tolerance and an open-armed welcome here either. Church schools, whether Church of England or Roman Catholic, usually insist that parents manifest an **enthusiasm for religious worship** before a child is accepted.

Many of the best Catholic schools (primary and secondary) insist on five years' devout family worship before children are accepted (and for good schools that are free, competition is rife, so why shouldn't they?). If you are lapsed, you will need to start **thinking about re-awakening your religious fervour** about five years before enrolment to ensure you beat the admissions system.

How We Beat The System

Sally failed her 11-plus in a Midlands county with the grammar school system. Rather than accept a place at the high school, she was baptised a Catholic and was able to secure a place at the free Catholic secondary school.

MOVING FROM STATE TO PRIVATE

In some cases, parents who can afford private education, but have sent their children to state primary schools, are opting to send them to fee-paying secondary schools. This involves a huge amount of effort for parents, as senior schools are on the lookout for the brightest state pupils. Your child must be doing well academically if you want to make the move into the private sector, and preparing your child for the entrance exam can be hard work. (NB It's a good wheeze in areas with grammar schools to do it the other way round: get your children up to speed in the private system then have them sit the 11-plus to avoid crippling school fees at secondary stage.)

State schools don't give good advice about the private sector. They'll have everything on secondary state schools, but nothing on the private fee-paying ones. Make the most of the Internet (most private schools now have a website). The Girls' Day School Trust and the Independent Schools Information Service are good sources of information. Your town hall also has to provide information on all schools in the borough. But you can only beat the prospectus flannel by asking other parents what they think, or consulting an excellent source: **The Good Schools Guide** (Lucas Publications, £22), now in its seventh edition, has unbiased reviews and frank answers to the questions all parents ask. Visit their website at <u>www.goodschoolsguide.co.uk</u>. You will need to subscribe to access most of the information, but it's a small price to pay for finding the right school.

Exams for private schools

Sarah Kilby has an 11-year-old daughter who has just passed her exam into a sought-after South London high school. She says:
- You will need to **employ a tutor** to help your child through the exams to get them into the private system, and start thinking about it in Year 5. They need to be taught how to take exams, work at speed, answer the questions effectively, and enhance their non-verbal reasoning. But only do it if you are convinced your child is bright, or

you will be subjecting them to seven years of academic hell which they will not be able to cope with.

- Enter them for a school you don't care about, but which holds entrance exams early in the academic year. This will give your child **practice in a formal exam**, something they don't have in most state schools.
- Any **extra-curricular activities** such as sports, music, languages – anything not covered in school – need to be coached privately so your child has interests they can talk about at interview.
- Make sure your child wears his or her **prefect badge** when they go to sit the entrance exam.

Interviews for private schools

- Encourage your child to read a **really unusual book** – we chose Christy Brown's *My Left Foot*. All the other children will have read *Sabrina the Teenage Witch* or *Goosebumps*, and your child will really stand out from the crowd when asked what he or she has read. It works a treat!
- If your child is asked to choose a subject or bring in an object and talk about it, **persuade them to talk about a team or group event** that they've done. (You'll need to use a bit of parental influence here with their choice – these sort of events show they can work as a team.) Encourage them to talk about an unusual hobby perhaps, something off the wall, like fishing. Avoid anything to do with a project they have done at school, but choose something they can talk about naturally and with genuine enthusiasm.
- When you're looking round a school, write down every last thing the head says in a notebook. They **give away secrets** – 'We look for girls/boys who are...' – which might be useful in the interview. Listen carefully enough, and they will invariably tell you what's in the exam.
- Never forget they are spying on you as much as you are spying on them. Dress up (though not too glamorous), have confidence and **don't be cowed by them**. You're the parent (destined to pay through the nose) not the pupil.
- **Look at other parents** – they are as important as the teachers. You'll be at the school gates with them for years – are they the type who will become friends?
- **Visit a day school at home time.** Look at the children's behaviour as they're leaving – are they stimulated, uncontrolled, orderly? Check out the parents as well. Talk to them while they're waiting to find out what they think about the school and whether they feel it's satisfactory for their children.
- Find out from the head **details of staff turnover**. If staff are coming and going at an alarming rate, it may not say much for the kind of relationship the head has with the staff. Be suspicious if a large number of the staff are recent graduates. Newly qualified teachers are cheaper to employ than more experienced ones – if that's the case, where's all the money going?
- **Make yourself known** to the headmistress. If you have a glamorous job, write on company headed paper when corresponding with the school. Heads are star stuck and any possible influence or favours you can provide will ease your child's route into the school.

- **Ask questions at meetings** when the head addresses potential new parents. He or she will get to know your face.
- Work as a team – have your partner fix the teacher on a subject during interview, whilst you do a **sift through the school work on show**. Look at the books at the bottom of the pile, which is where the less brilliant pupils' work will be hiding. Play good cop, bad cop too. One of you ask a soft question, then the other move in on them with a trickier one. That way you'll have a better idea of what the school is really like.

PRIVATE SECONDARY SCHOOLS

'Teaching would be fine if it wasn't for the parents.' *An anonymous private school teacher*

Paying for your child's education does not necessarily mean it will be a good one, but chances are it will be better than most state alternatives. You can be more choosy about finding the right school for your child; whether it be an academic hothouse, or a school that will benefit non-academic all-rounders.

Most private secondary schools have 'feeder' prep schools, and it is from these that they glean their intake. If you have your eye on a particular senior school, **work right back to the primary stage** (even the nursery) and secure a place there for your child.

Go round the schools a year early, when your child starts Year 5. Most hold open days in the autumn. You can then get a feel for what they specialise in, and if nothing else, it will help you to find the right tutor for extra coaching. At worst, this is pushing your child. At best, you're giving them the best possible chance.

Don't give up: even if a place is not immediately available, spaces can come up mid-year and even mid-term (people may leave or move away), so keep calling until you make yourself a pain in the neck.

A school's only as good as its head

Beware of the private or state schools with a head who has been there a long time or is approaching retirement age. Also beware of schools run by a young head who seems very ambitious: he or she will be wanting to make a good impression quickly and will then head for a more important headship. Beat the chance of a head change within a short time of your child being there by **looking at schools with a newish head** who has put in about 12 months to two years.

Never believe a word you're told about a school. **Parents always have their own reasons for liking or hating a school**. Look at their children. They might be impossibly difficult and deserve the strict regime that their parents resent.

Or, they might not be as bright as their parents think which is why they are struggling to keep up. Balance out the arguments, then make up your own mind.

Halve your fee burden by educating your child in the state system up to the age of 11 or 13 (common entrance ages vary depending on the school), then putting them in for the entrance exam to an independent school. But, as already mentioned, most senior schools are 'in bed' with a feeder prep school. Ring up the school you have in mind and find out which other schools their intake comes from. You may discover an excellent state primary which has success at common entrance stage. Primary schools will often send you details of where their pupils go on to at secondary stage.

Once you're in

The joy of being the one who signs the cheque is that **you can put pressure on** in areas you are not happy with – in some private schools this seems to be the lack of extra-curricular activities. The pressure of looking good on the independent school league tables seems to have blinded some institutions to giving children other interests. If you are not happy, lobby the school and encourage fellow parents to do the same.

You can influence **social teaching** in schools too. Several schools are slow, for example, to pick up on the early signs of eating disorders – an area of girls' development which is increasing alarmingly. Check up on pastoral care and encourage the school to have speakers who will come and talk to girls.

Results tricks

Private schools play a crafty game at results times. Often they offer children places and demand an immediate acceptance and deposit payment before the 11-plus results or other private school offers come through. This leaves parents in an impossible situation. You may have to bite the bullet and pay a deposit – it may be three or four hundred pounds, but what is that compared to the saving on fees if your child is accepted in to a good grammar school? Failing that you will have to fall on the mercy of the school by asking for a holding delay, and then you can wait to see if your first choice comes through. However, private schools do communicate with each other and even if you make a contingency for a deposit, the word will get round that you have accepted a place.

Fee-paying schools are under a contractual obligation to educate your child as well as possible. This puts the onus on them to teach your child to reach his or her potential. State schools can claim penury and lack of resources when they fail their pupils. As a fee-paying parent, you can demand that your children get all they deserve.

Independent schools belonging to the **Independent Schools Council** (ISC) are now regularly inspected by the Independent Schools Inspectorate. (Their counterparts in the state system are inspected by Ofsted.) Reports are made available to parents. Schools not within the ISC will be inspected by Ofsted (see page 4).

BOARDING SCHOOLS

The nature of boarding education has changed over the last few years, but this is no thanks to the quantum leap in the cost. The leading public schools are now charging in the region of £16,000 a year (2001), and that is before you invest in the uniform, laptop computer, mobile phone, music lessons and school trips (usually skiing in some exotic location). Undoubtedly the best of these schools are amongst the best schools in the country, for facilities and the quality of the staff.

The irony is that because fee-paying boarding schools are charging so much, they have priced themselves out of the market for most parents. Only 15 schools in the country are now 100 per cent boarding, and **there are boarding places to be had** even at the most academic schools. If you are keen for your children to board, this fact alone might ease entry. Alternatively, you could enrol them for **weekly boarding**, or they could attend as a day pupil. You will still be getting the best of the facilities.

You may believe that single-sex education yields better results, and there are compelling arguments to support this theory, which can be a problem as increasing numbers of boarding schools go co-ed. Opt for one of the small number of schools that are experimenting with teaching children separately at senior level.

FACT: It's not just that girls are better academically than boys at all ages and all subjects; they perform better in general. Since 1995, girls have outscored boys at ages 7, 11 and 14 in English tests. In 2001, 55 per cent of girls achieved five or more top-grade GCSEs (A* to C) compared with 45 per cent of boys. (*Department for Education and Skills, October 2001*)

PAYING SCHOOL FEES

'If you think education is expensive, try ignorance.' *Derek Bok*

FACT: Approximately 7 per cent of children in education are at fee-paying schools.

If you opt for the private sector, school fees are likely to be the second biggest outlay of money in your lifetime after buying a house. And the pain can go on for years and years if you have three or four children. To add insult to injury, fees are predicted to rise by up to 7 per cent this year (2001/2).

According to the Independent Schools Information Service (ISIS), two thirds of parents of children in private education are paying from their own income.

That is a huge burden given estimates that suggest the total cost of primary and secondary schooling, plus university, is in excess of £200,000 per child. That cost is based on average fees around the country and assumes the child is a day student. Choose a more expensive school and add the cost of boarding plus an allowance for inflation in the future and **you could be looking at £300,000** or more.

The only way to beat the system is either to give birth to a prodigy who will win scholarships all the way through, or to **invest wisely from day one** (and that means birth). Even if you exploit the state system at primary and secondary stage, there is always the cost of university. The National Union of Students says that student living expenses in London in 2001 amount to more than £6,000 (almost £5,000 outside of London) a year.

Whilst the cost of primary private education might come out of income, focus on ways to ease the impact of the fees when they start to escalate – usually from the age of seven or eight with a further big hike at 11 or 12.

In the past, **endowment policies** have been a favourite: designed to mature over the period and cover the cost of school fees. This is neither the most tax efficient nor cost effective way to fund schools fees.

Some independent schools have a **'composition scheme'** where you pay school fees in advance – effectively buying fees at today's prices. The advantage to you is the discount it brings – from 1 per cent upwards, depending on how long before your child joins that the money is deposited. The disadvantage is that if your child fails to pass the entrance exam, you may not get back all that you handed over. Check that the fund can be taken to another school if you change your mind.

Specially designed policies for school fees can be a trap. Whatever you put in place financially should be able to benefit you – the parents – even if circumstances change and the money is no longer required for private education. Even if you aren't allocating money just for school fees, maximise your ISA allowances and invest in assets that will make use of your capital gains tax allowances in the future.

Use lump sums: sometimes a school will allow you to pay future fees in advance if you have a lump sum. But it's not unheard of for schools to close (comparing the number of pupils over the last three or four years might be an indicator of a school in trouble), and you will be left high and dry if you have paid a wodge of fees in advance. Better to put the lump sum in an account which pays high interest (a 90-day postal account for example) and withdraw fees each term.

A useful investment for school-fee planning is **zero dividend preference shares** issued by split capital investment trusts. They are low risk and do not produce regular income, but you are in line for a specific pay-out at a certain point in the future – ideal for the more expensive later years of education.

Pin down grandparents: money invested on behalf of the children, and which comes from someone other than yourself is more tax effective as it takes advantage of the child's tax allowance. It does depend very much on individual circumstances – your parents may be blessed with lots of grandchildren – but grandparents may have money to spare.

These websites might help:

> www.isis.org.uk
> www.prosper.co.uk
> www.clarkeandpartners.co.uk
> www.inter-alliance.com
> www.swallow-financial.co.uk.

Investigate bursaries or scholarship funds set up by schools themselves, especially those hit by the **loss of assisted places**. There are even trusts set up by philanthropists that enable needy children to obtain a private education. These charitable trusts usually only pay out in exceptional circumstances. (These may include the death of the breadwinning parent when the child is already at a school, essential boarding need due to disability of a parent, or a child with a learning handicap that cannot be catered for in the state system.) Look for *The Educational Grants Directory*, *The Directory of Grant Making Trusts* and *The Charities Digest* in your local library.

It's normal practice for schools to ask for fees a term in advance. Don't be cowed: write to the governors asking if you can **pay monthly by direct debit**. And ensure you are clear what the school means by a term's notice of withdrawal, or you may be paying when your child has actually left the establishment. If the reason you are taking your child away is because of some breach of contract on the part of the school, you won't want to forfeit the money or leave your child in a school which you have become unhappy with. The trick is to **get the school to ask you to remove your child**. If it is the school's request, you are legally absolved from either giving notice or paying the term's fees.

Look out for **quirky scholarship:** these are often granted to the children of clergy, medics, single mothers and those associated with a City livery company. Choral scholarships are worth considering too, but they do not cover full fees and the choristers are expected to sing for their supper.

FACT: If you live in Richmond, Newbury, Reading or the City of London or your name is West, you may be able to obtain a bursary to Christ's Hospital, Horsham, a charitable foundation school with a very unusual entrance procedure. The West education endowment gift, was established in the early 18th century via a bequest from a childless couple called John and Frances West, and supports 60 children. Any child living in those areas or who can prove they are in some way linked to the West family (now 250 strong nationwide) can apply for a bursary – which is means-tested.

For **music scholarships** read *Music Awards at Independent Schools* by Jonathan Varcoe from the Music Masters and Mistresses Association.

If you have three or more children going through one school, approach the governors for a **job lot discount**. You may get an emphatic 'no', but it is worth a try and it's not unheard of for discounts to be granted. In the words of a well-known supermarket, every little helps.

UNIFORM

Private schools are inclined to clean up when it comes to uniforms. Many (like Eton) have an exclusive uniform which can only be purchased from their outfitters, but for others, particularly the day schools, **you can find suitable clothes in high street shops** (British Home Stores, Woolworth's and Marks & Spencer are all good sources). Even sports shorts and cricket whites are available cheaper on the high street. Talk to parents with children already at the school. They will be able to tell you what you can get away without buying (schools often charge a small fortune for wool overcoats for example), and what can be substituted with cheaper imitations.

If you have only one child to put through the school, make use of the **second-hand uniform sales**. These bun-fights usually happen about twice a year, and you will need nerve and sharp elbows. Arrive early (it can be worse than the January sales) to make sure you are not left with just threadbare blazers to choose from, and be prepared to fight the crowds for the best bargains.

Be quick off the mark too with **parents whose children are about to leave the school**. You can often buy their entire uniform at a cut-down price.

Thankfully **state schools** have a more relaxed view of uniform, many now favouring sweatshirts and grey or black trousers and skirts. **School uniform suppliers often charge over the odds** for these and, excepting uniform which has a school badge, you can usually buy everything in the right colours from high street shops.

HOME EDUCATION

'The parent of every child of compulsory school age shall cause him to receive full-time education suitable:
(a) to his age, ability, and aptitude, and
(b) to any special educational needs he may have, either by regular attendance at school or *otherwise* (our italics).'
(The Education Act, 1944, section 36, as amended by the Education Act, 1996, section 7.)

The critical words here are 'or otherwise'. If you really have run up against a brick wall trying to get your child into your preferred school, there is nothing to stop you from educating them at home.

You don't:
- need permission to educate 'otherwise'
- have to tell the LEA
- have to have premises equipped to any particular standard
- have to be a qualified teacher
- have to cover the same syllabus as the school
- have to follow the National Curriculum
- have to plan your curriculum in advance at all
- have to keep to school hours, days or terms
- need a fixed timetable
- have to give formal school-type lessons in a classroom.

As long as what you provide is adequate and suitable for your child's age, ability and aptitude, and the education is 'efficient and full-time', you can **beat the shortcomings of the education system** by taking it into your own hands. Plus, if you can prove that you are providing pupils with everything they need, there is nothing to stop you taking on other children as pupils. You are not functioning as a school, so health and safety, and insurance issues may not apply.

In the intimate environment of home, 'lessons' can take a shorter time, so your education day will be over sooner. But though timetables are not necessary when educating at home, it does help to **make a distinction between 'learning time' and 'home time'**.

Home-taught children may encounter problems when entering main stream education. **Socialising may be more difficult** (especially when school children have established groups of friends) and ironically your child may well be ahead of his or her peers in interactive social skills with adults. Make sure your child has an active social life with other children, as well as being involved in groups such as Cubs/Brownies, sports teams and so on. Precocious children may be bullied.

Home learners needn't follow the National Curriculum either, but if you intend to send them to school at some stage, **they will need to be up-to-speed with the Key Stages**, so they do not fall behind. You can **keep abreast of the National Curriculum** via websites such as www.ace-ed.org.uk, www.learn.co.uk or the National Grid for Learning at www.ngfl.gov.uk.

Education Otherwise is an invaluable organisation that helps parents who educate their children at home, including information about deregistering your child from school, and dealing with the LEA. You'll find the address at the end of the chapter.

'He wants to learn'

Nicky Kenward educated her son Alfie at home until he was ten, two years ago, and ran a home educators' group of about 40 families:

'We taught him at home right from the start and we shared the teaching with others in education groups. I was a teacher – which is actually a disadvantage because you never quite get away from the feeling of being in a classroom. You have to let your own child break all the rules you ever learnt about teaching because schools aren't child centred – they teach from where the education system says they ought to be. If you have taken children out of school, it's because you disagree with the system and I certainly did. I'd seen a lot of wasted intelligence; kids who had gone through the system and failed.

'The answer to knowing what to teach your children is to ask yourself what are you teaching your children now – they are learning when you read to them, doing colouring, looking at insects in the garden. With Alfie we role-played a lot, what he called "the imagine ifs", he dressed up in costumes all the time. I lived with Darth Vader for four years! Alfie did eventually ask if he could go to school, and I should have said I would let him go when he could keep up with other children. He had life skills, knew how to be with adults, but was behind with the Key Stages of the curriculum. So when he went to school he was behind his age group, but his headmaster said he was only behind in what's seen as conventional education. He was streets ahead in socialisation, and the ability to cope with the world – if anything he's precocious, always questioning the world. All his teachers say he wants to learn. But he was bullied by the other kids in the school for not fitting in with convention and had a baptism of fire. He lost confidence and went from being a kid who was popular in the education groups to the one who said I'm not liked.

'On the plus side, I still think a lot of time is wasted in school just moving about (which obviously doesn't happen at home), and I don't think kids come out of school with skills for life – the ability to pick up the phone – and you can teach that at home. Subjects are too compartmentalised and at home you can take a subject and really investigate it from all angles. I would do it again, but you should home educate for the right reasons. Not out of snobbery about schools and other children (a mentality which is rife in home educators), or because you want to control your child's development and design the child you want. Kids will be kids and you must let them be that. It's a question of balance.'

SPECIAL EDUCATIONAL NEEDS

If your child has a learning problem, you need to **be in the system and exploiting it**, rather than beating it. Most local authorities have very good special needs back up, and you may be better off in the state system than the independent one.

All children are assessed for development pre-school at regular intervals, and you can ask the **advice of your health visitor** up until your child is five. It is the duty of the health service to inform the LEA (Local Education Authority), and give you information about any voluntary organisations that could offer further advice. If your child is under two, you can ask the LEA to assess their needs. If they are over two, you or the school can ask for a **statutory assessment** which is a detailed examination, with progress reports and information on any special help that has already been given. As parents, you are given 29 days to agree to the assessment while the LEA has six weeks in which to tell the parents of a statutory assessment. Your health visitor can also refer you for special hearing tests or speech therapy.

You can ask a school for information on its policy towards children with **special educational needs (SEN)**. The school's annual report should include information on this policy. The school should have an SEN co-ordinator, arrangements for special provisions and information on how the school works with parents to cope with a child's problems. If they haven't, you should want to know why.

A statement of special educational needs sets out what your child requires and the special help that is needed to meet those requirements. As a parent, **you have the right to say what your preference is regarding the school that you would like your child to attend**. The LEA must respect those wishes if the school is a state school and provided that it is suitable for your child's age, ability and SEN, and your child's presence will not detrimentally affect the efficient education of other children already at the school. Visit www.ace-ed.org.uk, which has useful resources on all areas of education.

> **FACT:** 10 per cent of the UK population has some degree of literacy difficulty and up to 4 per cent, including 375,000 school children, is severely dyslexic. The prevalence is the same in both sexes. (*Dyslexia Institute*)

Private schools can be slow to recognise learning difficulties like dyslexia, and not very encouraging to affected children. This attitude comes from concern about how the school will appear in the league tables: a poor achiever can pull down a class achievement average. You are paying the fees, so you can insist upon support, but you may be better moving to a school better equipped to cope or one in the state sector.

Gifted children make up 5 per cent of the child population. They also have special educational needs, but special needs are recognised by law only if there is a learning *difficulty*. Attempts are being made to redress the balance. The Mensa Foundation for Gifted Children runs courses for talented children. The National Association for Gifted Children (NAGC) is a national charity that supports such children and their families.

EXCLUSION FROM SCHOOL

Has your child been excluded from school?

Children may not be able to attend school regularly for a variety of reasons: illness, pregnancy, behavioural difficulties, a fixed period exclusion (suspension) or permanent exclusion (expulsion). But section 19 of The 1996 Education Act reads:

'Each local education authority shall make arrangements for the provision of suitable education at school or otherwise than at school for those children of compulsory school age who, by reason of illness, exclusion from school or otherwise, may not for any period receive suitable education unless such arrangements are made for them.'

In other words, the LEA (Local Education Authority) must make arrangements to educate the child either at school or elsewhere.

'Suitable' education is defined as 'efficient education suitable to the age, ability, aptitude and to any special educational needs the child (or young person) may have'. LEAs decide what is suitable education out of school for a particular child in line with their own policies and 'the efficient use of resources', but they should consult with you as parents. In other words, LEAs are obliged to arrange some form of education for your child and must ensure that these arrangements are suitable for their needs.

Illness

A child can be asked to be absent from school when suffering from illnesses such as German measles (which is not serious but can be dangerous if the child comes into contact with a pregnant woman). For conditions such as headlice, which isn't an illness but is very contagious, the school has the right to ask the child not to return until he or she has been treated. In fact, if the infestation is chronic, the LEA medical officer may ask to see the child and has the power to suspend them.

Sick children should be able to benefit from as much education as their illness allows. Depending on individual circumstances, this could range from little or no provision for a child who is seriously ill or injured, to a full timetable for other children. Ask your LEA to make sure your child isn't missing out.

Pregnancy

Pregnancy should never be a reason for exclusion from school. Schools, LEAs and social services departments should work together to provide support for mothers of compulsory school age, both during the pregnancy and after the baby is born. They should try to keep the pupil in her school if possible (unless personal or medical circumstances make other arrangements necessary), and to return her as soon as possible to full-time education. Pregnant girls who receive education out of school during their pregnancy should remain on the school roll during this time to enable them to return to the school after the birth if they choose to do so. A girl should stay in education during pregnancy, and your local LEA should make sure she gets the care and support she needs.

After the baby is born, there should also be provision of childcare for teenage mothers. For mothers in further education, look for a Further Education college with a crèche.

FURTHER EDUCATION

Getting there

In 2001 over 100,000 children, between the ages of 18 and 21, were in higher education, and the Government plans to increase that figure even more. That's great news in that it creates a more qualified workforce, but it means stiff competition to get into the course you want at the university or college you fancy. Be quick off the mark in applying (entries must be in by mid-December the year prior to entry) by doing it online through www.ucas.com, the website of the **University and Colleges Admissions Service**.

One route is to apply for a more unusual course (Chinese for example) and then to **swap courses** once you have entered the college or university. Don't be led too much by the league tables (published annually in many national papers). **Some lower league universities excel** in certain departments, even if they are not winners overall, and examination of the figures shows that the percentage differences in the tables can be as little as 0.1 of a per cent.

Passing your exams

Getting through the exams is a rather important consideration when it comes to getting into higher education. Here are some useful tips:
* **Fill in the gaps.** Ensure your lesson notes are in a good state and there's nothing missing. That way, you'll find it much easier to make revision notes later.
* **Find a proper working space.** You can't revise properly sitting on the sofa. If you've got a desk, clear it up and make sure it's got all the stuff you need – like a lamp, stationery and a supportive chair.
* **Get planning.** Work out how much revision you need to do, make a revision timetable – and stick to it.
* **Spend some cash!** Stock up on pads and pens. With good stuff to work with, revision won't seem so bad!
* **Cut to the basics.** Turn your class work into easy-to-follow revision notes. Writing down the information will help you to understand and remember it.
* **Don't push yourself too hard.** Do a set amount of work each day and take regular breaks. Try to revise just two subjects a day. And ...
* **See your mates.** Exams don't mean you have to become a hermit. Have a group revision session – test yourselves and talk through any bits you find difficult.
* **Test yourself.** On websites such as www.learn.co.uk, there are test papers on all core subjects with advice on where to find more information on the subject.
* **Get some fresh air.** If you get tired or stressed, stop revising for a while and

go for a brisk walk. The fresh air will do you good and the exercise will boost your energy levels. Even stop and watch TV for a while.

- **Use cue cards.** Write down a basic outline of what you've learnt on small cards. Use lots of concise lists and diagrams. Read them through whenever you get the chance – like on the bus home.
- **Ask for help.** If you're worried about exams or revision, talk to your parents or your teacher. They are there to help.
- **Don't panic!** The worst thing you can do is stay up all night. Read through what you have been revising, then get a good night's sleep. It's an effective way for your brain to sort through what you have learnt.

For children to make the right choices regarding further education, exploit the careers advice given in schools. Most should have plenty of information about colleges and universities; if they don't **they should do the donkey work for you.**

Be informed: **arm yourself with plenty of information** by using bookshops, your library and the Internet with sites such as The Further Education Funding Council's website at www.fefc.ac.uk. Most colleges and universities have their own websites too.

Poor results – and how to avoid them

University and college places are dependent on exam results. You can either wait for the disappointing piece of paper in August (and the ensuing agony of the UCAS Clearing House policy), or prepare in advance by putting your child through a **tutorial college or crammer**. These colleges teach GCSE, A-level and AS-level courses on a full-time basis, or, usefully, provide Easter revision courses for pre-exam cramming. Courses can be expensive (up to £3,000 a year), but because they are geared towards an intensive programme of work, can be very effective. Contact the Conference for Independent Further Education on 020 8969 0324 or visit the website at www.cife.org.uk. For more information see the websites of two colleges: www.mpw.co.uk and www.dld.org.uk. Check they cover your child's syllabus, though.

These sort of colleges often have a more relaxed approach to education (no uniform, less restricted timetables) and would be a **good option for children who have lost the enthusiasm to learn** and need a more laid-back routine – or, in other words, children who are disruptive and hell-bent on beating the school system.

Helping hand with homework. You can make a real difference to your child's results by being on hand when they are doing homework. At GCSE and A-level, coursework sometimes makes up a substantial chunk of the overall mark (30 per cent of the marks in English Literature and 20 per cent in English Language are derived from coursework, and marks on art courses can be 100 per cent from coursework). For homework advice try www.standards.dfee.gov.uk/homework/ , www.eduweb.co.uk and www.freecampus.co.uk.

Funding – it doesn't all stop at 18!

Oh, for the days when there were grants for further education, regardless of income. Tuition fees seem to be here to stay and unless you want your children to start their working lives with an albatross of debt around their necks, you need to make provision for what could be the **high cost of further education** in the future. The maximum tuition fee contribution has risen to £1,050 (2001), but students can apply to their LEA (Local Education Authority) for help.

The good news is that **you can apply for help** within the first four months of the start of the academic year if you are finding that you can't cope. Help from the LEA is assessed on parental income. If the combined income is less than £17,805 (in 2001), there need not be any contribution towards fees from you. If your parents earn over £17,805 then they will be asked to contribute.

Students with siblings at university? The LEA will take this into account and be more gentle with parents' bank balances. There are some courses where the maximum tuition fee is £520 and they are:
- placement years that last one full year
- part-time first degrees
- initial teacher training courses (if it is not your first degree – then no contribution is needed)
- a year spent studying overseas as part of your course. Schemes such as Erasmus, which is an organisation set up to assist students wanting to study in the EU, need no contribution, for example. (See UK Socrates-Erasmus Council under Useful Addresses.)

Taking an NVQ and working at the same time? You might be able to get income tax relief. Check with the local tax office.

Loans

These are familiar to every student these days and are as much a part of life as freshers' week. Every year the system changes slightly. Unlike before, 75 per cent of the maximum loan entitlement (2001) does not depend on the family's income (before the entire loan didn't). Loans are payable in three instalments at the beginning of each term.

When funds are really short

Beat the financial burden of being a student. If you are down to your last half-penny there are means for acquiring extra funds. These include:
- career development loans
- access funds
- hardship loans
- NHS loans (for students taking medical, though not doctor's, courses)
- scholarships (The ideal guide for these is *University Scholarships and Awards 2001* by Brian Heap, Trotman, £11.99.)

Most of the above will only be granted if you can prove that you have exhausted all other means of financing your course. **Look too at a career in the Forces.** The Army, Navy and Air Force will often fund students through university so long as they then pursue a career with them on leaving. Some companies now do this as well.

Open a bank account with your child. Don't leave the negotiation up to your son or daughter. **Banks are keen to open accounts for students** (it may be worth their while once the student is earning), but they can come down very hard on students who run up overdrafts, unless they have already arranged an interest-free overdraft in advance. The contents of your child's bank account is between him or her and the bank, but you may be able to persuade your son or daughter to let you have some say in it. Likely as not it will be you who is contributing any credits anyway!

Away from home

Safety is more of a consideration now they are away from home too: you can **beat the chances of accidents and loss of equipment** by making sure bikes, cameras and laptops are properly insured. They may well be covered on your home contents insurance but you need to check. Mobile phones are worth the investment too, because it will enable you to keep in touch with your offspring.

For down-to-earth advice on life as a student, visit www.studentuk.com, which has advice on every university in the country (what they are really like) as well as information on grants, loans and landlords.

Mature students

You may not have to fund yourself through college as a late learner. LEAs can award **mandatory and discretionary grants**. Mandatory grants are for students taking full-time courses such as degrees, diplomas and BTECs. Discretionary grants are available for Access courses, A-levels and full-time GCSEs.

If you are interested in further education or going on a course, check if there is funding available. If you are on benefit, **you may be eligible for government-funded training** for work; you can get the information from your local library or Training and Enterprise Council (TEC). If you are unable to get a grant, apply for a career development loan which can cover up to 80 per cent of the course fees; childminding fees are sometimes also taken into account. The local TEC will have information.

Weird and wonderful education laws

Take music lessons if you go to North Carolina; it's against the law to sing off key.

In Arkansas (which by law must be pronounced 'Arkansaw'), the law states that school teachers who bob their hair will not get a pay rise.

In California, animals are banned from mating publicly within 1,500 feet of a school.

If a child burps during church in Nebraska, his parents may be arrested.

Anyone 14 or older in Indiana who profanely curses, damns or swears by the name of God, Jesus Christ or the Holy Ghost, shall be fined between $1 to $3 dollars for each offence, with a maximum fine of $10.

USEFUL WEBSITES

www.dfee.gov.uk (Department for Education and Skills)

www.learndirect.co.uk (Information on finding a college course)

www.ucas.com (University and Colleges Admissions Service)

www.cife.org.uk (The Conference for Independent Further Education)

www.bda-dyslexia.org.uk (British Dyslexia Association)

www.dyslexia-inst.org.uk (The Dyslexia Institute)

www.goodschoolsguide.co.uk

www.isis.org.uk (Independent Schools Information Service)

www.deni.gov.uk (The Northern Ireland Department of Education)

www.wales.gov.uk (The Welsh Assembly)

www.totalwales.com (Welsh Schools' performance tables)

www.scotland.gov.uk (The Scottish Executive)

www.ace-ed.org.uk (The Advisory Centre for Education)

USEFUL ADDRESSES

Advisory Centre for Education (ACE)
1b Aberdeen Studios
22 Highbury Grove
London N5 2DQ
Tel: 020 7354 8321
Email: ace-ed@easynet.co.uk
www.ace-ed.org.uk

Boarding Education Alliance
Anne Williamson
c/o Cohn & Wolfe
30 Orange Street
London WC2H 7LZ
Tel: 020 8460 4357
Email: annwilliamson@classic.msn.com
www.boarding.org.uk

Childline
Freepost 1111
London N1 1BA
Helpline: 0800 1111

Daycare Trust
Shoreditch Town Hall Annexe
380 Old Street
London EC1V 9LT
Tel: 020 7739 2866
Email: info@daycaretrust.org.uk
www.daycaretrust.org.uk

Department for Education and Skills
Sanctuary Buildings
Great Smith Street
London SW1P 3BT
Tel: 020 7925 5000
Email: info@dfee.gov.uk
www.dfee.gov.uk

Department of Education for Northern Ireland
Rathgael House
43 Balloo Road
Bangor
County Down BT19 7PR
Tel: 028 9127 9279
Email: deni@nics.gov.uk
www.deni.gov.uk

Education Law Association
39 Oakleigh Avenue
London N20
Tel: 0130 3211570
Network of solicitors specialising in education law

Education Otherwise
PO Box 7420
London N9 7SG
Tel: 0891 518303
www.education-otherwise.org

General Teaching Council for Scotland (GTC)
Clerwood House
96 Clermiston Road
Edinburgh EH12 6UT
Tel: 0131 314 6000
Email: gtcs@gtcs.org.uk
www.gtcs.org.uk

Girls' Day School Trust (GDST)
100 Rochester Row
London SW1P 1JP
Tel: 020 7393 6666
Email: s.wheatley@wes.gdst.net
www.gdst.net

Girls' School Association (GSA)
130 Regent Road
Leicester LE1 7PG
Tel: 0116 254 1619
Email: gsa@webleicester.co.uk
www.schools.edu/gsa/

Headmasters' & Headmistresses'
  Conference (HMC)
130 Regent Road
Leicester LE1 7PG
Tel: 0116 285 4810
Email: hmc@hmc.org.uk
www.schools.edu/hmc/

Incorporated Association of Independent
  Schools (IAPS)
11 Waterloo Place
Leamington Spa
Warwickshire CV32 5LA
Tel: 01926 887833
Email: hq@iaps.org.uk
www.iaps.org.uk

Independent Schools Information Service
  (ISIS)
Grosvenor Gardens House
35–37 Grosvenor Gardens
London SW1W 0BS
Tel: 020 7798 1500
Email: national@isis.org.uk
www.isis.org.uk

Local Government Ombudsman
21 Queen Anne's Gate
London SW1H 9BU
Tel: 020 7915 3210

Mensa Foundation for Gifted Children
Mensa House
St John's Square
Wolverhampton WV2 4AH
Tel: 01902 772771
Email: mensa@dial.pipex.com
www.mfgc.org.uk/mfgc/

Montessori Society
26 Lyndhurst Gardens
London NW3 5NW
Tel: 020 7435 7874
Email:
   mariamontessoriamiuk@compuserve.com
www.montessori-ami.org

National Association of Head Teachers
1 Heath Square
Boltro Road
Haywards Heath
West Sussex RH16 1BL
Tel: 01444 472472
Email: info@naht.org.uk
www.naht.org.uk

National Association for Gifted Children
  (NAGC)
Elder House
Elder Gate
Milton Keynes MK9 1LR
Tel: 01908 673677
Email: nagc@rmplc.co.uk

National Childminding Association
8 Masons Hill
Bromley
Kent BR2 9EY
Tel: 020 8464 6164

Ofsted
Alexandra House
33 Kingsway
London WC2B 6SE
Tel: 020 7421 6744
www.ofsted.gov.uk

The Scottish Executive Education
  Department
Victoria Quay
Edinburgh EH6 6QQ
Tel: 08457 741741
www.scotland.gov.uk

The Welsh Assembly, The Public
  Information and Education Service
The National Assembly for Wales
Cardiff Bay
Cardiff CF99 1NA
Tel: 02920 825111
www.wales.gov.uk

University and Colleges Administration
  Service (UCAS)
Rosehill
New Barn Lane
Cheltenham GL5 3LZ
Tel: 01242 223707
www.ucas.ac.uk

UK Socrates-Erasmus Council
R&D Building
The University
Canterbury CT2 7PD
Tel: 01227 762712
www.ukc.ac.uk/ERASMUS

Finance

'No one can earn a million dollars honestly.'
William Jennings Bryan

The only way to beat the financial system is to possess lots of money. But if you were not lucky enough to be born with a silver spoon in your mouth, you'll have to find your own way to riches. You could either rob a bank (bit risky), land yourself a lucrative job (becoming head of a multinational blue chip company or famous pop star should do the trick), strike oil in your back garden or marry a tycoon. Failing that, you could make what money you do have work very hard indeed. Manage to achieve a balance between a sensible rainy day savings plan, an element of risk and an eye for a bargain and, above all, make sure it isn't those nice people at the Inland Revenue who are benefiting from your labours.

BILLS, BILLS, BILLS

It is possible you could go through life without having to pay bills, but you might have to live in the Arctic Circle and catch your own food. Those little brown envelopes that fall with such comforting regularity through the letter box are as much a part of life as traffic jams and bad head colds. But like good comedy, **the secret of painless bill paying is timing.** Settle your bills on a monthly basis, by standing order or direct debit (which sometimes come with savings), and stagger quarterly and annual payments so that they don't all arrive at once. Pay all your bills on time, especially credit cards, or you will be throwing away good money on interest charges. Arranged overdraft fees are less than credit card APRs (Annualised Percentage Rates).

Direct debits can only be used to pay commercial organisations, not individuals. Also, you are not in charge of how much is taken from your account, the organisation doing the debiting is ... so keep an eye on the figures.

Offer to pay cash: professionals like painters and builders will often offer you discounts for cash. Provide them with crisp tenners and you can negotiate 5 or 10 per cent from the final bill. Also ask for a discount if you pay a bill by return of post.

A cheque will be honoured by the bank if there is enough money in the holder's account. But payments can be made even if you are overdrawn by making sure the cheque card number is written out on the back of the cheque; the bank is obliged to honour the cheque up to the limit of the guarantee card even if there aren't enough funds in your account. The same applies to **charge cards**, which have a guaranteed figure (usually published on the reverse of the card) and is often either £50 or £100. If you are overdrawn, you can use your charge card to obtain cash at a supermarket checkout without the risk of it being refused at an automatic teller machine (see page 30). However, please be advised that it is a criminal offence to sneak through payments when you are overdrawn.

In the good old days of gentlemen's banking, it paid to deface a cheque, or screw it up so it couldn't be read magnetically and the information had to be put in manually, thus giving you a day's grace before money was debited from your account. Today, however, cheques are scanned, and damaged cheques are keyed in manually *but at the same time*. The only way to **buy yourself time** is to post a cheque rather than pay it in at a branch or 'omit' to sign the cheque, which will then have to be returned to you. You can also delay a cheque being debited from your account by writing in a slightly different number in the figures box than you have put in words. Again, the cheque will be returned for you to amend.

And for those of you north of the border, retailers in England are not obliged to accept Scottish bank notes. Mind you, neither are Scottish retailers obliged to accept English notes.

There is a big difference between a quote and an estimate. An estimate is what the company thinks will be the charge for the product or service. A quotation is a fixed price given by a company or an individual for a product or service. It is a legally binding contract between you and the supplier. So if you are going to place an order, get a quotation first, preferably in writing. However they can invoice you for a different sum depending on their final costs for supplying you. But they must justify the amount they are charging and have informed you in writing of the additional costs before presenting their final bill.

If you pay a deposit, you may think that it's the only thing you will lose if you cancel. Quite often, that's the case. However, legally you have entered into a contract with a company and you could therefore be liable for the full cost. **Protect your interests** by checking before you send any money.

When sending a cheque to end a financial dispute, write **'in full and final settlement'** on it and any adjoining correspondence. Once the cheque is cashed it is more difficult for the grievance to be pursued.

The dreaded VAT

Many businesses have an annoying habit of quoting a price without VAT. Whenever you enquire about a price, **make sure you have calculated the 17.5 per cent VAT** on top, or you'll be in for a nasty shock. Can you beat it? There are advantages to using companies or traders that don't charge VAT (a company has to register for VAT if its annual turnover is greater than £52,000), though if they don't earn enough to qualify, it may be because they aren't good enough to earn enough money – if you follow the logic! If you're dealing with a trader such as a carpenter or electrician, always ask whether they give a **'discount for cash'**. They beat the system by making cash disappear into their pockets and out of their books so they have a VAT/tax saving – why can't you share in that saving? Do take care that you are not doing anything which may be consisered fraudulent.

Save time and money: you can now file your VAT return online up to 12 midnight the day before it is due. Go to the Electronic VAT Return Service (EVR) at www.hmce.gov.uk.

Utilities – or money down the drain

Type your annual gas, water or electricity bill into the search engine of www.buy.co.uk, add your provider and your method of payment. It will tell you the best deal currently on offer should you wish to change. It also has a mobile phone tariff calculator.

Many of the utilities companies offer **customers discounts** on shopping, restaurants and holidays, via linked promotions. You can make quite a lot of savings. Shop around for what suits you.

Consider paying for your utilities by **direct debit**. All gas and electricity suppliers offer some kind of discount to customers who pay in this way. You can pay monthly or quarterly, but discounts sometimes only help people who pay monthly. This system allows you to spread your money throughout the year which is helpful, especially in the winter months (although you're effectively 'lending' them money in the summer). Discounts are also sometimes on offer from utilities companies for prompt payers (i.e. if you pay within ten days of the bill being issued).

Customers opting for **dual fuel** can sometimes be offered discounts. Dual fuel means taking two utilities, such as gas and electricity, from the same supplier. Check with your utilities company what is available.

Gas and electricity tokens and keys work out as more expensive ways of paying for fuel. However, they do make you aware of how much you spend on gas and electricity and may be a way of encouraging you to cut down. This can be helpful if you're on a tight budget and can't afford to get a huge bill.

If you live in a house with a high rateable value, but don't use much water, **opt for a water meter**. If you live in a house with a low rateable value and use a lot of water, stick with paying the old way.

You can ask to **have a water meter installed, free of charge**, if you want to pay your water bills like this. Not every property is suitable (flats with communal pipes, for example) but it's worth asking your water company. If you feel you should have one but the water company refuses, you can appeal to OFWAT (Office of Water Services). Once you've had a meter installed, you have a year in which to change your mind if you want to.

Water companies have the right to impose water meters on certain households:

- farms
- if you have a pond or a swimming pool that holds over 10,000 litres (2,200 gallons) and refills automatically
- if you have a power shower
- if you have a bath that holds over 230 litres (50 gallons) – three times the average
- in certain cases, if you have garden watering equipment, such as a sprinkler system, that is left unattended.

It won't cost you anything to **change your electricity or gas supplier**, the pipes and technical bits and bobs are all the same. The only difference is who sends you the bill. Just make sure that your meter is read by your new supplier and that you've given your old supplier 28 days' written notice.

BANK ACCOUNTS

You are under **no legal obligation** to have a bank or any other account, especially if you are paid in cash. You can simply use the Post Office and pay bills by postal order. It's not as simple as having a bank account, but it keeps you off everybody's mailing lists.

Using the Post Office as a bank: it won't save you money but it's often much more convenient, especially if you live in a rural area. At time of going to press, you can make withdrawals and deposits at the Post Office if you bank with Alliance Leicester, Barclays, Cahoot, The Co-operative Bank, Lloyds TSB and Smile.

Live off the bank. Open a cheque account with enough funds and arrange an overdraft facility (some banks will offer a free overdraft of around £50). You can then live within this facility without paying charges and are effectively being funded by the nice people at the bank.

Oh joy! **Your account is mistakenly credited with money.** Oh sadness, it's not yours to keep … so don't spend it. The bank can take it back whenever it wants to.

If you **lose your cheque book**, let the bank know straight away so that they are then liable if any of your cheques are used fraudulently. If you don't tell them, you will be the one who has to pay up if your cheques are used.

If your cheque book is stolen, let your bank or building society know straight away. You won't have to pay up if your signature is forged on any subsequent cheques. However, if your cheque guarantee card is stolen at the same time, you could be liable for any loss. You actually have a contract with the bank which states that the cheque book and card will be kept separate.

Banks will often place **a hefty early repayment charge** on your fixed-term loan if you decide to pay it off sooner than originally planned; i.e. before the agreed repayment date. But check your loan agreement. Some banks calculate the early repayment charge solely on the final outstanding balance, while allowing you to make larger than agreed capital repayments along the way and without extra charge. So, leave £1 outstanding in the account while you pay off the larger amount, and when it comes to the repayment charge, you'll hardly notice the cost because it will be calculated on the measly £1.

Writing **'account payee'** or 'a/c payee' across a cheque means you are protected against the cheque being transferred to a thief's account (*Cheques Act, 1992*). Most banks and building societies print these words on their cheques.

If you come across an old passbook that relates to a long-forgotten bank account, you can still find out if there's any money left in it. Contact the British Bankers Association (020 7216 8801 or look on their website: www.bba.org.uk) and ask for their **Dormant Bank Accounts** leaflet.

Check out the free give-aways from banks and building societies. **Don't be afraid to switch accounts.** But always keep one account open, your oldest one – for those questions when form-filling, 'have you had a bank account for more than three years?'.

It won't have escaped your notice that bank branches are now mixed into one homogenous mass and you will have to call a central number to make any account enquiries. You can be bullish and simply **ask your branch to reveal their secret number** (especially if you have a business account), but as one HSBC bank manager says, 'the irony is, most enquiries can be answered better by the operators at the central call centre'.

When you call your bank or insurer, hang on the line and **don't use the touch tone phone options**. The switchboard will assume you don't have a touch tone phone and you will be answered more quickly.

Use an automatic teller machine (ATM) of the bank you bank with and money will be debited quicker than if you use the automatic teller of a bank that has a reciprocal agreement. However, the bad news is that banks are working very hard to tighten up loopholes. They are all in the process of setting up **'real time' systems** – i.e. if you take out money from a machine at 9am, your account will be debited at 9am.

Put payments on your credit card and you have an automatic 30-day **free overdraft facility**. But pay off the full amount when the credit card bill comes in, and arrange a temporary overdraft facility with your bank if funds are short. It's cheaper than paying a credit card company APR.

Want to complain about your bank? It is worth following up complaints. To find out what you can complain about and how to do it, visit www.bba.org.uk/media where you will find a sample draft letter. You can also complain to the banking ombudsman at:

The Banking Code Standards Board
33 St James's Square
London SW1Y 4JS
Tel: 020 7661 9694

Money from the hole in the wall

As of January 2001 charges were abolished for customers using the automatic teller machines (ATMS) of another bank. However, beware of 'convenience' ATMS, which you often find outside village shops or off-licences. These machines sometimes impose a transaction charge. Better to **use the 'cash back' facility** offered by shops and supermarkets.

Very naughty and thoroughly illegal, but you have to admire his cheek:
Mr X detached pre-printed slips from his bank paying-in book. He then went to several branches of his bank and replaced the blank paying-in slips with his own. Several customers filled in the slips, unwittingly depositing money into his account rather than their own. He was caught.

Whilst banking by telephone or on the Internet will not actually save you money, companies like First Direct (who at the time of going to press have one million customers) are able to offer **keener interest rates** thanks to their lack of overhead costs (i.e. branches). It also means you can find out your balance at 3am on Christmas Day if necessary.

Cut down on paperwork by using Internet financial services. Some companies, such as the Egg credit card and The Co-operative Bank communicate with customers by email.

TAXES

'Death, taxes and childbirth. There's never any convenient time for any of them.' *Margaret Mitchell*, Gone with the Wind, 1936

FACT: Over 36 million people in the UK pay £5.8 billion per annum in unnecessary tax.

Beat the accountants: the Inland Revenue has produced a free CD-ROM for personal computers which has the basic eight-page tax return on it, as well as the supplementary pages for employment and the first year for self-employment. The disk also does calculations for you. Contact the Inland Revenue on 0845 9000 404 for a free copy.

You can download tax calculation software free on the Internet: try www. taxcalc.com and www.e-taxchecker.com, www.digita.com and www.SA2000. co.uk. Some do not include all the supplementary pages so check first.

Get a 10 per cent discount by filing your tax return on line, Go to www.inlandrevenue.gov.uk and register. It only works, though, if you owe money, not if the Inland Revenue owes you.

Oh yes, don't forget the accountant: **firms will always offer you the first meeting free of charge**. Use this and visit a few. And use the ability to visit your local Tax Office. They will sit down and help you prepare your own tax return completely free of charge. The Inland Revenue (number on your tax return) will also answer questions about tax over the phone free of charge, which your accountant would charge for.

If your accounting year runs alongside the tax year, this is called **fiscal accounting**. It's fairly straightforward, but it does mean that you only have a short time to do the accounts before filing your return. Earn yourself more time by choosing to have a different accounting period.

Choose your own accountancy date so that it ties in with your least busy period. If your business is seasonal (you might run a hotel or be a professional Father Christmas), delay taxation by choosing a year-end just before the busy, profit-making time.

Accountants hate receiving messy jobs, and **will charge you for the pleasure** of tidying it up. A couple of extra hours by you putting together organised accounts, or doing any investigative work they require, will reduce your fee. Likewise, avoid sending in your accounts at their busiest time (November to January). If you do, you'll probably get a rushed job and will have to pay an extra amount.

In 2002–3 the personal tax allowance is £4,615. If you have income below this amount **don't pay tax unnecessarily** or have tax deducted by your bank. Fill in an Inland Revenue form R85 (you can also get them from your bank or building society). The same applies to students doing summer jobs. Fill in P38 which declares you expect to earn less than the personal allowance in the year.

Trading accounts

Whether you are a limited company, partnership or sole trader, take certain measures to avoid a potentially **costly Inland Revenue investigation:**

- If any figures appear strange or inconsistent with previous years, nip the query in the bud by explaining the reason in the 'white space' on the tax return.
- Disclose those items that are not allowable for tax such as entertaining, personal travelling etc. Show them being claimed in the face of the accounts then show the taxman you are disallowing them. This demonstrates goodwill. The alternative of not even putting them in your accounts leaves the Inspector wondering where you've hidden them.
- National Insurance Contributions for **self-employed people** are dependent upon certain levels of profits per your accounts. Include certain figures to bring profits down, whilst having no effect on the tax situation

e.g. entertaining, depreciation on computers and other office equipment.

- To **bring tax levels down**, at the end of a VAT quarter and at the end of your accounting year, delay income and accelerate expenses.
- If your partner isn't working, pay them a small amount through your business, which is under the £84 per week tax and NIC threshold. **This saves tax by diverting income into their hands** and uses their tax-free band.
- If you are a successful sole-trader, and paying some tax at the higher 40 per cent rate, consider bringing your partner into the business with you as a partner. She/he may work for you in some way anyway. You will need to make a couple of administrative changes **but the tax saving can be up to £7,000 each year**.
- In a partnership earning more than £160,000 per year? **Bring non-earning spouses into the partnership** to split the tax liability.
- For people who are in a working partnership, beat the accountant's fees. There are tax return forms specifically for you. Each partner fills in their own eight-page form as well as any supplementary pages. Also, one partner is nominated to fill in a return on behalf of the whole partnership.
- Partnerships should always have a written agreement. **Beat acrimony and problems** on the death of one partner by making sure your agreement is watertight. For example make each other's spouses consignees on cheques.

Be aware that there are two methods of claiming back an allowance for the fact you've **used your own car for the benefit of your business**. Choose the method that gives the best result:

- If you are an employee and use your own car, the Inland Revenue 'Fixed Profit Car Scheme' mileage rates dictate exactly how much you can claim as a tax-free allowance.
- If your employer reimburses you below these rates, you should recover the balance by making a claim on your tax return.

Since April 2000 **expenditure on computers** qualifies for 100 per cent write-off in the first year.

Investigations – or guilty until proven innocent

If ever you are subject to an Inland Revenue investigation *always* **respond asap**. It reduces suspicion in their minds, which must have been there for them to have opened the enquiry (though the IR does do random investigations). Remember, in this instance, you are guilty until you can prove your innocence. If you can't deal with the entire question at the same time, reply to those parts that can be answered and promise the rest of the information as soon as you are able. There is always room on your tax return to explain that your income went down because you joined a religious commune for a year.

Dates and payment

Miss the final date for your tax return and you will be charged with a fixed penalty of £100 (as of 2001). If you still haven't sent it in six months later it will be another £100. If the Inland Revenue consider your case to be serious enough, they'll charge a further penalty of up to £60 a day. Mind you, the penalty cannot exceed the tax due. Keep an eye on the tax return filing dates, and check with your own office – ask to speak to an Inspector, not just a clerk as they will not know the full picture!

At time of going to press, **a late-filing penalty was still avoided** as long as your return was in their letter box by 7am on the morning of 2 February – giving you nearly two extra days to file. However, be aware that by 28 February, the element of the outstanding tax that relates to the previous tax year carries a 5 per cent surcharge if unpaid. So, make sure you know how the bill is split and clear this older part first.

Let the Inland Revenue **do the calculations free** for you: have your tax return for the previous tax year in by 30 September.

The return filing date will be 31 January or three months after it was issued, whichever is the later. So, if the Inland Revenue was late in issuing your return, **you could have an extended deadline**. Always read the notes on the front page of the return. The payslip you receive is blank. You can decide if you want to clear the whole balance or not. Sometimes this may be a cheaper/easier way of securing finance.

Read the methods of payment on the payslip – **buy an extra month of credit by paying the tax bill on your credit card**.

When you send in your tax return, if you are being asked to make **'Payments on Account'** for the next year, you can ask for these to be reduced. The Inland Revenue hardly ever refuse – you will have to give a reason, but this can be achieved by completing a form SA303.

Made a mistake?

FACT: A recent audit of 40 tax offices carried out by the Revenue in April 1999 found that some offices calculated over 50 per cent of tax bills incorrectly.

You can claim a rebate on your taxes up to six tax years later if you find you've made a mistake on your tax return. If you find out that the mistake was made by the Inland Revenue, you can claim for any year up to 20 years ago; and you may also be due compensation.

If you think there's been a mistake on your tax return, contact your local tax office. If you have to take things further, go to the Regional Controller (your tax office will have the details). If this fails, take it a stage further. Ask an impartial Adjudicator to deal with your complaint. Call 020 7930 2292 (or go to www.open.gov.uk/adjoff/) for further details. The final resort would be to go to the Ombudsman (address at end of chapter).

Things to write off against tax

If you are an employee (or 'how to milk your employer'):
- You can get tax benefits for **business bicycling:** claim capital allowances and a certain amount per mile if you use your own bike to and from work – the bike and helmet provided by an employer can be tax free too.
- Be relocated – up to **£8,000 of removal expenses** paid to you by an employer will be tax free.
- Your employer can provide you with a **mobile phone, a computer** (up to the value of £2,000) and **season ticket interest-free loan** ('benefit in kind' which, if you borrow less than £5,000, will be cheaper than borrowing money on an overdraft or credit card) and after all that there is a 15 pence per day tax exemption on **luncheon vouchers** provided by your boss.

If you are self-employed:
You can set far more off against tax (well there have to be some benefits to the lonely world of self-employment).
- Claim your **travel expenses** – especially if you work from home.
- Keep a note of **heating and electricity costs** – you can claim a percentage of home heating bills if you work there.
- You can set the **whole cost of a computer** against tax this year and during the next two years, and the same exemption applies to software and Internet-enabled mobile phones.

Your children have a personal tax free allowance each year (£4,385 in 2001). But the revenue only lets them earn £100 a year tax free within this allowance if the money came from you. Better to ask grandparents to give them cash if the income is going to be greater than this. **Use their personal allowance once they are at university:** look into the possibility of buying them a house or flat in their university town in their name so that rent received from housemates can go towards their personal allowance.

Employing a nanny? Avoid being fined (up to £5,000) for paying them cash in hand. Set up your nanny as a 'one person personal service company' – that way you can save £2,500 on a net annual income for your nanny of £11,700.

This part of the tax return is really at the inspector's discretion, and your cheek!
More unusual claims have included:
- A bouncer who claimed for plastic surgery to have his face re-built when on the wrong end of a brawl.
- TV presenters who claim for a hair-do, dentistry, make-up etc. (People in TV generally can claim a portion of their TV licence.)
- Actors who claim cinema tickets as research, as well as any items they need

to purchase to 'get into character', such as alcohol when playing a drunk, nightclub expenses when playing a party animal etc.

- Holidays are always a favourite claim – the artist who needed to go to Tuscany to paint his chosen type of art, the writer who 'needs' to travel to Mozambique to find himself and a bit of solace.

A word of warning: tax *avoidance* is legal but tax *evasion* is illegal. So be clever, not stupid.

FINANCIAL ADVISERS

Financial advisers get huge commissions for signing you up. But turn the situation to your advantage. **It is a competitive market** and many advisers will actually give you part of their own commission in order to attract you. This may be in the form of a cash payment or in the form of them subsidising more attractive terms (for you) in the agreement. Haggle – it's worth it.

When you use a financial adviser **only choose an independent one (IFA)** and go for one who charges on an hourly or fixed rate, whilst reimbursing you the commission. IFAs receive commission for selling you products. Can you be sure that an IFA who receives this commission him or herself will offer you the best product if he or she can earn double the commission on another product?

Consult the cyber adviser

The Internet is the place to get free advice, to gen up on the latest finance news and to give yourself a financial health check – without having to part with fat commissions.

Investigate sites such as:

www.financial-planning.uk.com
www.ftyour money.com
www.investmentguide.co.uk
www.fool.co.uk
www.sort.co.uk
www.mrscohen.co.uk.

CREDIT – OR BUYING ON THE 'NEVER NEVER'

FACT: Britons today owe £13 billion on their credit cards.

Loans

If you need a loan when you're buying a new car, **look at the APR**. It's supposed to be the most reliable guide to comparing loan deals. You will want a low APR, but also remember that this may exclude extras such as insurance.

Go for an unsecured personal loan rather than one that is secured against the car. Payment protection will cover your payments in case of illness, injury or redundancy. If you are turned down for a loan, don't give up. Every lender has its own lending criteria; you may well be accepted elsewhere. Always shop around for the best deals.

But don't let a shop assistant force you into signing a credit agreement in the shop. Take it home and think about it first. In any event you are entitled to **a cooling-off period**.

Cut your credit card bills by moving your debts to the card that charges the lowest APR and gives you an interest-free period. Then ask for your credit limit to be reduced. In fact some credit card companies and banks reduce the APR if you transfer all your credit and store cards to their card. Credit card companies can be sneaky in that they will claim you are a 'valued customer' and up your credit limit. When funds are tight, ask them to return it to its former level.

Keep on the move

Apply for new cards and use them only during the cheap introductory rate (which is usually 0 per cent APR for the first six months). You can then move to another credit card at the end of the six months.

Use the Internet for information about lenders – www.moneyextra.com is a great website when it comes to looking for comparative financial information. Without asking you to register, it can find you a new mortgage, as well as the best deals on credit cards, deposit and current accounts, ISAs, insurance and personal loans.

All that glitters...

Banks will want to sign you up for their gold card accounts, flattering you with your importance. Beware! High interest rates on overdrafts and fees can outweigh the benefits. **Store credit cards can carry astronomical rates** making them one of the most expensive ways to borrow money.

If you have bought an item using your credit card from **a company that subsequently goes bust**, you can get your money back from the credit card company as long as the price of the item is more than £100 but less than £30,000, and the credit advance is up to £15,000. This protection does not apply to charge cards, debit cards or most gold cards.

When you buy something on credit, **the goods are yours** even though you are still paying for them. If the goods become faulty, continue to make the repayments while you complain. You could lose your rights if you don't keep your side of the bargain. If you pay over one third of the credit price on goods but then fail to repay the rest, the company can only reclaim the goods with a court order.

Charge cards (such as American Express, Diners Club) are different from credit cards (like Visa and MasterCard):

- you can't borrow money on a charge card
- there is no spending limit
- retailers accepting them have to pay for the privilege
- the full balance has to be paid each month.

Get wise to offers made by store cards. You may find goods are insured against accidental damage or the card may have a rebate system if the goods you have purchased on your card are marked down in a sale shortly afterwards.

Credit ratings – or beating big brother

You can be refused credit simply because you aren't on the electoral roll or because you are living at an address where somebody already has a bad credit rating. Credit reference agencies carry information on the financial dealings of practically every adult in the country. These agencies are the ones companies and banks turn to when you've applied for a loan, a mortgage, credit or when you want to open a bank account. Anyone subscribing to a credit reference agency will only be given like-for-like information; for example, credit card information to credit card companies and so on.

As an individual, **you are entitled to know** if a lender has contacted a credit reference agency, whether you are refused credit or not, and you can see the details that the credit reference agency has on you. You can check whether everything is up to date and that the information is correct. The agency has 28 days to make any corrections.

For any complaints about a credit reference agency, contact:

The Office of Fair Trading
Fleetbank House
2–6 Salisbury Square
London EC4Y 8JX
Tel: 0845 7224499

To check your credit rating, call Experian on 0115 9768747.

The great credit card scam

In January 2000, a breathtaking fraud was unearthed in South London involving a group of Russians. To steal account holders' information, the Eastern Europeans employed waiters who wore credit card swipe machines on their belts, whilst working in top London hotels and restaurants. The waiters would then re-swipe customers' credit cards on to a tiny machine, also on their belts, and the information would be downloaded through a computer to a blank card's magnetic strip. Using fake holograms the gang were able to reproduce near perfect fakes of Visa, American Express and MasterCard cards.

The fake cards were then sold on the black market for £300, giving a month's leeway before the cardholder noticed the fraud. Two of the waiters were apprehended but jumped bail.

DEBT AND SAVING

FACT: The amount of outstanding consumer credit in 1998 was £101.7 billion – that's over £1,700 per UK citizen.

FACT: There is an average of over 72,000 court summonses for debt each year by County Courts in England and Wales.

Is that permanent overdraft beginning to get you down? Try these strategies:

- For a fortnight record every single penny that leaves your purse or pocket. Then put **10 per cent of your weekly income** into a separate account and don't touch it…no matter what. If you earned £15,000 (after tax) a year, you'd have £1,560 stashed away at the end if it.
- Cut out one £30 meal a month, and you would save £360.
- Smoke 20 fags a day? Give up and you'll have a healthy £1,500 in your pocket at the end of the year.

Pay off debts in order of priority, and let your other creditors wait. Losing your home would be a huge problem so **always pay your mortgage**. Then pay the gas, electricity, water and council tax. Followed by credit and store cards.

The time not to pay off your loans is when you are charged a lower interest rate on your debt (student loans for example) than the interest you can receive on a savings account or another type of investment. (See the Education chapter for more information on student loans.)

You don't always have to pay for overdrafts… if the bank knows what to expect and it's only for a couple of days or so. If you know that you're going to get overdrawn, call the bank and explain the situation. If told in advance and given guarantees that you'll clear the overdraft quickly, a bank won't always charge.

All my worldly debts I leave for you

If you have a joint account and your partner vanishes off the face of the earth, you are liable for any debts. Make sure you are also aware of your household money movements, if your partner is the bill payer. (See the Law chapter for more information on matrimonial matters.)

ISAs (individual savings accounts) were introduced on 6 April 1999 and replaced TESSAs and PEPs. They are meant to encourage people to save, using a combination of three types of tax-free investment:

- a savings account
- life insurance
- stocks and shares.

A mini ISA offers just one of these elements (ideal for a deposit-type account) while the maxi ISA offers all three. You can't have a mini and a maxi ISA in one tax year or two mini ISAs of the same type. Unlike TESSAs, which ISAs replaced, you won't lose the tax-free benefits by withdrawing cash in the first five years. There are, however, limits on how much you can invest in an ISA in any given year. As of 2001, you can invest £7,000 in a maxi ISA in one year. Or, with a mini ISA you can invest either £3,000 in cash, £3,000 in stocks and shares or £1,000 in life insurance.

FACT: Over 54 per cent of the adult population has little or no savings. (*The M&G Great British Saving Survey*)

How to make your money grow

Officially called 'compounding', here's how to earn interest on your interest:
You have £1,000 in savings earning, say, 6 per cent interest per annum. At the end of the year you will have earned £60. Next year you will have earned 6 per cent on £1,060, with a total balance of £1,123.60. By the third year you will have earned £67.42 in interest, with a total of £1,191.02. Save £10,000 in an account paying 6 per cent, leave the money alone and within ten years you will have £17,908.47 gross.

MORTGAGES

'In the midst of life we are in debt.' *Altogether New Cynic's Calendar*

FACT: Each year more than 32,000 properties are repossessed for failure to meet mortgage payments. (*1999 figure*)

Lenders are falling over themselves to part with their money. **Shop around for a mortgage.** Let the companies know about the incentives you've been offered by their competitors – they might waive some charges. You can haggle over legal costs and so on to get the set-up costs down too.

You can get **a 100 per cent mortgage** but the interest rate will be high. There will be other costs involved such as solicitor's fees, an application fee, surveys and so on. A deposit will help get the interest rate down and help with all those extra charges. It might mean tightening your belt for a year, but it's worth it in the end.

Don't be too perfect: your credit rating will be checked by a potential mortgage lender. If you have never had a loan or used a credit card, they have no way of knowing if you are a trustworthy borrower and so may not be keen to lend to you. Be pure as the driven snow in your repayments of loans, so your credit rating is good.

FACT: A recent NOP Research Group survey found that 75 per cent of borrowers had no idea what the rate of interest was on their mortgage.

Not all lenders will credit extra payments until the end of the year, so the interest charge won't be reduced until then. **Ask your lender to credit your repayment to the capital sum immediately** or put the money into an interest-bearing account until the end of the year and then use it to pay towards your mortgage.

Some mortgages offer 'baby breaks' where you can reduce your repayments while you're on maternity leave. Look at taking out a flexible mortgage, which gives you some leeway to be, um, flexible!

Mortgages online

The Internet has come into its own here, with potential borrowers able to key their financial information and borrowing needs into search engines, which can then come up with a list of borrowers, rates and other mortgage information. Try sites such as www.eloan.com/uk, www.charcolonline.co.uk, www.emfinance.co.uk, www.flexemortgage.com, www.moneysupermarket.co.uk.
Or look at www.thegoodwebguide.co.uk/chan_mone for impartial reviews of good finance websites.

PENSIONS

Be prepared, the **state pension is likely to grind to a halt** sooner or later, and we will all have to provide for our own old age. But if you are about to retire and find you have enough funds, **you can defer your state pension** if you want (and can afford) to. The gains are not huge, however. For every seven weeks it's deferred, its value increases by 1 per cent.

FACT: By 2008 there will be more retired people than children.

Beat penury: **make sure you are ahead of the game** by joining your employers' pension scheme and/or making contributions as early as possible into a personal pension plan. If you would like an annual income of £30,000 on retirement at 65, at today's interest rates you will need to be contributing £416 per month at the age of 30.

From October 2001, **employers with over five employees** are obliged to provide a company pension plan. Make sure your employer is complying.

You can actually have as many pension schemes as takes your fancy, so long as your contributions do not exceed the percentage permitted by the blessed Inland Revenue. The amount you can contribute in any one year varies from 17.5 per cent if you are under 35, to 40 per cent if you are over 61. Find out the percentages by logging on to www.inlandrevenue.gov.uk.

Getting the most from your pension: a story

Imagine you are 36 at the beginning of the tax year. Your age-related percentage is therefore 20 per cent. You can choose a 'basis year' of income to calculate your pension contributions (though you will need to provide proof). So, say the basis year you have chosen is a year in which your earnings were £20,000, the maximum total contribution to your fund in the tax year is therefore £4,000 (£20,000 × 20 per cent), inclusive of tax relief.

Your kind employer has agreed to make a total contribution of £500 into your personal pension scheme during the year, which leaves a balance of £3,500, inclusive of tax relief at basic rate.

Make the most of it by paying a further £2,730 to your personal pension scheme and the nice Inland Revenue will add a further £770 in tax relief (assuming a basic rate of tax of 22 per cent). This would result in a total contribution in the year of £500 + £2,730 + £770 which equals £4,000 (20 per cent of your earnings in the basis year).

There used to be a system called **'carry forward'** which was withdrawn with effect from 6 April 2001. This allowed you to bring forward unused tax relief from up to six years earlier and make a higher contribution in the current year. However, there is also a system called **'carry back'** which allows you to ask the Inland Revenue to treat a contribution you are making now as if it had been paid in the previous tax year. This means that, if you had not already paid your maximum contribution in that earlier year, you could make up the shortfall by a contribution now.

Using your pension to help your dependents: you can allocate some of your pension contributions for term life assurance. This will provide your widow, widower or dependents with a lump sum if you die before your pension has started. These contributions will count towards your overall contribution limit, however, so the amount you can pay towards your own pension will be less. For contracts that started before 6 April 2001, you can, if you wish, pay up to 5 per cent of your earnings for term life assurance. For contracts starting on 6 April 2001 or later, the rules are different. The maximum you may pay towards term life assurance is 10 per cent of the amount you are paying towards retirement benefits. For example, for every £100 you pay towards your own retirement benefits, you may pay another £10 to a term life assurance policy under the scheme.

Can't afford a pension or not earning?

Stakeholder pensions came into effect in April 2001, and are a tax efficient way for anyone, even non-earners, to make contributions to a pension. Funds are invested by an insurance company and the amount you can invest each year is capped, but they work in a similar way to personal pension plans.

INSURANCE

(See the Housing chapter for more information about house insurance.)

Keep a note of when insurance policies need renewing and always **shop around for a better deal**. It often helps to use the services of a broker who can do the compare-and-contrast donkey work for you. An insurance broker is free – they are paid commission by the insurance company. It is worth offering to pay a healthy excess on your policies (especially motoring) to bring down the cost of your premiums.

Ask for several quotes for household insurance. **Some companies will match quotes you have been given** (especially your bank if you have a good banking record with them).

Put aside time to **go through your insurance policies**. You may find that you are covered twice in areas like personal injury, but not covered at all in others. For example, your bag or briefcase may well be covered on your house insurance. If your keys are stolen, you should claim on your building insurance policy. You will be changing the locks and these are considered to be part of the fabric of the building by insurance companies. Some companies give you free cover for loss, theft or accidental damage on items purchased with their credit card over a certain value. Cover can often last up to 100 days for items bought here or abroad.

You don't necessarily need to buy an extended warranty for electrical goods. They can be expensive and involve very strict terms and conditions. If something is going to break down, it often does in its first year … when you are already covered by the normal store warranty. It's risk versus cost.

Sometimes it pays to be a woman, sometimes it doesn't. Women get offered cheaper premiums for motor insurance, because men tend to drive faster cars, and are behind the wheel more often. Ergo they have more accidents. Insurance companies are particularly wary of boy racers aged between 17 and 24. A 21-year-old man living in Manchester could pay £417 to drive a Peugeot 205 1.1L, with a £350 excess. A woman of the same age would pay £332 and a much lower excess.

Life insurance also favours women, with women living an average of 81.5 years, men 77.4 (*Government Actuaries Department figures, 2000*). Women pay more for income protection cover because they suffer more minor illnesses (mainly musculoskeletal problems and mental anxiety), and men pay more for critical, life-threatening illness cover. But **when it comes to annuity rates, it pays to be a man**. Annuities are heavily weighted against women because of their greater life expectancy. A man aged 65 with a £100,000 pension could receive £9,089 a year before tax. A woman of the same age would get £63 a month less for the rest of her life (*The Annuity Bureau*).

Medical insurance

Health insurance premiums have doubled in the last ten years. Because of this, many people are choosing to pay for treatment on a one-off basis. This has led to a **dual pricing policy** where a hospital will quote one price if you say you don't have medical insurance and another – up to 50 per cent more – if you do. Some insurance companies are suggesting that customers get round this disparity by initially paying for their own operations and they will then reimburse them, often within 24 hours. Shop around. (See the Health chapter for more information.)

Dental cover can be especially misleading. If you pay a monthly premium of, say, £14, it amounts to £180 per year. That is more than two fillings a year. Work out how much dental work you have had over the past few years. Is it worth it? Find a dentist too who will treat your children free (many will treat them until they are around 20 years old).

Complaint against your insurers?

You can appeal to a higher authority. If your insurers are part of the **Insurance Ombudsman Bureau** scheme, an independent assessor will look at your case and has the power to award up to £100,000 against the insurance company (£10,000 a year in permanent health insurance cases). If the insurers are not part of the scheme, you can contact the Personal Insurance Arbitration Service; the arbitrator looks into the details of your case and makes a binding decision. You will need your insurer's consent to go to the Personal Insurance Arbitration Service.

Insurance Ombudsman Bureau
135 Park Street
London SE1 9EA
Tel: 0845 600 6666

Personal Insurance Arbitration Service
Chartered Institute of Arbitrators
International Arbitration Centre
24 Angel Gate
City Road
London EC1V 2RS
Tel: 020 7837 4483

Sometimes, **loss adjusters get involved in insurance claims**. Their job is to find out how much insurers should pay towards the cost of a claim. They help negotiate the claim on behalf of the policyholder, you, and they will be paid by you. Normally, they are only called in when the claim is rather complicated, but appear more and more often as insurance companies tighten up on claimants. Make sure you are on site when they make a visit to assess a claim and that they fully understand the details of your claim.

STOCKS AND SHARES

'A broker is a man who takes your fortune and runs it into a shoestring.'
Alexander Woollcott

The stock market is an interesting system to try and beat. Though the overall trend is towards growth and many people have made millions, many more have lost their shirts. **It's just sophisticated gambling.** A share is a small stake in a business. If you're thinking of buying shares, look at the business, not the share price. Research a business that you think might be a good bet. And don't get too out of your depth; stick to businesses that you know and understand. Read companies' reports and accounts – not exactly gripping stuff, but useful if you're considering investing in them.

Taxpayers will have to **pay income tax** on dividends from shares and capital gains tax on any money made from selling shares over the Capital Gains Tax threshold. You can avoid this by putting shares into an ISA, although there is a limit on how much you can invest in an ISA in any given year (see page 39).

Playing safe

The value of shares can go down as well as up, but there are ways of minimising a downward trend. **Spread the risk** by investing in shares through collective investments like unit trusts or investment trusts. Unit trusts are usually managed by a high street bank that has a large portfolio of stocks and shares. An investment trust is a fund set up as a company in which you invest by buying shares in it. The fund then uses this money to buy portfolios of shares in other companies.

It pays to **think long term** when dealing with shares – invest for at least five years but more likely ten. You may have to wait a while until your shares rise. As with any gamble, put a figure on particular shares – how much will you let them drop before you sell them?

Spotting the trend

Keep an eye on what's happening in the high street, the items in people's shopping baskets, the cars people are driving. If you can spot a trend, you should consider getting some shares in a company related to it. The share price of Psion, for example, went through the roof and paid early investors handsomely. Then the bottom fell out of the market. The skill is knowing when to sell!

Most analysts value companies according to the **P/E Ratio** (price divided by earnings per share). The higher the PE the more expensive the share. But if earnings are growing rapidly, the PE should fall rapidly as you work out forecasts for growth. If earnings do not grow, the share price will obviously react accordingly. Different sectors of the market are rated in accordance with growth potential, and an example would be high tech companies in 2000 when almost everything shot up in the hope of massive earnings potential, even the very poor performers.

Another strategy could be to identify and buy **'bombed out shares'** – those of companies who, at the prevailing share price, could be vulnerable to a bid. The share price should then take a leap.

School fees

If you're a parent with school fees to pay, have a look at **zero preference shares**. They're low risk, tax efficient investments which generate predictable lump sums on set dates in the future. Each has a finite life – usually four or five years – during which time no dividend is paid, so there's no income tax liability. Returns aren't guaranteed but issuers provide a 'hurdle rate' for each zero, which indicates the rate of growth required to pay investors in full. So far, no zero has ever failed to deliver its promised yield. (See also the Education chapter for school fee options.)

Internet sharedealing

> **FACT:** According to some stockbrokers, investors who switch to Internet dealing tend to increase their activity fourfold.

Pity the poor stockbrokers. Everyone has become an expert thanks to the Internet, and by 2003 online sharedealing is expected to be the largest activity on the most popular Internet sector. If you are smart and stay on the ball you can beat the commission system.

Try one of the following:
- **Order Routing** – where you email your instructions to a broker who makes the sale or purchase for you
- **STP (Straight Through Processing)** – where you deal directly with the market using the website of the stockbroker hosting the service. It is certainly cheaper this way (you avoid commission), but surveys have shown that online traders do no better than the traditional means. And what you don't get is the advice of a broker.

Look at the following sites:

www.dljdirect.co.uk
www.etrade.co.uk
www.stocktrade.co.uk
www.tdwaterhouse.co.uk
www.schwab-worldwide.com/Europe
www.caves.co.uk

as well as the online sharedealing facilities of banks like Halifax, NatWest and Barclays.

Cashing in

Certain hotel and restaurant chains give **discounts if you are a shareholder**. Purchase the required minimum (around 200–400 shares depending on the hotel chain) and enjoy your room being upgraded (subject to availability on arrival), 10–15 per cent off food and drink as well as reduced room charges. Early check-in and late departure are often also available.

Make sure you use up your **capital gains tax allowance** every year by 'bed and breakfasting' – selling shares at the end of the financial year and buying them back at the beginning of the next.

DISCOUNTS AND BENEFITS

Everyone likes getting a discount and some people seem better at achieving this than others. **Luck or skill?** With a bit of work, most of us can get some form of saving on items or services. Getting a discount usually involves a bit of give and take. In other words, the company giving the discount will want to get something out of it: for example, cash up front rather than having to wait for you to pay later.

Like haggling in a Moroccan market, **don't show how much you want the item** if you're trying to get money knocked off it. A salesperson is less likely to give you a discount if he or she knows you just can't live without the item. They will hold out until you give in!

Timing is of the essence

Sometimes, companies and suppliers have **very quiet periods of trading**, so any business is therefore welcome at that time. Try and find out if a supplier is in one of those quiet times (or make enquiries to find out when that time is). They'll be keen to get your business (and your money, even at a discount) just as much as you want what they're offering. An example of this is car salesmen who want to shift used cars from the forecourt before the next registration and the next wave of used trade-ins come in.

Give a company the impression that you are considering buying from their competitors but that, for a discount, you are prepared to buy from them.

The one downside about discounts is that you tend to get what you pay for. In other words, if you manage to knock the price down too much, **you won't necessarily get the full quality of service.** Everyone has got to make a living. However, it is within your rights to demand that goods are of good enough quality, and check that you can return them if they are faulty.

Thank heaven for small mercies

If you're a petite size or have small feet, have you considered **buying children's clothes** and shoes? You don't pay VAT on children's clothes so you can save money. Kids' T-shirts and trainers look great on smaller women (and men), and with children becoming more fashion-aware by the minute, you can stay in style as well as save the pennies.

Make the most of the sales. Sales are a means for shops to get rid of old goods before the new season's stock comes on to the shelves. If you aren't too fussed about being state of the art, you can get last year's style washing machine, for example, and make a significant saving. Buy shop soiled or ex-display goods too, and haggle over the price.

In supermarkets look out for **three for the price of two** or buy-one-get-one-free offers. They are usually on popular brands anyway, so you will be making a saving, so long as you really want three packs of choc chip cookies.

Antiques often show the trade price (marked with a 'T' in small letters) on the price tag. Don't pay full price, offer the trade amount and stick to it.

Get what you deserve

Single parent who is finding it hard making ends meet? The **Working Family Tax Credit** allows you to work over 16 hours per week, claim a benefit (if you're on low income) and get financial assistance for up to 70 per cent of child care costs, as well as entitling you to retain your child maintenance payments from the father.

If sickness forces you off work for a long period of time, how will you be paid? Some employers continue to pay full wages for six months. However, by law, they only need to pay just over £52 a week at the moment for that period. Are you covered for that? Be prepared – **think about health and sickness insurance**.

Tips if you are self-employed and working from home:

- You must keep paying your National Insurance contributions to qualify for the full state pension and benefits. Self-employed people currently (2002) pay a weekly contribution of £2 plus 7 per cent on any profit up to a maximum of £1,180.
- Home workers can claim a portion of the costs of their mortgage or rent, heating, lighting and telephone against income tax. Capital expenditure, on computers for example, is also deductible.
- If your anticipated self-employed income for the next 12 months is more than £52,000, you must register for VAT with your local HM Customs and Excise office.
- There is no holiday or sick pay for the self-employed. But permanent health insurance will pay you an income if you are ill or have an accident – usually paying out after four weeks of incapacity.
- Make sure that your office at home is not used exclusively for business or ensure that you don't receive clients at home. It could be argued that it is a change of use of your property.

MARRIAGE AND MONEY

'Never marry money. Marry where money is.' *Anon*

FACT: 'Will you marry me?' Those words are worth about £3,500 each, as the cost of the average wedding tops £14,000 (*Weddingplan, 2001*). And it's getting worse. It is estimated that the average cost will rise by 8 per cent each year and by 2006 will be nearer £20,000.

Do it on the cheap: a register office wedding, including notice of marriage (now compulsory), fee for the registrar and marriage certificate will cost under £100 (2001).

Marry in the provinces: the cost of venues and catering in the capital will set you back about £2,500 more than if you were to marry in, say, East Anglia.

All my worldly goods...

So, if the average cost of a traditional wedding in the UK is around £14,000 in 2001, that means that if you overrun your budget by just 10 per cent, you'll have to find another £1,400. **Prepare a budget and stick to it.** Any changes along the way and you'll know exactly where you stand financially and can adjust accordingly. Prepare a provisional budget, listing items that are of importance to you and that you want in your wedding; posh frock or posh venue? Drinks on the house or guests to pay for their own? Going over budget somewhere means you'll have to find the surplus from elsewhere. It's not a bad idea to build in a contingency sum of around 10 per cent of your final cost.

To amass enough cash for your wedding, you would need to save £500 per month for the next two years. Save or borrow: **the reasonably cheap way to raise a lump sum** is to add it to your mortgage. At a standard variable rate of 7.74 per cent borrowing an extra £14,000 would add £90 to your monthly mortgage payments. But on an interest-only mortgage, over 20 years, that would amount to £21,000 in terms of total interest charged – one and a half times the cost of your wedding. **A personal loan is a cheaper option.** With an APR of 10 per cent on a £14,000 loan, it would add £3,500 to the cost of the wedding. Pay £300 per month and the debt would be cleared in five years.

Plan ahead: if you have daughters, **it is worth putting aside a small sum** each month earmarked for their nuptials. Even if you have sons, these days in-laws are often expected to make a contribution.

All the best laid plans...in case something should go wrong on your big day, budget for **standard wedding insurance** as soon as you know the date of your wedding. A plan like this usually covers the following risks:
- cancellation
- wedding attire
- wedding presents

- photographs/video
- loss of deposits
- public liability

There are usually four main exclusions in such policies:
- circumstances known to you when you took out the policy
- disinclination of you or your partner to marry
- lack of funds (other than redundancy after the policy is taken out)
- the first £25 of each claim.

Marriage and money facts:

- Married couples are taxed separately.
- You are only liable for your spouse's domestic debts if your accounts are in joint names or if you have joint credit cards. So play it safe and keep your accounts separate.
- After 6 April 2000, the married couple's allowance is only available if one spouse was aged 65 or over on 5 April 2000.
- If you're married and one of you isn't paying tax, swap savings into the name of the non-taxpayer and have the interest paid gross.
- If you are not working, pay investments into your name so that you and your partner can take full advantage of your personal tax allowance.
- Likewise, make sure your spouse uses their capital gains tax allowance each year by gifting money or shares to them.
- Property and money exchanged between husband and wife will be exempt from tax.
- In fact, money can be shifted around a family in a very tax efficient way. Make use of the tax-free gifts you can give children (up to a set amount), who are non-taxpayers. You will, however, have to complete a tax return for them if they have investments.
- If you're not married and your partner dies, you are not entitled to a widow's pension. Unmarried partners can't insure against each other's death. Beat the potential loss by insuring your own life and make your partner the beneficiary.

(See Inheritance on page 53.)

(See the Law chapter for more information on matrimonial issues.)

A NEW BABY

FACT: It is estimated that the first 16 years of a child's life will cost £68,000.

Babies are expensive. That little bundle of joy can cost between £3,000 to £6,500 in its first year. Try to **pay off any loans**, credit card bills and so on before the baby arrives.

Make a will. **If you die intestate**, your partner will get your personal belongings and an initial sum of money while your child will get the rest (see Inheritance on page 53).

Make the most of your **legal right to maternity leave**, but take too much time off work and it could affect your pension, especially if you are in a company scheme. If you can, try to make up additional voluntary contributions while you are on maternity leave. Working mothers are eligible to 18 weeks maternity pay, which is taxed and paid automatically through their employers. For the first six weeks, it's worth 90 per cent of the mother's average weekly earnings in the eight weeks before she stopped work. It then drops to a flat rate (£59.95 in 2001) for the next 12 weeks. But even if you have no intention of returning to work, do not hand in your notice until you are on maternity leave because you are still entitled to statutory maternity pay.

When it's worth being 'in the system'

Women who have given up work or are self-employed should claim several weeks of **maternity benefit** from the Benefits Agency (provided they have paid National Insurance contributions).

Men are now able to take three weeks' **unpaid paternity leave**. Find out from your employer if you can tag this on to an annual holiday.

You can claim **Child Benefit** for a child until they reach the age of 16 (or later if they are still in full-time education). It's a slightly larger amount for the first child. By claiming Child Benefit, you also get National Insurance credit towards your basic state pension to cover the period when you're not working.

Can you have it all? Have your baby in your early twenties, and give up work to look after it, and you could lose *over half* your lifetime earnings. So leave having your children until your late twenties or early thirties, take the statutory maternity leave (six weeks) and you can reduce this loss to about 5 per cent of your lifetime earnings.

Babies and pensions. If a 26-year-old stops work for six years, she could reduce the ultimate value of her personal pension by a quarter. Beat this shortfall by investing money in an ISA or Stakeholder Pension (see Pensions on page 40) or invest money, whilst you are still earning it, in a share portfolio. For advice on maternity and finance call the Maternity Alliance on 020 7588 8582.

MENTAL HEALTH

No laughing matter, but a costly one unless you can take preventative action. If your partner is suffering from a degenerative mental disease, such as Alzheimer's, it will cost upwards of £450 to obtain a Court of Protection Order from the Public Trust Office to take control of their financial affairs (particularly important if endowments are due to be paid out, for example). It is a sensitive issue, but wise to try and persuade your partner to **grant you power of attorney** before they are too ill to be able to organise it. Solicitors charge around £100 for this and there will be a further cost of around £75 to register it with the Public Trust Office. (See also Health chapter.)

LIVING ABROAD AND OFFSHORE BANKING

If you have lived or earned money abroad, you can either leave it in a foreign bank account or move it to a foreign bank's branch here when you return home. You can also open a foreign-currency account with a UK bank. Your money will earn interest at the rate of the country it is from. You can then change your money into sterling when you need it or the exchange rate is good.

Consider too an offshore bank account, which can be denominated in any currency and switched into sterling at no transaction cost. Interest is paid gross, and you have to declare it on your tax return.

Living and working abroad? **Expatriates Contingency Tax insurance** covers you against having to pay UK tax if you have to return home early for any reason. It's worth getting insured against kidnapping, deportation and so on too. Sounds funny, but you won't be laughing if it happens.

MONEY-MAKING SCHEMES

Can one get rich quick? If there was an easy answer, you wouldn't need to read this book (and we wouldn't need to write it!). But if you are prepared to take the risk:

Buy Premium Bonds: the odds of winning a prize in the monthly draw (smallest prize £50, top prize £1 million) are 21,000 to 1 for each £1 bond. Your investment has to be a minimum of £100 or a maximum of £20,000. There are 500,000 prizes each month. Application forms are available from any Post Office or call the National Savings helpline (0645 645000).

Play the National Lottery: though it has become a national pastime with over 50 per cent of adults buying tickets each week and with annual sales of £4,983 million (up to March 2001), the odds of winning aren't quite as good as with Premium Bonds. The chances of winning the jackpot are around 14 million to 1. The odds of winning a prize (minimum £10) is 54 to 1 for each £1 entry. However, if you don't win a prize, you've also lost your stake ... pure gambling and not exactly a savings plan!

If you think that, like lunch, the **FTSE All Share stock market is for wimps**, you can choose to ride the shares roller coaster. No pain, no gain. Learn about buying and selling options (which each give you the right, though not the obligation, to trade in 1,000 shares). You will need about £20,000 to get started, and a broker like www.mybroker.co.uk or www.investinoptions.com. You will then need to open a US dollar margin, or debt account with $2,000 and be assessed to make sure you are sophisticated enough to cope.

Find out about new share issues – the best are initial public offers (IPOs) when a previously privately-owned company offers shares for the first time. There are no broking charges, and IPOs are usually under-priced. Try www. webshareshop.co.uk, www.stockacademy.com and www.nothingventured. com. The downside? IPOs usually involve small companies (market capital less than £100m) which can be volatile. Remember Lastminute.com?

Visit and use www.carpetbaggers.com if you are looking for the next building society windfall.

Buy to rent: property is still the money maker it always has been, and lenders are now keener then ever to give mortgages to landlords wanting to build up a property portfolio. To find out more details see the Housing chapter.

Just buy: there is no **capital gains tax** on the profit from the sale of your main property. So buy in a down-market area, do up the house, sell it at a profit, buy in a more expensive area, renovate the house and so on. This was the real money spinner for Yuppies in the booming 1980s, but it only works in a buoyant housing market.

Join the queue. Remember Amway? A US company, Amway is one of the success stories of **pyramid selling (or network marketing** to give it the proper name) and allegedly has annual sales of $7 billion. You find a product (with Amway it is cleaning products, vitamins and cosmetics), and become a recruiter by selling the product to, say, six people, who each find six people to sell to who each find six people and so it goes on…Money trickles upwards and you, at the top of the pyramid, receive commission on all the sales transactions beneath you and hopefully retire to the Caribbean very quickly. For the sales pitch, visit www.amway.com (or, for an unsolicited view, http://skepdic.com/amway.html), and for down-to-earth advice on pyramid selling visit www.gurujeff.com.

On the Internet there is potential money to be made when you move to an ISP (Internet Service Provider) which offers free shares for using its service or for referring others. See http://registration.totalise.net, but in view of the topsy-turvy fortunes of the Internet, there are no guarantees.

What about being paid to surf? **Some Internet advertisers will actually pay you to view their adverts** (done with a viewbar – a small window that displays their adverts). What they really want is for you to refer others and earn the commission on their viewing time. Don't book your dream holiday just yet.

For the ultimate scams, seek the advice of Anil Bhoyrul and James Hipwell, whose book *City Slickers: How to Make a Million in 12 Months* is published by Blake Publishing Ltd, at £5.99. The pair were fired from their finance column 'City Slickers' in the *Mirror*, for allegedly dealing in shares they had tipped. The book offers basic advice on the stock market as well as 'stock-picking, information gathering, transactions and moneymaking techniques' (*Amazon*).

Find a billionaire and persuade him (or her) to marry you.

HOW *NOT* TO MAKE MONEY

'A fool and his money are soon parted.' *Thomas Tusser*

Endowments – the pariah of financial products. These have had a very bad press for being expensive whilst trapping people into poorly performing stock market investments. An equity ISA or unit trust is a safer bet.

Variable rate mortgages – the only people these benefit are the lenders. You'd get a better rate with a different mortgage from the same lender.

Personal pensions – hidden charges can gnaw away at your initial investment. Stakeholder Pensions, introduced in April 2001, will be a better choice, though there are limits to the amount that can be invested (see page 41).

National Savings – give a notoriously feeble return on your investment. The ordinary account pays less than 2 per cent. Cash ISAs or another savings plan would be a far better bet.

Keeping your cash under the mattress. The only interest will be from the moths.

INHERITANCE

(See the Law chapter for more information about wills.)

At the time of going to press, an estate can be valued **up to £242,000 before tax is due** (nil-rate band). After that it is taxed at a whopping 40 per cent. Home values are included in a deceased person's estate. House prices on the up can push you into the tax net.

Don't let the Inland Revenue benefit from your demise

Gift assets like property to your beneficiaries (these transfers must be unconditional) and, as long as you survive for seven years after you have made the transfer, you will avoid them having to pay inheritance tax (IHT). Die within seven years and the value of the gift will be taxed incrementally.

Are you a grandparent? As before, if you live for seven years after making a 'gift' to someone, no tax is due so it's a good way to give money to your children and grandchildren.

Transfers between a husband and wife (living in the UK) are exempt from IHT, so **leave everything to your spouse**.

One way of using the allowances to maximum effect is for married couples to avoid leaving everything to each other – but for each to leave assets up to the nil-rate band to their children or grandchildren. In this way, both nil-rate bands will be used. If this is not done and everything is transferred to the survivor on the death of the first spouse, only one nil-rate band is available on the death of the second.

Cut the value of your estate by giving away gifts of up to £3,000 per year (2001) – this applies per person so a married couple could give away £6,000 – and can be carried over to the next year if not used (for one year only, however).

Give to charity. Gifts to British charities are tax-free while you are alive or as a bequest, regardless of size (so you could leave your potting shed to the National Trust). The same applies to gifts to established political parties, and if you are feeling very grand, you can make a bequest to the nation tax-free.

Tax on life assurance proceeds can be avoided by writing the policy in trust for the beneficiaries. When you take out life assurance, the salesman should explain this in full and provide the appropriate forms.

WILLS

As stated in the Law chapter, **you are doing no one any favours by dying intestate** and you leave an unholy mess for your nearest and dearest. So the best way to beat the taxman is to make a will. The rules on intestacy are sobering, and knowing them should at least galvanise you into action. (The following apply to England, Wales and Northern Ireland, except that in Northern Ireland children under 18 can make a will.)

* If you are married with no other living relatives, your spouse will inherit your entire estate.
* For those of you who are married with parents and siblings, your spouse will get the first £200,000, personal possessions and half of the rest. The other half will go to your parents (if they are still alive) or be split between your siblings.
* If you are married with children, your spouse gets your possessions, the first £125,000 and an income from half of the remainder for life. The other half is inherited by your children.
* If you are divorced, the children you had with your ex-partner will inherit (not the ex-partner).
* Beware if you are living with someone but not married: they will not automatically be recognised as beneficiaries in law. Children born together have a claim on your estate, but you could leave a partner in financial difficulties if you are the breadwinner.

In Scotland, your spouse gets rights to your house up to the value of £110,000, furnishings up to £20,000 and cash up to £30,000 (£50,000 if you have no children), or a percentage of everything valued above this. Your children get the rest. **So beat the Scottish system**, where in theory your children could receive nothing, by making a will and stating your intentions for your estate.

At time of writing, **we don't think you need money to get into heaven.**

Weird and wonderful financial laws

In New York, it is considered a misdemeanour to arrest a dead man for being in debt.

In 1981, officials in Georgia, USA, stumbled upon a law that allowed pensions to Confederate widows. That week, the last widow died, and they repealed the law.

A Minnesota tax form requested that you fill in the date of your birth and your date of death.

In Denmark, a stripper tried to claim her breast implants as an expense by stating that they were 'tools of the trade'. It was disallowed.

In America, you cannot sue the federal government without the government's permission.

One man in his will left his overdraft 'to my wife – she can explain it'.

A man, anticipating marriage, gave money to his fiancée to pay off her debts. She married someone else and refused to pay back the money. The US tax court held that, although a loan resulting from theft is tax deductible, a loss from misrepresentation is not. They treated the unfortunate man as an accomplice to fraud.

USEFUL ADDRESSES

Banking Ombudsman
70 Gray's Inn Road
London WC1X 8NB
Tel: 020 7404 9944

Building Societies Ombudsman
Millbank Tower
London SW1P 4XS
Tel: 020 7931 0044

Credit Reference Agency
Experian Ltd (formerly CCN Group)
Telbert House
Telbert Street
Nottingham NG1 5HF
Tel: 0115 941 0888

Credit Reference Agency
Hire Purchase Information plc (HPI)
Equifax plc
New Street
Salisbury
Wiltshire SP1 2TB
Tel: 01722 422422

Inland Revenue
Tel: 0345 161514

Insolvency Service
1st–2nd Floor
Ladywood House
45–46 Stephenson Street
Birmingham B2 4UP
Tel: 0121 698 4000

Insurance Ombudsman
City Gate One
135 Park Street
London SE1 9EA
Tel: 020 7928 7600

Insurance Ombudsman Bureau
135 Park Street
London SE1 9EA
Tel: 0845 600 6666

Investment Ombudsman
4th Floor
6 Frederick's Place
London EC2R 8BT
Tel: 020 7796 3065

National Debtline
Tel: 0121 359 8501

Office of the Data Protection Registrar
Wycliffe House
Water Lane
Wilmslow
Cheshire SK9 5AF
Tel: 01625 545745

Office of Fair Trading
Fleetbank House
2–6 Salisbury Square
London EC4Y 8JX
Tel: 0845 7224499

Office of Water Services (OFWAT)
Centre City Tower
7 Hill Street
Birmingham B5 4UA
Tel: 0121 625 1300

Pensions Ombudsman
6th Floor
11 Belgrave Road
London SW1V 1RB
Tel: 020 7834 9144

Personal Insurance Arbitration Service
Chartered Institute of Arbitrators
International Arbitration Centre
24 Angel Gate
City Road
London EC1V 2RS
Tel: 020 7837 4483

Personal Investment Authority
Ombudsman Bureau
Hertsmere House
Hertsmere Road
London E14 4AB
Tel: 020 7216 0016

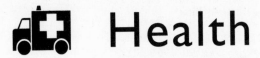 # Health

'Be careful about reading health books. You may die of a misprint.' *Mark Twain*

Live a healthy lifestyle, with plenty of good food and exercise and, with a bit of luck, your only brush with the medical profession will be the occasional visit to the GP for a minor ailment.

But it's a unpredictable world, and at some time or other we all have an encounter with the health service – even if it's only to give birth. Alongside education, healthcare is the biggest issue on the political agenda, and though the NHS has pledged to cut outpatient appointment waiting lists to three months and inpatient appointments to six months, this won't happen until 2005. The only way to get the best out of healthcare until then (and possibly after) is to understand the system, then find out how to beat it.

WHAT ARE YOUR RIGHTS?

The 1992 Patient's Charter gave everyone rights which include:
- being seen as an outpatient within 13 weeks of referral from a GP
- being seen within 30 minutes of the time given for an outpatient's appointment
- being given a clear explanation of any proposed treatment, including risks and alternatives
- choosing whether to take part in medical research or student training
- having access to your health records or notes
- being given information on local health services, including what to expect and maximum waiting times
- a bed within two hours of admission to a casualty department
- being guaranteed admission for treatment by a specific date of no more than two years after being put on a waiting list by a consultant
- an operation within 30 days of a postponement
- having complaints investigated, with prompt full replies.

Since then **the present Labour Government (2001) has set certain standards** which they expect the NHS to achieve. These include:
- all emergency ambulances arriving within 14 minutes in urban areas and 19 minutes in rural areas
- being assessed immediately when going to a casualty department
- having a specific appointment time and being seen within 30 minutes of it.

Whether these targets have been achieved nearly ten years on is a matter of opinion (and ammunition for the Opposition benches) but the bottom line is that, if these targets are not achieved, you have the right to complain.

Need to see your medical records? The Access to Health Records Act, 1991 gives you the legal right to see those records written on paper after November 1991, and the Data Protection Act, 1984 gives you a legal right to see any records held on computer. Write to your GP or dentist for non-hospital records or your local health authority who hold your hospital records. If you were treated privately, whoever treated you will have those records. You should expect to be given access to your records within 40 days. You should be able to see records made within the last 40 days free of charge. The holder can charge up to £10 to show you older records and/or send photocopies.

The system does ensure, however, that **parts of your medical records could be withheld** if whoever holds them thinks that seeing them could seriously harm your physical or mental health.

You can see **your children's records**, but you need to have their consent. For very young children you can make a case to see them if you think it is in their best interests.

Living as a traveller. By the very nature of their nomadic lifestyle, travellers and gypsies choose not to be tied to one place for very long – one way to beat the system – but this can create problems when it comes to healthcare. These people can often slip through the net and proper care (such as dental or ante-natal) and follow-up treatment is often difficult to maintain. Nomadic people have rights, but these need to be reformed. See www.cf.ac.uk/claws/tlru/conf-summary.html to find out about new proposals put forward by the Traveller Law Research Unit which covers healthcare issues.

Health Facts:

- If you suffer from a stroke, make sure you are not in England. If you live in the South West, you have only a one-in-three chance of getting into a specialist care unit. If you live in Scotland, Wales or Northern Ireland, the chance is more than twice this.
- More people have heart attacks on a Monday morning than at any other time of the week.
- On a waiting list? You can find out how your local hospital is performing. Go to the Department & Health website at www.doh.gov.uk/performanceratings. Hospitals are categorised with a star rating from three stars to zero.
- 20 per cent of private healthcare revenue is from people funding their own treatment.

BEATING THE MEDICS

'**Even if you have a sympathetic GP, you've only got an appointment of seven minutes to win them round.**' *Jeff Braterman, British Homeopathic Association NHS Co-ordinator*

FACT: If you want to be seen quickly, live in Poole, Dorset, where 99 per cent of inpatients were admitted within 6 months. Don't live in the Surrey and Sussex Healthcare Trust area where only 51 per cent were. (*Department of Health, 2001*)

Unhappy with your doctor? You can **change your GP** anytime without having to give a reason, though it's a good idea to get a new one lined up before you leave your old one. Get recommendations from friends and ring up the practice to ask to be put on the doctor's list. It also works the other way round: your GP can drop you without explanation or because their patient list may be full. Your local Health Authority (details in your local phone book) is required by law to produce a list of local GPs, showing their age, sex, date of qualifications, what services their practice provides and who works there.

Before **choosing a GP** you are entitled to a look around and an interview. Some practices are more negative towards older patients, so if you are older, investigate this aspect before signing yourself up. Similarly if you are interested in alternative therapies, ask the GPs their view on referring patients for these or if there is a partner in the practice who specialises in them.

A dentist can also strike you from their practice – but not without giving you three months' notice.

Make sure you are in the right hands 1: avoid seeing a lecturer, see a consultant. Lecturers are academics and won't be as experienced in surgery.

Make sure you are in the right hands 2: try to fall ill or have an accident at any time other than the beginning of August. This is when the new medical students start work in hospitals (and when the consultants go on holiday).

Confused by what you're being told, or worried you will forget? You can **take someone with you** when you go in for a consultation. It helps to have another pair of ears to listen to what's being said (there can be a lot to take in at once) or even get them to take notes for you.

Doctors are not allowed to touch you without your permission. If you are a woman and your doctor is male, ask for a female member of staff to be present during an examination. If you're having surgery, you will be asked to sign a consent form, which asks you if there is any procedure you don't want doing. If it doesn't, and there is, write your amendment and then sign the form. If the doctor or surgeon then ignores your request, they would be committing an offence (of 'assault and battery') and would have to pay compensation – unless their actions can be justified in that it was immediately necessary to save your life. (See the section on Personal Injury and Compensation in the Law chapter.)

Want the best place in the ward? During a stay in hospital, make sure you get a bed by the door. Blame claustrophobia or a liking for a through draft. The food trolley will reach you a good half-hour before it gets to the other end of the ward, by which time the food will be, at best, lukewarm.

Just because **a teaching hospital trains doctors** does not mean you have to have a gaggle of them around your bed when you are examined. If you don't want to be on display as an educational exhibit, you are entitled to ask them to leave.

'I demand a second opinion'

A second opinion is not a vote of no-confidence in your doctor, but an entitlement. If you are told the same thing twice, it will help you adjust your preconceptions about your illness. **You have a right to a second opinion,** so make sure you ask if you want one. Barging in and demanding one could be offensive. Point out to your doctor that you just want reassurance; you're not questioning their judgement (even if you are).

Slow getting a second opinion? **Take matters into your own hands.** Call out a doctor in the evening. Most areas now have what's called a 'doctor's co-operative' for out-of-hours visits. So it's almost definitely not going to be your regular doctor who comes to see you. You will get short shrift, however, if your condition is only minor. You can also make an appointment to see another GP in the practice.

How We Beat The System

Chris Ottewell from Bristol found a successful treatment abroad:

'In 1995, I began to get earache and headaches. I went to my GP in 1996, who initially thought it was just earache, but referred me for a brain scan in 1997. It turned out I had an acoustic neuroma (AN), a brain tumour which was non-malignant, but at the rate it was growing would eventually kill me. I was offered radical brain surgery. I was horrified, both by what I heard about the risk and the side effects of surgery and by the fact that my ear would have to be destroyed to get at the tumour. I was put on the waiting list.

'Nine months later my parents heard an interview on the radio with a woman from Wales who was being treated for AN in the States. We managed to track down her email address and I got in touch. I started to investigate the treatment on the Web and found out that there was another way to treat my tumour. I emailed Dr Lederman at Staten Island University Hospital, and then we talked on the phone. He does a very precise radiotherapy which doesn't involve surgery. I bought my scans from the NHS for

£25 and sent them to him by email. On the strength of the scans he said he could treat me. I rang and arranged treatment and flew over, all within six weeks. It was fast and easy – I didn't even need to take time off work. My balance is back to normal, my hearing has improved and the tumour is shrunken. The market cost of this kind of treatment is $25,000, and there are charitable foundations that can help pay some of these costs.

'Sixteen months after diagnosis the operation on the NHS came through. Now I am campaigning to get this treatment available over here – it is actually much cheaper than surgery – about a quarter of the cost.'

WAITING LISTS

'The art of medicine consists of amusing the patients while Nature cures the disease.' *Voltaire*

FACT: Pay to go private in Germany instead of in the UK. One in five German hospital beds are empty. Prices for a cataract operation there are around £975 (compared with £2,500 here) and for a hip replacement £5,500 (£8,000–12,000 here). What's more, the NHS is now paying for patients to go to Europe for treatment.

It is your GP who refers you to a hospital consultant, who will then schedule you for an operation or suitable treatment. You then become a figure on a waiting list **but check that you are actually on the waiting list**. You might be 'under review' to see if your condition stabilises or improves, and this is a way that waiting-list figures are massaged to appear shorter than they actually are.

The early bird catches the doctor. Most hospitals book appointments in hour-long blocks. They will give six people, say, a three o'clock appointment. From there on in, it's first come, first served. So, **arriving just five minutes early may save you an hour's wait**.

GPs often allow a certain number of appointments outside normal surgery hours, so don't be fobbed off with 'there are no appointments' from the receptionist. **Insist on being seen today** and arrive at the end of surgery.

You don't have to take all the advice you are given as gospel. **Ask about other treatments** (your GP has a budget and the treatment he or she is suggesting may be the cheapest option). Enquire if your doctor has got written information about them so you can read them in the comfort of your own home, and always ask for a phone number of a support group so you can call for more information.

If your complaint or illness is something you've never come across before, ask your doctor or consultant if you can **talk to another patient with the same condition**, or if there is a support group. Exploit the information your GP practice or hospital holds.

Get expert opinions **if you are suffering from an unusual condition**, by asking to be referred to a teaching hospital. The doctors here are usually more up to date with the latest treatments and research.

Find another health authority: some health authorities have better success rates, lower costs or reduced waiting lists than others (including the one you live in). You can ask your doctor to refer you there. Doctors often presume that the patient would rather be treated locally and so won't refer you to a hospital outside your area even if it can offer better care. If you don't mind travelling, go back to your doctor with some quotes and you may get your hospital waiting time reduced. In 2001 *The Sunday Times* published a Good Hospital Guide. Go to www.sunday-times.co.uk.

Pay to be seen privately for the initial consultation – you will be seen within two to three weeks – then ask to be transferred on to the NHS waiting list. That will by-pass the initial consultation waiting time and put you onto the list quicker.

Alternatively fund yourself completely for a **one-off private treatment** – you don't need health insurance.

Ring around **consultants' secretaries** – they often know more than your GP. Then once you are on a waiting list, call the consultant's secretary daily and ask if there are any cancellations. This will remind her that you are available at short notice – and hopefully making a nuisance of yourself will get you seen quickly.

Go to Accident and Emergency (A and E) **during** *EastEnders* **or** *Coronation Street*. Wait until after them and you'll have a longer wait– as people wait to watch it before they go to hospital. Also try to avoid Friday and Saturday nights, when A and E is overflowing.

Have you a chronic condition and **been on a waiting list for an operation for months?** Some people have tried going to an A and E department and saying it's too painful to bear any longer. It may help bump you up the list, but A and E is very busy, and you'll get short shrift if you're faking.

Could any part of your health problem be **blamed on your working conditions?** If your job could be a causative factor, then you could get a private appointment paid for by the firm you work for – as in law, employer's responsibilities are getting greater. Although it is necessary to prove negligence on the part of the employer, back pain is particularly hard to disprove. (See Personal Injury in the Law chapter.)

Have your health problems checked whilst buying the groceries. Some large supermarkets have in-store clinics where you can pay for a one-off consultation. Also use the services of the pharmacist. Many are trained to give consultations on mild ailments.

Wait outside the surgery to see the receptionist in the morning before the phone starts ringing. You'll have the upper hand to get a quick appointment.

Surgeries' financial years run April to April. **Report your problem before April** and you have a much greater chance of getting it seen to in the next 12 months, before the money starts to run out.

As you are prioritised in order of need on a waiting list, **report any worsening of your condition** to your doctor immediately, and also let them know if you become pregnant. It is all evidence to accelerate your treatment.

To speed up the waiting time for **private infertility treatment**, what about payment in kind? Payment for donors to infertility clinics is about to be abolished, which is likely to cause a shortage in donors. Clinics may be more inclined to speed up your treatment if the fertile person in the couple is willing to donate sperm or eggs.

For minor complaints, or if you are unsure whether to call out a doctor, you can call NHS Direct on 0845 4647 or through the Internet at www.nhsdirect.nhs.uk. Alternatively, you can visit other general medical sites such as www.askyourpharmacist.co.uk or www.surgerydoor.co.uk. The Internet is a valuable source of information on medical matters, but proceed with a certain amount of caution and common sense. Use only reputable sites that are written or checked by named, qualified medical professionals and avoid sites sponsored by commercial organisations. Your GP has your medical records and seeing you in person will result in a more accurate diagnosis.

Find out where the queues are: **The National Waiting List Helpline** (020 8983 1133) has access to consultants' lists at hospitals around the country, and can tell you the average waiting time for inpatient appointments and outpatient procedures. **The College of Health Helpline** can also give you information on waiting times in hospitals around the country (Tel: 020 8983 1133).

How We Beat The System

Lucy Vernon's grandfather had a novel way of beating the visiting hours:
'My grandfather ran a huge grocery business and always used to go to work in a white coat. If he ever wanted to visit anyone in hospital, he'd just walk in whether it was visiting time or not. Everyone assumed he was a doctor and he came and went as he pleased.'

FACT: A 2001 report by the British Medical Association recognised that the NHS could not survive in its present form, and that patients will have to pay privately for a growing amount of healthcare, including expensive drugs and treatments.

A little knowledge

'People don't wait any more for their doctor to give them information.'
Markella Boudioni, Patients' Association

Want to know who's best? Contact local support groups for your medical condition. They should be able to tell you which hospitals, doctors and surgeons are the 'best' in that area of medicine. Again, in 2001, *The Sunday Times* published a Good Hospital Guide. Go to www.sunday-times.co.uk.

You can also help yourself by **educating yourself in your illness**. The Internet and most of the large number of support groups have up-to-date information on treatments and where you can get them. They provide invaluable emotional support as well. GPs do not have the time to research every illness in great detail, so you will need to do a certain amount of research yourself.

COSMETIC PLASTIC SURGERY

'A plastic surgeon is one who has credit card facilities.' *Mike Barfield in* The Oldie

It's no coincidence that it's movie stars who have plastic surgery. They are the ones who can afford it. Cosmetic plastic surgery is very expensive (nose reconstruction – or rhinoplasty – costs about £2,700 and breast reduction between £4,000 and £5,000). However **you may be able to have treatment on the NHS** if you can convince your GP and consultant that the size of your nose/bust is causing you mental distress and depression, or in the case of large breasts, shoulder and neck pain. Play it up if necessary. 'Cosmetic surgery is a great drain on resources,' says one plastic surgeon, 'and only a few health authorities will allow it. In fact, most are thinking of banning it altogether. You will need to find a doctor with a sympathetic ear.'

Your plastic surgeon should be a member of the **British Association of Aesthetic Plastic Surgeons** (BAAPS). Call the General Medical Council to make sure that the surgeon of your choice is on the specialist register of plastic surgeons. You can get a full list from:

BAAPS
35–43 Lincoln's Inn Fields
London WC2A 3PN
Tel: 020 7405 2234

Whatever surgery you're contemplating, find out how often the surgeon has done the operation. Have they always gone smoothly or have there been law suits? **Ask to speak to former patients** and look at before-and-after pictures.

Get ahead with your research: surf the Internet. www.plasticsurgery.org is an American site but very comprehensive in the subject matter and patients' questions and answers it covers.

MAKING A COMPLAINT

There are good systems in place concerning complaints against the medical profession or local health authority. The following will make sure your complaint is effective:

Successful complaints are quick ones. The system won't take you seriously if you wait ages before grinding your axe. Try first to resolve a complaint or problem informally (i.e. go to the medic direct/write to the practice manager in a GP practice) before starting the more formal complaints' process. Be prepared for a long haul. It can be a time-consuming process which, sadly, is unlikely to be resolved quickly. Stick to your guns.

Always keep copies of letters and documents. Make the most of your local **Community Health Council** – a good place to start when it comes to getting help and advice. The CHC is the local watchdog, checking on what happens in the local health services. You can find their number in the phone book.

Before you can bring in the Health Service Commissioner (see below), you should approach the relevant NHS authority and be able to show that the problem that occurred has caused you injustice or hardship.

The **Health Service Commissioner** is the ombudsman for the NHS. The service is free and totally independent of the NHS. They can investigate whether the local health authority or trust has provided the proper service or not, or has been guilty of maladministration (not following the proper procedures, giving the wrong information). The Health Service commissioner is independent of the NHS and the Government. However, the commissioner will not usually consider a complaint if you have not tried to resolve the matter through the NHS complaints procedure. Contact the commissioner at:

The Health Service Commissioner for England
11th Floor
Millbank Tower
London SW1P 4QP
Tel: 020 7217 4051

If you have a complaint about a family doctor, dentist, pharmacist, optician or member of their staff, you should talk to the local NHS Trust or health authority. GPs, dentists and so on are independent of the NHS, but offer their services under contract to the health authority. If they don't uphold that contract, the HA can intervene. You'll find details of your local HA in the phone book or on your NHS medical card.

Put **a complaint about a family doctor** in writing to the general manager of your local HA or NHS Trust as soon as possible. For dentists, the complaint should be made within six months after the end of the treatment which caused the complaint or within 13 weeks after the problem came to your notice – whichever is sooner. Late complaints can be dealt with in certain circumstances (for instance, if you were too ill to do anything about it). The HA can't award compensation; you would have to pursue that in the courts in which event there is a longer limitation period.

You can **get information and advice about pursuing compensation** from a solicitor specialising in such cases or from Action for Victims of Medical Accidents. The AVMA will give basic, free advice and put you in touch with a specialist solicitor.

> AVMA
> Bank Chambers
> I London Road
> Forest Hill
> London SE23 3TP
> Tel: 020 8291 2793

(For cases of personal injury as a result of medical malpractice, see Personal Injury in the Law chapter.)

FACT: If you are the driver of a car in a road traffic accident and the victim claims compensation against you and is paid, the NHS Trust who treated them is entitled to claim £354 against your insurance as the driver. An emergency treatment fee may also be charged by a doctor attending the scene so claim it back from your insurance company.

MEDICINES AND PRESCRIPTIONS

Who is entitled? The following are entitled to free prescriptions:
- People aged 60 or over
- Children under the age of 16
- Young people aged 17 or 18 in full-time education
- People or their partners in receipt of income support, Job Seekers' Allowance, working families tax credit or disabled person's tax credit (if the difference between the maximum amount of credit and the actual award is £71 or less)
- People named on a current NHS Low Income Scheme Full Help certificate (HC2)
- Expectant mothers and women who have given birth to a live child or a child stillborn within the past 12 months
- People with one of the specified medical conditions listed in leaflet HC11. (These include conditions needing continuous surgical dressings or appliances, forms of hyperadrenalism which need situation therapy, some forms of diabetes, myxoedema and epilepsy, and prescriptions for people with a continuous disability.)
- War disablement pensioners.

Get your contraception free. All contraception is free through your GP except, curiously, condoms which are only free when you obtain them from a Family Planning Clinic (look in the phone book for your nearest branch).

Make the most of exemptions. You are also exempt from paying for dental care if you are pregnant and an NHS patient, and for 12 months after giving birth. Make sure you have as much dental treatment as you can within the period of exemption.

How We Beat The System

Treatment to make you smile
Whilst she was pregnant, Angela complained that the bridge of teeth at the front of her mouth was moving and causing problems. Her dentist took an impression of her mouth and submitted the request for dental work to the local dental board. They agreed the work was necessary and she had over £500 of dental work with a bill to pay of just £60.

One way to get **free treatments and prescriptions** is to become part of a drugs' trial. Make sure you get as much information about the drug as possible (i.e. any possible side effects or risks), and you are allowed to pull out of the trial at any time. You should be shown the results (although bear in mind that this could take years).

Beat the cost of expensive medicines, lotions and treatments – go for the unbranded 'generic' version of the same things. These are perfectly good, serviceable products and considerably cheaper, but just don't make as much profit as the higher profile branded goods. The letters BP (British Pharmacopoeia) and BPC (British Pharmaceutical Codex) on the products are your indication of quality.

The following generic non-prescription products are just a few of the ones available at chemists where there is a qualified pharmacist in charge; most are still considered to be drugs. **Save money when buying medicine** by taking the branded product to the chemist and asking if there is a generic equivalent.
- Acetone – removes nail polish
- Acetylsalicylic acid mixture – aspirin in a plain pack
- Aqueous cream – as effective as moisturiser
- Ascorbic acid – vitamin C
- Benzoic acid ointment – an acne-reducing cream
- Blackcurrant syrup – tastes just the same as a certain popular blackcurrant drink
- Boric acid lotion – same formulation as other eye lotions
- Calcium tablets – unbranded
- Cascara elixir and castor oil – laxatives
- Oil of cloves – relieves toothache
- Co-codamol tablets – codeine
- Cod-liver oil
- Eucalyptus oil

- Ferrous fumarate and ferrous gluconate – cheaper than iron tablets from vitamin companies
- Hydrocortisone cream – dermatological cream
- Liquorice lozenges and liquorice extract – relief of peptic ulcers
- Lysol – disinfectant
- Menthol and menthol eucalyptus inhalation – helps relieve colds and sore throats
- Olive oil – traditional remedy for earache
- Purified talc – cheaper than branded talcum powder
- Sodium bicarbonate
- Thiamine – Vitamin B
- Zinc and castor oil cream – traditional ointment for babies' bottoms.

Cheaper traditional medicines include:
- Witch hazel – relieves sprains and bruises
- Calamine lotion – relieves minor skin rashes and irritation
- Cream of magnesia – relieves acidity in the stomach and also acts as a mild laxative
- Plain senna tablets – do wonders for constipation
- Kaolin – deals with diarrhoea
- Iodine – an effective skin disinfectant
- Lanolin – as good for dry skin as an expensive cream (some people may have an allergy to it, however, so aqueous cream is a good alternative).

Too busy to get to the chemist? Log on to www.pharmacy2u.co.uk to get prescriptions dispensed and to order over-the-counter medicines and treatments. Over 10,000 items are available and if your prescription is received by 12 noon, the medication will be delivered securely to your door next day.

There is **no standard charge for an eye test** – so shop around for the best deal. If your work involves you regularly using a VDU for continuous spells of an hour or more at a time, you are entitled to ask your employer to pay for an eye test, plus further tests at regular intervals. If tests show you need glasses for the VDU work, your employer will have to pay for a basic pair of frames and lenses.

COMPLEMENTARY MEDICINE

You can get **complementary therapies on the NHS** – there are even five homeopathic NHS hospitals. Contact the British Homeopathic Association for details, go to your GP with the facts and ask for a referral.

You can get **alternative therapies on the NHS** – but it may depend upon where you live. Homeopathy, massage, aromatherapy, reflexology and shiatsu are all available. If you are interested, go with the details yourself and suggest it to your GP, as he or she may not themselves be aware of what is on offer. When selecting your GP, you are entitled to see their qualifications. A GP with qualifications in an alternative therapy is much more likely to refer you for treatment in one if you ask.

How We Beat The System

Jeff Braterman battled to receive homeopathic treatment:

'I have moderate to severe chronic eczema for which my GP could only prescribe steroids. I wanted to try homeopathy, because I knew eczema doesn't respond well to conventional treatment and taking steroids long term has side effects. My GP was sympathetic, but didn't think she could refer me for homeopathic treatment – apparently the Primary Care Group for our area 'discourages' such referrals. But I heard of something called 'out of area treatment' where in special cases a GP can refer a patient for treatment at a place with which they do not have a service agreement. The GP's clinical decision on each individual case should be the one that counts, and my GP was supporting my referral.

'I wrote to the Chief Executive of the Primary Care Group in person, asking him to clarify for me in writing what the position was. They wrote back to say that they do discourage these type of referrals, but in the end the decision rests with the GP. So I went back to my GP with the letter from the Primary Care Group, and she was able to refer me for homeopathic treatment.

'I've now been in treatment for a year. I've made a real improvement – my eczema is mild now, it no longer causes me embarrassment, and it is not itchy any more. Emotionally I feel a lot happier and more optimistic, and I'm delighted that I don't have to take steroids.'

Many **practitioners of alternative treatments have no system:** in fact, there is no legal requirement for alternative practitioners to be registered. However, many do belong to organisations which set levels of competence for their particular area. But don't be fooled by lots of letters after a practitioner's name. It might indicate years of study, but it could equally be the result of a weekend course.

Nor is there any legal requirement for them to have **insurance**, so protect yourself by checking first.

You can **get information on therapies** and their practitioners from The British Complementary Medicine Association or the Institute of Complementary Medicine (addresses at the end of the chapter).

HIV AND SEXUALLY TRANSMITTED DISEASES

The results of an HIV test or other sexually transmitted disease are confidential and won't be sent to your doctor or anyone else, so you can stop any mention of a test appearing on your medical notes. If you go to a genito-urinary clinic for testing, **you can even use a false name**. HIV testing involves a simple blood test which you can get at a sexual health clinic or genito-urinary clinic. Blood is checked for the HIV virus as well as chlamydia, gonorrhoea and hepatitis.

There will be a genital examination for warts and herpes. Pre-test counselling will be offered as will a full sexual health screen and post-test counselling. Results are usually available within a week, although you may be able to find a clinic which offers same-day testing or results within three days.

The National Aids Helpline (0800 567123) will have a list of genito-urinary clinics as well as support groups.

HIV and life insurance. Having an HIV test won't affect your life insurance if you've tested negative. Existing policies are unlikely to be affected. You are advised to declare your status if asked. If you become HIV positive before organising life insurance, there are specialist insurance agencies who may provide some cover; contact the Terrence Higgins Trust on 020 7831 0330 for information.

HAVING A BABY

Maternity care within the health service is a system you can beat by experience. The third-time mother will be better at making the most of the facilities of the maternity unit and post-natal care, than the first timer who may be overawed by the whole experience. However, because hopefully you are not 'ill' (just exhausted!) after giving birth and with this advice, you can be more in control of your delivery and your hospital stay.

The Patient's Charter and maternity services

The Government has published a special charter for pregnant women and new mothers. This explains your rights and the standards of service you can expect to receive during pregnancy, the baby's birth and post-natal care. Among other things, it covers:

- your choice about who will be responsible for looking after you; where you have your baby; the type of care you wish to receive, for example whether you wish to have your care led by a midwife, GP or consultant obstetrician
- what information you can expect to have to help you reach decisions about your care including information such as appropriate tests before the baby is born (ante-natal tests); and
- the care of your baby.

These rights and standards are part of the Government's policy as set out in *Changing Childbirth*. You can get copies of the Maternity Charter from your GP's surgery, ante-natal clinic, hospital, Health Authority, Community Health Council and the local library. Or you can ring the National Health Information Service on 0800 665544.

> **FACT:** Of all women born in 1972, almost 25 per cent will remain childless at 45, compared to 16 per cent of those born in 1952. The birth rates across Europe have dropped by a third since 1965. In Germany and Italy, they have reached the point where they are actually lower than the death rates. (*The Salvation Army*)

To ensure your child is legitimate 1: you must be married before its birth even if conception took place out of wedlock. If you were married at the time of conception but divorced at the time of birth, this still constitutes legitimacy. If the father dies between conception and birth, his child is still born legitimate. But you can marry the child's father after the birth, and the child becomes legitimate retrospectively; you can re-register the birth and get a new birth certificate.

To ensure your child is legitimate 2: you must have the consent of your husband before fertility treatment. Even if the treatment involved donor insemination, the husband, not the donor, is considered to be the legal father of the child.

To ensure he or she inherits a title, your child must be legitimate. Legitimate and illegitimate children are treated exactly the same under the law, except an illegitimate child is not automatically entitled to British citizenship nor can he or she inherit a hereditary title.

Want to choose the sex of your child? NHS fertility clinics are forbidden from allowing parents to choose the sex of the child unless there is a risk of an inherited genetic disease that is gender specific. Use a private clinic which allows this option.

Feel you had the wrong start in life? A child can sue for damage caused while it was in the womb if that damage was caused by 'negligence' (perhaps from smoking, drugs or alcohol), and that includes the mother's.

For a birth not to be officially registered by law, miscarriage must take place before 24 weeks of pregnancy.

Expectant mother? You are entitled to free healthcare and dental care during the pregnancy and for the first year of the baby's life (see Medicines and Prescriptions).

We're all in the system right from the start. You have to register your child's birth within 42 days (21 days in Scotland) in person at the local register office (even a stillbirth), and it's against the law not to do so. Once registration has been completed your baby is officially 'in the system' – a number on a computer for life. Your baby will need to be registered for you to be eligible for Child Benefit or to register the baby with a doctor, and a birth certificate is critical for a child for him or her to be able to get a passport/receive National Insurance/be educated. It doesn't have to be you or the father who actually registers the birth – it can be an uncle, aunt, grandmother or even the hospital porter so long as he was present at the birth.

Decided you don't like your baby's name? If you realise that naming the child after every single player in your favourite football team was not such a good idea, you have a year to change the name without question. Contact your local register office.

Unmarried mothers have the same rights as a married one. The system allows you to claim financial support for the child from the father via the Child Support Agency. You can be married to someone else and still claim. You will start with sole legal control of your child, but the father has the right to acquire joint parental responsibility which can be agreed between the parents or sorted out in court.

Worried you will have no say in your child's upbringing? Unmarried parents can complete a form called a Parental Responsibility Agreement which gives them joint legal responsibility for their child. The father has an equal and independent say while the mother gives up her sole rights over the child. The agreement lasts until the child is 18. You can get the form from the local county court offices and it should then be sent to:

Principal Registry of the Family Division
First Avenue House
42–49 High Holborn
London WC1V 6NP

(For more information on matrimonial law, and adoption and surrogacy, see the Law chapter.)

Unless there is any medical reason for staying, **you can leave hospital within six hours of giving birth**. You will be under GP care and visited by a midwife for the first ten days after the baby is born, then by the health visitor. Maternity departments are notoriously stretched and you could be more comfortable (and cherished) at home.

Get the best maternity care by providing the essentials yourself. The NHS will give you the bare minimum for yourself or your baby, so don't expect it. You will need to provide nappies, cotton wool and other hygiene necessities, as well as sanitary protection and toiletries for your own comfort. Take in a store of snacks too. Hospital meals appear at odd times and you may need sustenance in between.

Get yourself a private room for you and your baby in an NHS hospital by paying for an 'amenity bed'. If possible, try to book in advance to be sure of getting one.

Beat hospital altogether. **You are entitled to a home birth** even for your first baby, if you request one, and a midwife is obliged to attend, though not a doctor. If a doctor is needed, they have to come when called, but not before. The majority of doctors will not recommend a home birth first time around for two reasons:

- because first deliveries can be the most difficult and complications may occur. It is better for the mother and the baby to be in hospital where the right care can be given. Home births work well in Scandinavia because the system is more geared towards it; there are more midwives per patient and teams of doctors ready to attend if necessary.
- because doctors these days work in an environment of defensive medicine and are terrified of litigation; that if the worst happened, patients would say 'my GP said it would be okay'.

Heart set on a Caesarean? Caesarean section is a complicated operation which has risks for the mother. For this reason doctors are not keen to recommend them unless they are 'medically indicated' – normally delivery would be difficult or dangerous. **Pay for private maternity care** and you are more likely to have a choice.

What are your maternity rights?
Ante-natal care
- The pregnant employee is entitled to paid time off work to attend ante-natal classes and appointments if it is medically recommended.
- The employee is entitled to their normal rate of pay while they are at the classes or appointment.
- An employer cannot unreasonably refuse to let the employee go and the employee does not have to attend these sessions outside their normal work hours.
- Though if an employee only works part-time it may be reasonable for her to arrange the appointments outside work hours if possible.
- After the first appointment the employer is entitled to a medical certificate stating that the employee is pregnant and also proof of the future appointment(s), such as an appointment card.

Post-natal rights
See the chapters on Work and Finance for your financial and leave rights after giving birth.

HEALTHCARE FOR THE ELDERLY

FACT: One in three women and one in five men is estimated to need care at sometime during retirement. Every year 130,000 go into care.

Whilst the NHS will pay for what is deemed to be nursing care, the bill for social or personal care (eating, washing and mobility) goes to the Department of Social Security (DSS). Patients are means tested and those with more than £16,000 in assets will not qualify for state funding. In fact the DSS can force the sale of the patient's property to recoup care costs. There's a grey area here too about what is meant by 'nursing'. A cancer sufferer needing medication will be looked after free. An Alzheimer's sufferer, who cannot be helped by medication, might have to pay his own way.

But in Scotland, the Executive has promised to fund long-term personal and nursing care for the elderly. The pressure's on for the same to happen in England and Wales.

Call in the troops – to counteract the proven covert restriction of services to older people, get in as many family members as possible to fight your case, proving your importance to the family.

Choosing a residential home for an elderly relative? Choose one in which a doctor has a financial stake. Conflicts of medical interest against financial interest often arise, and homes with doctors for owners are probably more sympathetic to medical arguments.

If you have been diagnosed with a terminal illness, **sign over power of attorney** at an early stage. This will allow relatives to take decisions on your behalf once you are unable to do so for yourself and will protect your interests, including your financial ones. (See the Finance chapter for more information.)

MEDICAL INSURANCE

FACT: One million people are seen in private hospitals, with 850,000 operations carried out each year. Nearly one in ten of us has private healthcare insurance.

Private medical insurance is **the sure fire way of beating the National Health Service**. It covers you for medical consultations, pays for operations and private hospital care and means you can avoid waiting lists. You have more choice about when and where you have your treatment. Patients who pay to be seen privately sometimes receive new (and better) treatment than is available on the NHS.

But the privilege doesn't come cheap. If you're young and fit, there are no financial benefits in taking out private medical insurance now. **The payments tend to rise the older you get**. So if you are contemplating taking out private cover, ask what the payments will be 10, 20 or so years down the line to see what you are letting yourself in for.

Premiums vary, so shop around. See if you can become involved in a company scheme, but beware: cover varies so **check the small print very carefully**. You may well have to pay an excess, and cover some of the cost of your treatment yourself (such as ordinary dentistry, childbirth, infertility treatments, injuries caused by a dangerous sport and so on).

Forewarned is forearmed. **There are no minimum standards of care in the private health sector.** Private clinics and hospitals are regulated only through the 1984 Registered Homes Act, which puts them on a par with nursing homes. Private hospitals have very little facility to deal with critical cases and in 2000 between 500 and 1,000 patients whose condition had deteriorated were transferred to NHS hospitals.

Permanent health insurance pays out a regular income if you are unable to work because of sickness or disability. Most policies pay up to 75 per cent (they can't pay more by law) of the sum you would have been earning, minus any state benefits you are eligible for and any other income.

But most permanent health insurance policies make you wait at least four weeks after you stop work before you can expect to receive payment.

Reduce your premiums by:
- extending this period for up to 26 or more weeks
- reducing the cover (i.e. less than 75 per cent) but you need to be sure that you have adequate savings or alternative income that you can call upon.

In a dispute? Most specialist health insurers are members of the **Personal Insurance Arbitration Scheme** – PIAS (address below). If you get into dispute over an insurance claim, you will need to approach them. However, you have to get your insurer's permission to do this. The PIAS decision is final so you can't go to court afterwards if you are still unhappy with the decision. So find a health insurer which is part of the **Insurance Ombudsman Bureau**, and you have more going for you. You don't have to get the consent of your insurers to approach the Insurance Ombudsman Bureau, their decision is not binding and you can still go to court afterwards.

DEATH

'There is no cure for birth and death, save to enjoy the interval.' *George Santayana, 1863–1952*

Death facts:
- The death must be registered within five days at the local register office.
- You will need the medical certificate, pension books, a pink form (Form 100) from a coroner if there was an autopsy, birth and marriage certificates, life insurance policies.
- The registrar will need to know the date and place of death, the deceased's last address, occupation and whether they were getting a pension or allowance from public funds. In return, you will receive a Certificate for Burial or Cremation (green form) unless you have an Order for Burial or Certificate for Cremation from the coroner; a death certificate if you want one for the will, pension claims, insurance policies etc; a Certificate of Registration of Death (for Social Services).
- If the death was of a stillborn baby, you will be given a Certificate for Burial or Cremation and a Certificate of Registration of Stillbirth.

The coroner will have to carry out a postmortem to determine the cause of death:
- if the doctor hasn't seen the deceased in the last 14 days
- if the cause of death isn't known

- if the death was suspicious, violent or unnatural
- if the death happened during an operation
- if the death happened while in prison or in police custody
- if it was caused by an industrial disease.

Death is deadly serious, but **don't be swept along by the bureaucracy** which surrounds it. If someone dies at home, the body needn't be removed immediately. A doctor will need to sign the death certificate, but you can get a nurse to help you lay the body out if you don't want funeral directors involved.

Not religious and want an alternative to a traditional church or crematorium funeral? Contact the British Humanist Association on 0990 168122 who will put you in touch with someone in your area who can offer alternatives.

Avoid the rigmarole of a funeral 1: If you are unwilling to dispose of the body, the local authority is obliged to do it for you (Public Health, Act 1984, Control of Disease, part 111, disposal of dead bodies, section 46), but they will send you the bill.

Avoid the rigmarole of a funeral 2: The law does not require you to use a church or crematorium. You could be buried in the back garden. But you will have to apply to the local planning authority and water authorities to see if they allow it (long, drawn-out process), and burial has to be at an adequate depth. A body in the garden tends to knock 10 per cent off the value of a property, and if a dear relative is buried under their favourite apple tree, you might find it hard emotionally to move house anyway.

Avoid the rigmarole of a funeral 3: Have your ashes scattered. In theory this can be done anywhere, though it is courtesy to ask permission if it is to be done on private land (golf courses are very popular). The Society of Allied and Independent Funeral Directors suggest you scatter the ashes early in the morning, and www.uk-funerals.co.uk sensibly advise you stand up wind as you empty the urn…

Avoid the rigmarole of a funeral 4: Leave your body to medical research. Make sure you inform your nearest and dearest, and include your request in your will. You can't avoid the whole thing completely though: medical schools are obliged to organise a funeral within two years of the death.

Avoid the rigmarole of a funeral 5: Be alternative. You can be:
- buried in one of 70 woodland burial sites around the country, in either a cardboard or wicker coffin or even a shroud. A tree or small marker will be put on your grave.
- buried at sea in one of two permitted sites: Newhaven or Needles Spoils Ground to the west of the Isle of Wight. You (or rather your next of kin) will need a Coroner's Out of England Form and a free licence from the Department for Environment, Food and Rural Affairs (020 7238 5872).

For more information visit www.uk-funerals.co.uk.

Can't afford the funeral? There are grants and loans to pay for funerals, up to around £600 plus disbursements which include cremation fees, doctor's fees and a contribution towards flowers. This won't cover all the costs though. A funeral with a hearse, one car and a crematorium service will be nearer £1,300. Ask the Department of Social Security for form SF200.

Make sure you are buried by the State: be on DSS benefit when you die.

At the time of going to press, no way has been found to beat death.

(For more information on wills see the Law chapter.)

Weird and wonderful health laws

Failure to flush a public toilet after use in Singapore may result in very hefty fines.

In Australia, children may not purchase cigarettes, but they may smoke them.

In Indiana, you can use it as a defence in court that, in the legitimate practice of your religious beliefs, you provided treatment by spiritual means through prayer to a dependent child, in lieu of medical care.

Thankfully, in Waterloo, Nebraska, barbers are forbidden from eating onions between 7am and 7pm.

There is a penalty of 20 krona in Denmark for failure to report when a person has died.

In Canada, citizens are not permitted to remove bandages in public, and the city of Guelph is classified as a 'no-pee' zone.

USEFUL WEBSITES

www.drfoster.co.uk (Independent guide to hospitals, produced with Boots the chemist. Includes broad information on waiting lists and performance)

http://surgerydoor.co.uk (A truly comprehensive health website for UK public and health professionals alike)

www.open.gov.uk/doh (Department of Health)

http://webmd.com (US site with help to find specialists)

www.onhealth.com (Chatty US health site)

www.netdoctor.co.uk (Medical information)

www.nhsdirect.nhs.uk (The NHS site for advice on medical problems)

www.nhs.uk/patientsvoice (The official site for the NHS with details of how to pursue complaints effectively)

www.askyourpharmacist.co.uk (Independent site for online consultations and advice)

www.bupa.co.uk (Health news and information from this leading private health insurer)

www.trusthomeopathy.org (Site for the British Homeopathic Association)

www.patients-association.com

www.patient.co.uk/selfhelp (List of UK patient support groups)

www.cancerbacup.org.uk (More than 2,000 pages of support for sufferers and their families)

www.hfea.gov.uk

See also *The Good Web Guide to Health*, published by The Good Web Guide, £12.99.

USEFUL ADDRESSES

Accident Line
The Law Society
Freepost
London WC2A 1BR
Tel: 0500 192939

Action for Victims of Medical Accidents (AVMA)
Bank Chambers
1 London Road
Forest Hill
London SE23 3TP
Tel: 020 8281 2793

Association of Community Health Councils for England & Wales
30 Drayton Park
London N5 1PB
Tel: 020 7609 8405

British Agency for Adoption & Fostering
Skyline House
200 Union Street
London SE1 0LX
Tel: 020 7793 2000

British Allergy Foundation
Deepdene House
30 Belgrove Road
Welling
Kent DA16 3PY
Tel: 020 8303 8525

British Association of Aesthetic Plastic Surgeons (BAAPS)
35–43 Lincoln's Inn Fields
London WC2A 3PN
Tel: 020 7405 2234

British Association of Cancer United Patients (BACUP)
Tel: 0800 181199

The British Complementary Medicine Association
St Charles Hospital
Exmoor Street
London W10 6DZ
Tel: 020 8964 1205

British Homeopathic Association
15 Clerkenwell Close
London EC1R 0AA
Tel: 020 7566 7800

British Medical Association (BMA)
Tavistock Square
London WC1H 9JP
Tel: 020 7387 4499

Child Support Agency
Helpline: 0345 133133

College of Health
The Data Protection Registrar
Wycliffe House
Water Lane
Wilmslow
Cheshire SK9 5AF
Tel: 01625 545700
www.dataprotection.gov.uk
Email: data@wycliffe.demon.co.uk

DoH Communications Office
Tel: 0541 555455
Can supply league tables and Patient's Charter

Principal Registry of the Family Division
First Avenue House
42–49 High Holborn
London WC1V 6NP

Funeral Ombudsman
26–28 Bedford Row ·
London WC1R 4HE
Tel: 020 7430 1112

General Dental Council
37 Wimpole Street
London W1M 8DQ
Tel: 020 7486 2171

General Medical Council
44 Hallam Street
London W1N 6AE
Tel: 020 7580 7642

General Optical Council
41 Harley Street
London W1N 2DJ
Tel: 020 7580 3898

Health Information Service
Tel: 0800 665544
Can supply information on your local
   Health Authority and local waiting lists

The Health Service Commissioner
11th Floor
Millbank Tower
London SW1P 4QP
Tel: 020 7217 4051

Health Service Ombudsman
Church House
Great Smith Street
London SW1P 3BW
Tel: 020 7276 2035

**Human Fertilisation & Embryology
   Authority**
Paxton House
30 Artillery Lane
London E1 7LS
Tel: 020 7377 5077

The Institute of Complementary Medicine
PO Box 194
London SE16 1QZ
Tel: 020 7237 5156

Insurance Ombudsman Bureau
135 Park Street
London SE1 9EA
Tel: 020 7928 7600

**International Stress Management
   Association**
South Bank University
LPSS
103 Borough Road
London SE1 0AA

Maternity Alliance
45 Beak Street
London EC2P 2LX
Tel: 020 7588 8582

Migraine Action Association
178a High Road
Byfleet
Surrey KT14 7ED
www.migraine.org.uk

National Asthma Campaign
Helpline: 0345 010203

National Childbirth Trust (NCT)
Alexandra House
Oldham Terrace
Acton
London W3 6NH
Tel: 020 8992 8637
www.nct-online.org

National Eczema Society
Information line: 020 7388 3444

National Foster Care Association
87 Blackfriars Road
London SE1 8HA
Tel: 020 7620 6400

National Register of Personal Trainers
Thornton House
Thornton Road
Wimbledon
London SW19 4NG
Tel: 020 8944 6688

National Waiting List Helpline
Tel: 020 8983 1133

NHS Direct
Tel: 0845 4647

Overseas Adoption Helpline
Tel: 0990 168742

Patients Association
PO Box 935
Harrow
Middlesex HA1 3YJ
Tel: 020 8423 9111

Patient's Charter
Freepost
London SE99 7XU

Personal Insurance Arbitration Scheme
Chartered Institute of Arbitrators
International Arbitration Centre
24 Angel Gate
City Road
London EC1V 2RS
Tel: 020 7837 4483

Housing

'Property is theft.' *Pierre-Joseph Proudhon*

It is said that we Brits are obsessed with the roof over our heads. Not surprising really, when the average property in the South East costs over £192,000 (Land Registry 2001). Buying property may be the most painful financial outlay of your lifetime, but it has also shown itself to be the safest form of long-term investment. Because we don't spend this kind of money too often though, it's important to get the details right. Be informed and you'll be armed against canny professionals and unscrupulous vendors; that way you'll get the best return on your investment.

LODGING, LEASING AND LETTING

If you're not on the property ladder (and are not tempted to put a foot on the first rung), renting is not necessarily flushing money down the drain. Know what you are doing and you can breeze through life with armfuls of rights and the smug expression on your face of one unburdened with the albatross of a mortgage around their neck.

> **FACT:** In the UK 2.1 million households rent through the private sector – that's 11 per cent of all housing and that figure is predicted to rise to 20 per cent in the next ten years.

There are basics to any rental agreement, which tenant and landlord are bound by law to observe, and you need to make sure they are included in your contract. These basics are so fundamental that they are considered binding whether they appear in the contract or not (in which case they are called 'implied terms'). This implied covenant applies to the lease of a dwelling for less than seven years. They are:

- The landlord has to keep in repair the structure and exterior of the dwelling (including drains, gutters and external pipes).
- The landlord must keep in repair and proper working order the installations in the dwelling for the supply of water, gas and electricity and sanitation and for water heating.
- If you are offering furnished accommodation, the furniture should comply with fire and safety regulations.
- If the landlord fails to uphold their duties and the property becomes a health

hazard, the local authority can apply pressure until the situation is improved. Local magistrates can order this to be done. As a last resort, you can appeal to your MP.

- Tenants must pay rent according to the terms of the agreement.
- The tenant is entitled to live free from disturbance by the landlord.
- However, if the landlord gives 24 hours written notice, they must be allowed access.
- Any improvements the tenants wish to make must be approved by the landlord.

As a landlord, you'll prefer an **'assured short-hold tenancy'** – all tenancies are now assured short holds unless the parties agree to the contrary, provided that the tenant is not a company. The landlord has a guaranteed right to repossess the property only, of course, after the period of the tenancy has expired.

As a tenant, you'll prefer an **'assured tenancy'** which gives the tenant several rights over the landlord. The tenant can stay on as long as the landlord can't establish a valid reason to require possession. The property has to be the tenant's main home.

Need **somewhere to rent** quickly? View a property as soon as possible and ensure that you have at least a month's rent and a deposit ready to pay out. Have references ready too from your bank, previous landlords and your employer, as your new landlord may wish to take them up. It will speed things up too if you have your own possessions insured or ready to insure.

Make sure you have the **upper hand on the contract**. Tenants have more rights now than ever before. You can stipulate that you want a clause in the agreement which allows you to quit the property for certain reasonable reasons (i.e. if your job moves location). The tenancy agreement should also include a term for renewal.

If you think you are **being charged too much rent** contact the Rent Assessment Officer (every council has one) who will be able to tell you if your rent is reasonable and around the going rate. Be aware, though, that you can only have your rent assessed when the lease comes up for renewal.

Paid out a **returnable deposit** to rent a flat or house? The rule of thumb is that letting agents keep the interest on your deposit once the amount is returned to you, but you can insist before you sign a contract that you wish to have your deposit back with interest at the end of the rental term. There may be a charge for this as the letting agent will have to strip out your interest from the pool earned on clients' accounts. Make sure your letting agent is a member of ARLA, the Association of Residential Letting Agents (01923 896555) who insist that its members take out professional indemnity insurance, have separate clients' accounts and join its bonding scheme.

If you are **leasing a property with a short lease** – jump in there. Most leaseholders have the right to buy the freehold. The shorter the lease, the more worthwhile it is to buy the freehold. This can bump up the market value by as much as 50 per cent. A landlord can sell the freehold to a third party, but use your right of first refusal.

As a landlord

Finding your property hard to let? Make sure it is furnished – small, unfurnished flats are more difficult to let and can cost more in lost rent money than it would cost to furnish and equip them. Ensure that furnishings are to the right British Standard (especially mattresses and suites) and that the furniture is simple but of good quality.

Beat the chances of a dispute. Always draw up an inventory and get both parties (you and your tenant) to sign it at the start of the lease. It protects both you and your tenant. Details don't have to be too minute, but note down the extent of wear and tear on furniture and fittings, cracks in the ceiling and so on. It saves arguing about things later.

HOUSING BENEFIT

A headache for the authorities and for the claimants, Housing Benefit is a system long overdue for reform. But until the powers that be do make changes, you need to understand the system and be armed with the right information.

Who can claim?

Housing Benefit is paid to people who have a low income (either workers or claimants) and who pay rent. It is paid whether or not you as a claimant are available for work. You can claim Housing Benefit if:
- you, or your partner, have to pay rent for the accommodation (house, flat, bedsit, etc.)
- you normally occupy that accommodation, or are only temporarily away from it
- your income is low enough.

Seek further advice if you think you have been wrongly treated, and you have savings worth less than £16,000.

Take documentation with you, such as wage slips and proof of rent, when you apply for Housing Benefit. Even if you don't have them all, take what you have got as soon as possible, as your claim for Housing Benefit will not normally start until they have your forms – even incomplete ones.

Beating the forms

The Housing Department will want to find out your relationship with other people (lodgers or boarders) in your home. They will want to know too if they pay you rent as the council may then be able to reduce the amount they pay you. You are allowed to live with whoever you wish, but if they can *prove* that you are cohabiting (living as a couple) they may reduce your payments. Your Income Support, Job Seekers' Allowance (JSA) and other benefits may also be affected. They will pay particular attention to different sex people living in the same accommodation, especially if there are two of you and/or you seem to have different bedrooms but no living room. They can even visit your home looking for things which prove you are a couple; they may ask whether you go out regularly in each other's company; look to see if you have the same food cupboards and cook together; or have only one tube of toothpaste. They may compare your form to those of others in your home who have claimed benefit to check you each give the same information. So compare what you have written before you submit your forms and make sure your stories match. Do be careful, however, that you do not do anything that may be fraudulent.

Home visits

Rent officers: a rent officer may visit your home to check how much Housing Benefit they estimate you should receive. He or she should give you seven days' written notice that they are coming, and you should let them in or risk having your Housing Benefit payments suspended until they can see the inside of the accommodation you live in.

Visiting officers: visiting officers visit your home to check you actually live there but, unlike rent officers, you do not have to let them in. Though you will have to prove you live there (driving licence; dole card or Income Support book; tenancy agreement; passport; bills), you can do this outside your home if you wish. These officers normally visit about once a year, depending on your council, and the only way they can suspend your benefit is if you don't show them adequate proof of habitation.

Problem landlords

If you are thinking of moving in: when landlords say 'No DSS' or 'No Under 25s', this is because they may have had a bad experience waiting for Housing Benefit to be paid. Have all the correct information and persuade them that you will get an interim payment after two weeks. If their concern is that you will not get full Housing Benefit, obtain a pre-tenancy determination to try to persuade them. You could also not tell them. Prove the amount you pay by either showing the Housing Benefit office a tenancy agreement or by showing them a rent book or receipts. Beware though – if you give your landlord's correct address, Housing Benefit may contact him or her. If you live with your landlord, officers may turn up at your home. Do also take care that you are not doing anything that may be fraudulent.

If they try to evict you: live in the same house as your landlord and you have very few rights. Live in a rented property, but not with the landlord, and they cannot evict you just because you are claiming or if you are in rent arrears awaiting Housing Benefit. You can demand an interim payment from the Housing Benefit Department, and if you are in arrears, your landlord will have to go to court to try and evict you. But don't feel you have to leave just because you are in arrears: landlords are not allowed to harass you. Seek advice from the Citizens Advice Bureau (which offers free legal advice).

Students: though most students cannot claim Housing Benefit either during term-time or during the holidays (see below), you can claim for Housing Benefit as soon as your course officially finishes.

As a student, you are entitled to Housing Benefit if:
- you are getting Income Support, or 'income based' JSA (Job Seekers' Allowance)
- you are a single parent who is getting (or could get) the single parent's premium
- you and your partner are both students and have a dependent child
- you receive a disability benefit, although seek advice first as simply receiving Incapacity Benefit may not be sufficient
- you are a pensioner who gets (or could get) one of the pensioners' premiums.

If you qualify, you will get Housing Benefit both during term-time and holidays. The Housing Benefit Department will probably speak to the DSS. Beware! If you haven't told the dole office that you are a student, be careful of what you tell the Housing Benefit Department as it could lead to your Income Support/JSA being suspended.

A good student housing scam: leave your course at the end of year one, claim Housing Benefit over the summer then sign up for the course again in year two. It is very likely, though, that the Housing Benefit office will swap information with the education department – in London they certainly will.

Rent reductions: if your council decides that the accommodation you are living in is too big for your needs, or is too expensive, they may decide to pay only a part of your rent (they cannot make you move). Beat the reduction by appealing against any decision, don't just accept it. People often do get more rent if they appeal. The council may say that your rent is unreasonably high compared with other properties in your area, but they must prove that there are similar tenancies available for a lower rent. Check they have compared like with like. Have they compared a private tenancy with that of Housing Association property? To reduce your rent, the council should just show the rent to be 'unreasonably high' – that is they should not just compare it with the lowest rent. Do some leg work yourself: make notes of rents in your area to support your case.

Away from home? You can be absent from home for up to 13 weeks and still get Housing Benefit for this period, even if you are not in this country. However, if you fail to tell the Housing Department that you are renting it out while you are away, or you are not coming back after 13 weeks, and you continue to claim Housing Benefit, this may be considered as fraudulent. You can be absent from your home for up to 52 weeks and still get Housing Benefit for the whole time if you are:
- a remand prisoner held in custody waiting for your trial or sentence
- in hospital
- abroad and receiving medical treatment

- away looking after a child whose parent is in hospital
- leaving home 'temporarily' because of fear of violence
- in rehabilitation or other residential accommodation.

Reviews: either you or the council can have your benefit claim reviewed, but if you receive a decision that you don't agree with, write to the council for an explanation. You can, in fact, ask for a review straight away if your case is urgent and the council has clearly made a mistake. The council should review your case within 14 days. If it takes longer, make a complaint.

Still disagree with the decision? Go to the Housing Benefit Review Board. You can represent yourself, but seek advice if you are not confident. You can call witnesses, but as the review board usually consists of two or three councillors, they may not be as independent as they are meant to be. Still not happy? You can have your case reviewed in court, but seek legal advice first. The Local Authority has a duty to pay the correct Housing Benefit, so if you suffer because of its failure (i.e. you are evicted), you can sue the authority. If your case is weak, the court may make you pay the legal costs of the council. Seek advice first.

Fraud: the council can accuse you of fraud if they think you knowingly made false statements or failed to report a change of circumstances. Don't panic!
- Listen to the accusations against you and ask questions. If they are relying on anonymous tip-offs insist on knowing what was said about you and who said it. Is their information correct? Is it reliable?
- Seek advice but make sure that the advice is confidential. Recent changes in the law mean that others can inform the authorities if they have evidence that you are making a fraudulent claim.
- Ask to have someone with you for support and to act as a witness.
- Don't sign anything you don't agree with.
- You have a right to remain silent – use it if they start pressurising you.
- Make notes of what they say and what you say.
- Get the names of the people who are interviewing you. They may be relying on tip-offs and have their facts wrong.
- Get advice from an advice or law centre or solicitor.

You may be asked to **pay back an overpayment** plus 30 per cent to cover the cost of taking you to court. There is a possible £2,000 fine or up to three months in prison if you are charged under one section of the Social Security Legislation. You can, in fact, also be charged with 'obtaining by deception', which is a more serious offence and carries a longer term of imprisonment. It may be better to go to court than pay back money you don't owe. Once you are cleared of fraud you can continue to claim benefit if you are still entitled.

If you want to **register a complaint**, it is always a good idea to keep copies of all your correspondence, forms you have completed, letters and so on. Always complain in writing and keep a copy of the letter – phone calls are hard to prove and can be denied. Keep details as brief as possible, but include dates and names of the people who dealt with you where possible. Inform the council what you are expecting from your complaint: e.g. compensation for loss. Your last resort? The Local Authority Ombudsman. He acts as a watchdog on local authorities and has the power to investigate the council. It may take time, but you can get results. Ask the council for the ombudsman's address.

MAKING MONEY ON PROPERTY

Letting

If you are letting property through an agency, check the terms and conditions. It's often cheaper to find your own tenants by advertising in free sheets and the local paper, then pay a manager to collect the rent. Agencies charge an average of 16 per cent of annual income plus lots of hidden charges.

Remember, if you are going abroad and want to let your house or flat, **ex-pat landlords have to pay tax** on their rental income. (See Second Homes on page 96.)

Buying to let

Though no investment is guaranteed to make you a fortune, property has showed itself to be a good investment in the long term. The Buy to Let scheme was introduced by the Association of Residential Letting Agents to help people who wanted to become landlords by purchasing property to let. The panel of lenders includes Halifax, NatWest and Woolwich who provide loans secured on the property to let. You are liable for tax on second properties, and will have the responsibility of tenants and as the freeholder, so seek the advice of a property solicitor.

How We Beat The System

Mary joined up with two partners to buy up flats in London to rent out:

'We found out some of the lenders in the buy-to-let market will lend to new limited companies, so we set ourselves up as one. Though we had no trading history, we put together a stonking business plan. Buy-to-let as an individual and you have to pay tax on the income (although you can offset quite a bit against refurbishment). As company directors, we put in capital in the form of a loan, and used it as deposits to start buying property with mortgages (in our case with Bank of Scotland). Obviously we have to pay corporation tax, but it's at a lower rate than personal tax.

'As the company grows and generates revenue, there will be a decent surplus of rent income over mortgage payments. We are paying ourselves back chunks of our original "loans" and there is no tax to pay on it as it isn't income as such. So without paying any tax at all, and with very highly geared borrowing, we have built up a property portfolio worth about £1m. At some point we will draw dividends from the company and be taxed in the normal way.'

Rent a room

> **FACT:** Currently (2001) the first £4,250 you receive in rent from a lodger renting a room in your house is tax free, so it's an easy way to make £81.73 a week without paying tax.

A lodger is a good way to earn a bit of extra income. Lodgers have no legal rights when they occupy your home, so you won't have to worry that they'll become a sitting tenant. It's a good idea to put all the letting arrangements in writing (how much rent and when it's due, deposit – if you require it and in what circumstances you'll return it – whether bills are extra and what restrictions you want – for example, house rules like smoking or overnight guests).

Land to build on?

If you have too large a garden, apply for planning permission to build on part of it. You can sell the land to a developer, but arm yourself with details of how much the land is worth, as developers are very canny. It is worth keeping a 'ransom strip' – usually a piece of land which provides access to the development site. It will give you a good financial bargaining tool.

HOUSE BUYING

The old adage that, next to marriage and bereavement, buying a house is one of the most stressful experiences in life is no lie. From the moment that you start scouring the local paper for a *bijou* property, you are on a roller coaster of hassle which ends with a nail-biting 'will they, won't they' of contract exchanging and signing. Unlike Scotland where the property buying system is more secure (your word is your bond), in England there is no certainty that your purchase or sale is successful until contracts have been exchanged and deposits paid (and even then, a purchaser determined to back out can forfeit their deposit). Make sure you know what conveyancing involves, and if necessary resort to some tried and tested house buying and selling techniques.

Surveys

You've found the house of your dreams. Make sure it is safe for habitation. There are three types of survey:

Valuation: this is required by the mortgage lender and is a check on the market value of the property as security for the loan. Such a valuation may be paid for by the lender and will tend to represent a conservative estimate of the market value. Any disrepair should be reflected in the value and, for this reason, many purchasers, who have not had structural surveys undertaken, have been successful in claiming against the valuer when major defects have been uncovered that prove the real value was materially less.

Home Buyer's Report: this is a low-cost compromise that should satisfy the requirements of most purchasers of smaller (suburban type) properties. It provides a check on the market value and the property's condition. The survey should pick up on any major defects or need for repair and maintenance, but is not recommended for older or larger properties.

Building or Structural Survey: this survey is usually conducted by a specialist building surveyor. It provides the most comprehensive examination of the building and reports on each element of the building's structure and finishes. Comments on building services are included based upon *visual inspection*. A detailed examination or testing of drainage, central heating, gas or electrical installations is usually undertaken by specialist contractors at an additional cost. Ask your surveyor whether he considers such tests to be necessary or desirable, and he will then arrange for them to be done. A good survey should automatically include a list of defects. However, if you want an estimate of the remedial costs, you will have to make a specific request. If you don't carry out a very detailed inspection, and later discover a catalogue of horrors, you will have no redress against the surveyor – visual inspection is just that. If you are buying an old property with its own septic tank, a CCTV survey is money well spent as the camera is attached to a cable, allowing you to investigate for leaks, cracking, root damage and so on.

N.B. Valuation and building surveyors are different disciplines within the profession, and you should check upon the status and experience of the surveyor who is actually going to undertake the work.

So your surveyor missed something important? You may well be entitled to compensation, but this is limited to the loss in value of the house (the difference between what you paid for it and what it might fetch with the defect taken into account). This may not equate to the cost of repair.

Surveyors' contracts are notoriously watertight (pardon the pun) and your survey will arrive with pages of 'conditions of engagement'. These are intended to define the extent of the surveyor's obligations to you. They will include the statement along the lines that the surveyor is unable to inspect woodwork or other parts of the structure or services that are 'covered, unexposed or inaccessible'. Part of the logic is that sellers are not too keen on a string of surveyors moving furniture, taking up carpets and making holes in plaster when they have still not sold the house!

This said, a good surveyor's experience will give him warning signals when things are amiss. Don't take the caveats in your report literally. You may find you have a basis of claim. A survey report is not an insurance policy and litigation on building matters is notoriously costly and difficult to prove for opinion evidence can be so subjective. **Beat the cost of claiming against a surveyor:** find a cheaper and speedier way of resolving the dispute than going through the courts. The moment you make a formal claim against a surveyor, his insurers will take control of the dispute, and their pockets are likely to be deeper than yours. Surveyors will frequently take a photographic record to supplement their notes. The purchasers who blow-torched their loft and made nail holes in the skirting boards as a basis for claiming damages against their surveyor were rumbled!

For advice contact the surveyors professional body, the Royal Institution of Chartered Surveyors at www.rics.org.uk.

Caveat emptor! **The burden is on the buyer** to make an inspection of a property. If you don't have a survey, and move in to find out the house is riddled with damp and death-watch beetle, you cannot claim compensation from the person you bought it from. It was up to you to make the enquiries. However, if the seller deliberately misled you, you could claim compensation. So there's a warning to sellers there too. If someone asks you something, don't make a wild guess or make your answer up. It could be held against you.

Seller's packs

The Government has mentioned introducing legislation that requires anybody selling a house to prepare a seller's pack before they can put the property on the market. Failure to do so will incur a fixed penalty fine. The pack will have to contain copies of the title documents, and leases (if any), planning and building consents, warranties and guarantees, local authority searches, a draft contract and a professional survey of the property by an accredited surveyor. It is estimated that the cost of preparing the pack will be about £700, although the Government is trying to reduce the impact on those in areas where house prices are especially low. Watch this space!

The hope is that the need for a seller's pack will reduce the number of properties available, because people uncommitted to selling won't put their properties on the market as a test. It may serve to increase prices, but trials do suggest that a greater proportion of sales will reach completion.

Steal a march on other house sellers by preparing a pack even now, and if you are a potential purchaser, ask if one is available. Check the dates on all the searches and the survey. You will not be covered should you suffer loss as a consequence of anything that post-dates the information provided. You may still need to get your own survey done.

The Sale of Goods Act, 1979 doesn't apply to property; in other words, **property does not have to be of 'merchantable quality'**. However, all new homes should be covered by a warranty – like the one from the National House Building Council (NHBC); this guarantees that they have been built to a certain standard. If not and problems occur, they should be put right by the builder.

The cost of buying a house (or beating your solicitor)

Solicitors should be as competitive when charging for conveyancing as any business. Don't immediately choose your family solicitor to do the work just because they handled grandpa's will so well: shop around for a keen price, and get a firm quote including stamp duty, land registration and so on. You should not need to pay out-of-pocket expenses either. Even use a licensed conveyancer to do the work. Since 1987, they have been allowed to set up in business alone or work for solicitors' firms, estate agents and building societies. Contact the Law Society (020 7242 1222) or the Council for Licensed Conveyancers (01245 349599) to get a list of those in your area, and get details of what is included in writing.

Do your own conveyancing: there has never been any reason why people shouldn't do the work themselves – there is a plethora of self-help books available to guide you through the process – and it will undoubtedly save you money on your moving costs. However, it does carry an element of risk. You may fall down where a property is leasehold or enfranchised (where leaseholders own a share of the freehold) because you will need to understand land law, planning law, trusts and contracts. Contracts are legally binding, and professional conveyancers are insured against error and subsequent losses.

Stamp Duty … and avoiding it

If the house you are buying is on the cusp of a Stamp Duty increment (1 per cent at £60,001, 3 per cent at £250,001, 4 per cent at £500,001 plus in 2001) make an offer excluding fixtures and fittings to keep the price below the threshold, and make a separate offer for these.

Don't rely on the word of the estate agent or the vendors. Find out how much they paid for the house or how much the house up the street was last sold for by contacting the Land Registry online at www.landregistrydirect.gov.uk. There is a small charge.

Buying a house … beat the crowds

- Be firm about what it is you want to buy and the price you can afford and stick to it. Have the necessary deposit ready and live in rented accommodation until the right property comes up, then you will be ready to pounce when the right thing comes on to the market.
- Renting shows you are serious and gives you a head start with the vendors when you make an offer.
- Many estate agents ask for a 10 per cent deposit on the house you are going to buy. Make sure this money is going into the client's account and offer £500 to show you are serious.
- Make an offer on a house in late winter. The housing market is most buoyant in the spring and autumn, and sellers are usually more desperate in the depths of winter. They are more likely to accept a cheeky offer. In one case buyers were offered a £7,300 reduction in the asking price if they completed before Christmas.
- Just because a house is 'under offer' it does not mean you cannot make a higher offer. A house is only sold once contracts have been signed.

- If you don't have to move, try offering less on the day of contract exchange. Desperate vendors could well accept your lower offer now you are this far down the line.
- Buy the cheapest house on an expensive street, not the other way round. You are then more likely to see a quicker increase in value.
- Where can you find out the local gossip? At the pub of course. Drop in there and chat to the landlord about the area in which you are intending to buy. They may well have information that doesn't appear on any sale details.
- Fixtures and fittings: ensure the purchaser provides a schedule of the fixtures and fittings they intend to remove or leave behind. Better be clear on the point than have an argument when you open the door to find the kitchen fittings gone and the garden denuded of plants.
- A contract is not legally binding until both parties have signed *and* exchanged it, so until then you can pull out of the sale at any time – though as a purchaser you may forfeit your deposit if you pull out after exchange of contracts.
- Go to auction. It takes a strong stomach as it can be nerve-wracking, but, if you are lucky, you can end up paying less than you would through a normal sale. This is the best bet when buying properties that are unusual or need renovation. You are obliged to pay a deposit on the fall of the hammer, so make sure you have funds available and a mortgage offer. But, do be warned that with auctions the purchaser commits themselves without the benefit of any searches or pre-contract enquiries.
- Look at buying an ex-business property. These do need money investing to refurbish them and you will need planning permission for change of use, but this is often reflected in the price. Estate agents consider the large, often listed, office premises properties as a white elephant and they can be a bargain – though in some cases we are talking millions!

> **FACT:** Stamp Duty on house purchases is set to be abolished in some parts of the country, especially areas where the housing market is stagnant. Win on two counts by buying a bargain in one of these areas (such as Thorntree in Middlesborough, Aston in Birmingham and Newnham in London) *and* saving money by avoiding Stamp Duty. Call the Inland Revenue Helpline on 0845 603 0135.

Online house buying

> **FACT:** Some estate agents claim that 70 per cent of their business is now done online.

The revolution in house buying over the Internet in the last few years has empowered the potential house buyer. **The advantage** with some websites is that you can contact sellers direct (paying a fee to the website) and cut out the estate agents' 1 to 3 per cent cut of the asking price. To evaluate websites, search them as a buyer and always read the small print on services offered to the seller.

Disadvantages include security and the lack of professional advice. Those that know suggest that if you are taking this route, you should always use a solicitor for the conveyancing. Don't attempt it yourself.

Websites include:

> www.assertahome.com
> www.fish4homes.co.uk
> www.winkworth.co.uk (London only)
> www.propwatch.com (Greater London only currently. A direct site encouraging bidders to contact each other via email to cut out the estate agent's fee)
> www.huntahome.com (UK wide)
> www.propertyfile.co.uk (UK and France)
> www.teamprop.co.uk (Database of nationwide estate agents)

Buying a house on a new brownfield development?

Developments in urban brownfield areas may be contaminated from its previous use. Since April 2000 local authorities have had to identify contaminated land which is a threat to health and, if the original polluter has gone, the current owners may have to do the cleaning up. **Get ahead of the game.** Before buying a property, don't rely on your solicitor or estate agent. Enter the postcode on the environment agency website at www.environment-agency.gov.uk to find out about flood or existing pollution risks, or check out the Landmark Envirosearch service at www.undermystreet.com (there may be a charge), which will do a search for you that covers past and present contamination, mining landfills as well as flood risk.

Looking for something a little unusual?

There are several organisations and charities that sell off their properties at a very commercial rate. These include:
- pubs
- breweries
- warehouses
- banks and building societies
- Church property (vicarages, redundant churches and other Church property including Church of England schools).

You can receive a list of redundant churches from the Church Commissioners on 020 7898 1784 or by visiting the website at www.cofe.anglican.org. Often these properties are on the open market, and there could be a saving. Generally, first-time **sales of vicarages and rectories are not liable for Stamp Duty**, so on a property of £500,000 there could be a saving of £15,000.

Be warned, though, some of these type of properties have a **covenant inserted into the contract** stipulating that the owners use a name that bears no relation to its former use. **There are also covenants** forbidding redundant churches to be used as places of worship, for any illegal or immoral purpose or as a theatre, betting or sex shop, fun fair or dance hall amongst others. Access should be granted to anyone wanting to visit the former church or to tend graves, and there are covenants protecting against the disturbance of tombstones and human remains...

FACT: In 30 years since 1969, when the Pastoral Measure for Alternative Use of Redundant Churches came into effect, only 189 out of 1,566 were changed to residential use, while 351 were demolished.

How We Beat The System

Sarah and David bought a former Church of England primary school in Shropshire:

'We bought the school, set on the side of a beautiful hill with magnificent views, from the parish council. The building was advertised and the estate agents representing the parish invited sealed bids by a certain day with a suggested asking price. They also tried to insist that bidders would have to commit to exchanging contracts within two weeks of the offer being accepted – basically meaning we had to have cash and accept all the terms of their outrageous contract. We completely ignored this, but they accepted our offer because it was £5000 more than the under-bidder – very naughty of them and, in the end, foolish. Five months later, when we were still negotiating, we dropped our price by £4,500.

'Permission had already been accepted for change of use, but not planning permission. You need plans for that and that was up to us – which is obviously a bit scary as you need to own the building to submit the plans. We used an architect whose speciality was churches, but he knew a thing or two about getting plans accepted for old converted buildings. We experienced no real problems with the planning department – though there was the odd scary moment over building regulations. But our contract with the parish council was a nightmare, and it took about five months to negotiate. Even now, if we build anything on any part of the playground, we are supposed to give the council a third of the value of that building – despite the fact that we own the freehold. In fact they tried to insist that we had to get permission from them as well as the planning department for any changes we made.

'The real problem was that the grassed paddock is a certified "open space". This does mean that no one can develop it, but strictly we shouldn't cultivate it into a garden. There's also a clause which states it is 'common ground' – so anyone can fly their kite on it, for example. While only the farmer next door and ourselves have access, it would be inconvenient if he chose to allow people over his land.

'Despite all that we love the house, it gives us plenty of space, and it was worth all the effort.'

People on your side

Save Britain's Heritage (SAVE) is a passionate organisation concerned with the protection of old and interesting buildings in danger of demolition. Its comprehensive website at www.savebritainsheritage.org tells you how to get a building listed, how to campaign to save buildings and how to form a pressure group. Call SAVE on 020 7253 3500 for more information.

The Society for the Protection of Ancient Buildings (020 7377 1644) runs practical courses for people who live in or want to buy an ancient building.

Contact too the **Scottish Civic Trust** (0141 221 1466) which has details of properties at risk and Ulster Architectural Heritage Society (028 9055 0213) which has a catalogue of listed buildings for sale.

Trouble getting a mortgage for an old building? Some mortgage lenders will demand that properties with original features (such as brick floors laid on earth) are 'modernised'. Don't give in: try lenders such as the Ecology Building Society (0845 674 5566) which are more likely to be persuaded to give you a mortgage on the property in its original condition.

How We Beat The System

After years of 'mismanagement', during which the island's population fell to a dangerously low level, the privately owned and run-down **Island of Eigg** in the Scottish Isles was put up for sale in 1993 for £2 million. Rather than let the island fall into the hands of an outsider, the islanders launched an appeal to buy the island for themselves. The Isle of Eigg Heritage Trust was set up as a legally established company with charitable status made up of four elected representatives from the local community, two from the Highland Council and two from the Scottish Wildlife Trust. The road ahead was a rocky one, with many setbacks, but as a result of donations (including an anonymous one of £750,000) and a grant from the Lottery, the islanders were able to bid £1.5 million on 4 April 1997. They took possession of Eigg on 12 June 1997.

Until 2001, Board meetings of the Heritage Trust were held approximately six times a year. The Trust is now moving towards quarterly meetings as management is devolved to sub-committees on the island. Regular meetings of Eigg Residents' Association are held on Eigg to ensure that the Trust is meeting the expectations of those living on the island. 'The rebuilding of Eigg's infrastructure will be a long slow process,' say the islanders, 'but with a feeling of security and stability beginning to return we are all looking forward to the challenges ahead. One thing we mustn't lose sight of is the fact that although we were successful – the land laws in Scotland haven't changed. Many other communities are still suffering at the hands of unscrupulous owners... We must make sure that the subject of land reform stays on the agenda until suitable legislation is introduced.'

(All information taken from Eigg ISA Magazine.)

THE MOVE

FACT: It costs upwards of £1,000 just to move from an ordinary three-bedroomed terraced house in London and the South East.

The cost of moving house can vary hugely, depending on the number of containers the company calculate your bits and pieces will take up. Get three quotes, but it is a false economy to use a company that is not a member of the British Association of Removers or the Guild of Removers. They are bound to comply with association guidelines. Make sure the company you choose is insured for loss or damage to any of your property.

Save yourself money on the move by doing the packing yourself. Ask for the cartons in advance, and ensure you wrap delicate items in plenty of bubble-wrap and tissue. Your goods will not be insured if you do the packing, but it's not rocket science to wrap things well and you could save a substantial amount on the cost. Check your insurance will cover you for breakages.

The cheapest removal company isn't necessarily the best. You get what you pay for and a more expensive firm will have enough people and boxes to move you efficiently.

…but you'll **get more out of your removal men** if you offer them a bribe like fish and chips if they will put in a couple of extra hours.

Reduce costs even further, if you haven't too much to move, by hiring a van and doing the whole job yourself.

SECOND HOMES

FACT: In Britain there are currently 200,000 second homes, and a further 300,000 let as holiday properties. A second home could be defined as 'a residential property that is occupied less than 91 days in any calendar year and that is not the occupier's only or main residence.'

In 2001 the Government announced plans to let councils charge, after consultation, the **full council tax for more second homes**. At the moment second homeowners get a 50 per cent tax discount, which costs councils an estimated £150m annually in lost revenue. This is a blow to second-homeowners, but consider the flipside. Country or seaside properties can command very large rents during the season (usually Easter to September). So long as you can oversee the rentals (or employ someone to do it for you), you can make enough money for the property to pay for itself.

Avoiding tax: with holiday homes just for family use, there is no tax implication in the purchase (though there could be inheritance tax due when you come to sell). Let the property even for part of the time, and you will need to declare any profit (or loss) to the Inland Revenue. With properties abroad or in Britain, you can offset any expenses involved and tax is only on the clear profit. Offset losses in the early years against profits later.

A little place on the Costa Brava? Coping with British systems is one thing. Getting your head around legal systems abroad is quite another. The basic rules of buying property abroad are:

- Take your time, and don't be tempted to buy on impulse or worse still an unseen property from a brochure. Time spent viewing an area you fancy is money well spent.
- Get independent legal advice and have a local valuer check the property before you commit yourself.
- Make sure you understand everything that is being said to you and have it put in writing.
- Budget carefully because there are extra costs (in Spain, for example, EVA, the equivalent of VAT, and notary fees will add 12 to 15 per cent to the total cost).

The National Association of Estate Agents has members who specialise in property abroad, and its Homelink service (www.naes.co.uk) will help you to identify estate agents in the UK and abroad who can help. It is important to get expert advice as there are often local rules and regulations that are very different from those in this country.

Beat the repayments: buy property abroad outright – some high street lenders do offer special mortgages for properties abroad, but such mortgages are affected by both fluctuating interest rates and exchange rates. You will need to put up a minimum deposit of 25 per cent on foreign loans and mortgages last an average of 15 years rather than our traditional 25 years. The Federation of Overseas Property Developers, Agents and Consultants can put you in touch with financial and legal experts to steer you through the obstacles.

HOUSE SELLING

Don't leave it up to your estate agent! An estate agent can introduce potential buyers to your house, but they can't be responsible for the contents. If you want to make a quick sale:

- Though an estate agent will suggest a price, do your own homework. From 1 April 2001, the public has been able to access information about how much properties were sold for, by postcode. Go to www.proviser.com, which has information from the Land Registry and tells you the local property prices across England and Wales by postcode. You can then judge if you are asking too much or too little.
- Make sure the house is clean and tidy and smells pleasant.

- When showing people round, let them go into a room first. It will seem bigger if there is no one in there.
- Put a big bunch of fresh flowers in the entrance hall – not lilies as they make some people sneeze.
- Send your children out for the duration of the viewing. They can be very indiscreet about the house's problems.
- Avoid patterned carpets which put many people off. Plain carpets also give the illusion of space.
- Cover-ups, like stone cladding, Artex or polystyrene ceiling tiles raise the suspicions of potential buyers as to what they are disguising.
- Make sure your house doesn't have a stupid name. 'Costalotta' or 'Up Yonder' may be quaint but will put off potential buyers.
- Adopt good taste: mirrored ceilings, garden gnomes, mock wishing wells and avocado bathroom suites should all go. Try to avoid clutter too. Let people see the fabric of the house, not be overawed by your personal effects.
- If you really are surrounded by clutter, arrange to have some of your things put into storage. This will make the house look bigger while you try to sell it.
- If your house has a history or a story (it may be haunted, have been used as a location for film or TV or have a beautiful interior) tell the local newspaper. They may run a story about it being on the market. Ask your agent if they have an in-house press officer or employ a PR agent. Don't be disappointed if at first you don't succeed – publications receive hundreds of press releases. Publication can take a while too – two weeks for weeklies and four to five months for monthlies – so publicity will only help sell your house if you plan well in advance. To find out historical information about your house try the Public Records Office online at www.pro.gov.uk or the British Association of Local History at www.balh.co.uk.
- There is no obligation to use an estate agent. You can save yourself their cut of the sale price by spending money advertising it yourself. Ask two or three estate agents to value the property for you or compare prices with similar properties. The cost of colour advertising in a local paper or magazine, radio advertising, or even the services of a PR agent can still be less than 1 per cent of the sale price. Have a sign writer produce a sale board for you so it looks professional.
- Put the asking price up by £1,000 and throw in a 'free' holiday for the successful purchaser – yes, this has worked!
- Keep abreast of the local school league tables. It will be ammunition in your sales pitch when you are selling a family house.
- Advertising your property should be part of your agreement with your estate agent. Only the very posh companies expect you to pay for advertising.
- If you deliberately mislead a purchaser, they can claim compensation. If a potential buyer asks you a question, claim ignorance rather than guess. It could be held against you.

BUILDING YOUR OWN HOUSE

'Architecture is the art of how to waste space.' *Philip Johnson, New York Times, 1964*

Though building land is scarce, **building your own house is by far the cheapest way to acquire a property**, as the results are usually worth more than building costs. Use the services of an architect (the word architect is a protected term and only a qualified architect can use the term). Contact the RIBA (Royal Institute of British Architects) at www.architecture.com for a full list of architects in your area. Architects can submit plans to the local authority and are aware of what is and is not acceptable in your area for development.

Save money, however, by submitting the plans yourself, and using the services of an architectural technician who will draw up your architect's plans for submission for building regulations at a lower cost.

If you are at home during the day, **you can save money too by running the job yourself** (rather than paying the architect to oversee it) and simply have the architect come round at odd intervals, paying him at an hourly rate.

Get an architect for a snip and make a contribution to charity. During Architecture Week (end of June each year), you can have a participating RIBA architect give you a domestic consultation for an hour when you make a £15 contribution to the charity for the homeless, Shelter. Visit the website to find your nearest RIBA member and to make an appointment. In the four years that the scheme has been running, the RIBA has donated £200,000 to the charity. Do the same in your business premises too with **Architect in the Office**. An hour's consultation costs a £50 contribution to Shelter.

If you are keen to get on with your development work, **you can start construction** before building regulations approval has been received from the council. Beware though that if they dispute anything in your plans you may have to stop work.

Building regulations can impose restrictions and conditions on your building work – for example, insisting on guards or restrictors on upstairs windows. Once the building has had its final inspection, you can then remove them.

Budget too for **a structural engineer** to make accurate calculations from your plans so the building is safe and properly constructed. If it's not done properly you may have difficulties when you come to sell and the property is inspected by a potential purchaser's surveyor.

PLANNING PERMISSION AND LISTED BUILDINGS (OR PROCEED AT YOUR PERIL)

Planning permission

You want to alter your house – what's the best policy with the planners?

It's always worth checking with your local authority to see whether an application is necessary or whether the improvements you want to make come within Permitted Development Rights:

- Planning permission is required for extensions to your home. But you can add either 15 per cent of the size or less than 70 sq m (750 sq ft) with certain conditions.
- Permission is required if you want to divide off part of the house for a self-contained flat or bedsit, but not if you want to let one or two rooms to lodgers.
- Permission is required if you want to put in a bay window, but not always for a window flush with the house.
- Permission is required for dormer windows, but not for roof or skylights.
- You can increase the value of your property with improvements which do not always need permission: greenhouses, sheds (up to a certain size), swimming pools, sauna enclosures and tennis courts.
- Tree houses can be tricky. Check the tree in question does not have a Tree Preservation Order, that your property is not in a conservation area and that the house is not listed. Choose a tree that is more than 5m (16 ft) from the house, and more than 2m (6.5 ft) from the boundary. The tree house must not be more than 4m high or overlook other properties. Too big and it might be considered an extension!
- Some local authorities have an Article 4 Direction withdrawing Permitted Development Rights. Call your local planning office, and check out the Department of the Environment website at www.detr.gov.uk/householders/guide.

Add value to your property by **selling it with outline planning permission**. Once planning permission is granted, it's valid for up to five years from the date of approval.

Give yourself a bit of privacy without planning permission by building a fence around your home up to 2m (6.5 ft) high where it joins neighbour's land and 1m (35 ft) where it joins a public road or pavement.

Don't take no for an answer: you can appeal against a planning refusal and it costs nothing to do so.

Planning permission is not usually required for small domestic conservatories provided they comply with the following regulations and are not listed nor in a conservation area:

- they are less than 30 sq m (320 sq ft) in floor area, built on to a domestic dwelling at ground level
- they are divided from the rest of the house by a door (a partition door or French windows are the most usual methods)
- they are glazed in compliance with safety requirements
- they are not within 1m (3 ft) of the boundary
- they are built with a roof and walls which are at least 75 per cent and 50 per cent glazed respectively.

Need more space without moving house?

You can build a wooden or brick-build annexe in your garden for a fraction of the price of an extension and, if it is not in a conservation area, at least 5 metres (16 feet) from the house and only for occasional habitation, planning permission may not always be necessary. You can also apply for **Agricultural Notification** (a cheaper and quicker process than full planning permission) if the annexe is to be built in your garden. Look out for advertisements in garden and homes magazines for these pre-fabricated buildings. Buildings that are not intended for habitation do not need to observe building regulations.

Look up ... and down

Attic and loft conversions are an obvious answer to a space problem, but think too about the ground beneath your house. A basement can increase the floor space of a house by half for a two-storey building. Add a loft conversion too and your house size can increase by 70 per cent. You will need planning permission, which can be hard to come by, but concern about urban density is making planners rethink basement development.

Listed buildings

There's no such thing as a listed façade or interior; buildings are listed in their entirety. So you will have to talk to your local planning authority before you start on any changes. Even minor works, such as painting, repairing gutters or replacing a window pane need to be checked out before you do anything. A building becomes 'listed' (Grade I or II) when it's architecturally important (in terms of design, decoration or craftsmanship); it's historically interesting (regarding our social, economic, cultural or military past); it has value as part of a group (such as a fine example of a village, square, terrace and so on) or it's old (all pre-1700 buildings that are close to their original condition are listed, as are most built between 1700 and 1840).

You can press to have your property listed if it is of architectural interest (see Grants for listed buildings, below), or have the area designated as a Conservation Area. This can be a double-edged sword, because changes to listed buildings are naturally very restricted.

The flip side is that many **buildings have slipped through the listings net** – they may have been earmarked for demolition due to lack of sewage facilities for example, some time in the past – which will give you a freer hand when it comes to building an extension or making other changes.

Grants for listed buildings

When buying an older property, talk to English Heritage about grants which you may be eligible to get for 'conservative repair' – though it stresses not for the 'wholesale reinstatement of lost or destroyed features'.

> English Heritage
> Customer Services Department
> PO Box 569
> Swindon SW2 2YP
> Tel: 0870 333 1181
> www.english-heritage.org.uk

Most councils now have a **conservation officer**. Talk to him or her about grants available locally for restoring listed buildings. They may assist you with roofing, masonry work and other critical conservation costs. It helps if you get your request in at the beginning of the financial year, and you'll also have better luck if you have a property of historic interest that is open to the public.

The Council for the Preservation of Rural England (CPRE) runs a comprehensive series of seminars on subjects such as making representations at a planning inquiry, how to object to a planning application and how to comment on and influence local development plans. These short one- or two-day courses have a very good reputation and take place at locations across the country. For details of this year's programme call the CPRE on 020 7976 6433.

Part of the Royal Town Planning Institute, **Planning Aid**, is a free, voluntary service offering independent professional advice and help on town planning. It is aimed at individuals, community groups and other voluntary groups who cannot afford to pay for private consultants. PA help people comment on planning applications, appear at planning inquiries, appeal against planning decisions and influence local plans. Find out more online at www.rtpi.org.uk/planaid.

FACT: A couple from Towyn, North Wales, successfully applied for planning permission from Conwy County Council to turn their three-acre garden into a cemetery with 600 plots, increasing the value of their home from £95,000 to £1 million. Could *you* cash in on the demand for more burial plots?

BEATING THE BUILDERS

'Building work is a bit like trench warfare – a period of frantic activity then an ominous lull in the proceedings.' *RIBA member*

Everyone has a bad builder story to tell and, like tax inspectors, the building profession is one of the most loathed. And justifiably so. Unscrupulous builders who have turned in shoddy work and overcharged their customers have pulled down the reputation of the whole industry. Having builders working in your house can be very intrusive, if you are at home during the day. And if you are out, you can open your front door to a scene of horrors that have happened while you were absent. Make sure you are in control of the situation so you are not taken for a ride and, if you cannot oversee the work, it is money well spent to employ an architect to run the job for you.

- Unlike the stock market, building costs only ever go up, never down. Make sure you have a contingency of at least 10 per cent for unforeseen costs.

- A quote is firm and binding, whereas an estimate is not. Once you have your plans, you need to put the job out to tender to at least three builders. The most expensive may not always be the best. Ask the advice of friends who have used builders. Were they happy with the work? Alternatively ask the local authority works department to recommend contractors.

- Once you have accepted a quote put it in writing to protect yourself, stating that you will only pay the final bill on completion of work to your satisfaction, that is fit for its purpose and carried out in a workmanlike manner using the proper materials. Agree to weekly or monthly evaluations before you pay in instalments. Do not pay the final amount until you are completely satisfied – this is your insurance policy.

- Your agreement with the builder constitutes a contract and should be signed and agreed by him. In the contract you can specify any details you have regarding how work is carried out. Do you mind them using your loo? Do you want the site cleared on completion? What are your feelings about the builders having a radio on while they work? This is also the time to decide whether or not you'll be acting as tea maker.

- Architects have a system called 'snagging' where they list defects at the end of the job. You can do this yourself, and present the builder with your list before settling the bill. You can wait three to six months until you have no more surprises.

- You can call in the building inspector if you need your complaints backed up.

- It pays to be on the ball. Keep a copy of all correspondence, because it will be ammunition in any complaints you have.

- Builders are responsible for work carried out by sub-contractors.

- Include a completion date in your contract. It will focus the builder's mind on the job. You are also entitled to include penalties if the work is delayed.

- Be a pain in the neck. You are paying for the work, so don't be afraid to keep asking what they are doing and why. An interested and involved client will keep the builders on their toes.

- Don't get caught out. Always use a builder, architect, surveyor etc. who is a member of a trade or professional association. This will help you in a dispute and it means they have to abide by association rules and standards. You are entitled to use their arbitration services too.

- You can claim compensation if the work done by your builders causes losses to your property, or for negligence or breach of contract for up to six years. But this may involve taking them to court yourself.

- Make sure your builder has indemnity insurance – insist on seeing a copy of it – but inform your insurance company that building work is taking place so you are covered if any other part of the property is damaged.
- Don't forget to increase your building insurance to cover the value of the newly built part of the property once it is completed.
- Does your builder suggest you pay cash to avoid VAT? Be wary. It may mean they are not a member of a trade association. On the other hand for small jobs, paying cash is a cheaper way to get work done.
- Need advice? Don't pay for it. Use the free services of the Trading Standards Office, Citizens Advice Bureau or Consumer Advice Centre.
- Once the architect signs the certificate upon completion, insurance responsibility passes to you, so delay it unless you are entirely satisfied with the work.

BEATING THE BURGLAR

If you have ever been burgled, you will know how painful it can be. Not only is it worth making sure your home is as secure as possible to deter uninvited guests, it can also help to keep your insurance premiums down. (Information from the Association of British Insurers – see their address at the end of the chapter.)

- **Doors**

Outside doors should have deadlocks which at least conform to BS3621. These locks can only be opened by key. A burglar cannot just use a plastic card to push back the tongue of the lock or break a glass panel and reach in to open it. Doors that you usually lock from the inside – for example the back door – should also be fitted with bolts. But locks and bolts are only as strong as the door and the frame to which they are fitted. So check the woodwork and replace it if it is at all weak or rotten. Double doors should have bolts (preferably security bolts with removable keys) at the top and bottom of both doors as well as a lock. On patio doors, additional security locks should be fitted to stop the sliding frame being lifted off the tracks. The sliding leaf of patio doors should be fitted on the inside. Make sure that doors are lockable from the inside because a burglar will look for a door to get out of the property with his bootie. Never leave keys in a 'secret' hiding place – thieves know all the hiding places. Leave a spare key with a trusted neighbour.

- **Windows**

Most burglaries are through windows. Key-operated locks should be fitted to all accessible windows – those on the ground floor and those near drainpipes and flat roofs. These locks are inexpensive to buy and easy to fit. Never leave keys in a lock – always take them with you.

- **Callers**

Check the identity of all callers. Before opening your door fully, ask to see their identity card if they claim to be officials. Don't be fooled by a uniform. Telephone their office if in any doubt. A door viewer or door chain will help you see who is at the door without opening it fully.

- **Going out**

A burglar can be in and out of your home in two minutes. So always shut and lock all windows – however short a time you are going to be away. Don't forget garages and sheds – they contain valuable items and tools useful to a burglar. Chain and padlock ladders, or keep them in locked sheds or garages.

- **Holidays**

Don't make it obvious that you are away – cancel the milk and newspapers. Ask a neighbour to keep an eye on your home, taking in any packages and removing mail from your letter box.

- **Property marking**

List your valuable items with serial numbers and a short description. Take photographs or videos of items such as jewellery and keep them with your policy. You will have a better chance of getting your property back after a burglary. Mark your property with a property-marking kit. Use your postcode and the number of your house. This will help the police to return your property to you. Your local Crime Prevention Officer will advise you for free and he can be contacted via your local police station.

- **Safes**

If you own valuable property you may prefer the added security of a safe. Before you buy one, consult your insurance company surveyor (they may insist on a certain type) or Crime Prevention Officer as to which type is best suited to your needs.

- **Alarms**

If you are considering installing an alarm, get advice from your insurers first before buying one. Many insurance companies insist that the installation of alarms is carried out by companies registered with the National Approval Council for Security Systems (address at end of chapter). Most alarms only warn that someone has already broken in. Your first priority is to stop them getting in at all.

- **Neighbourhood watch**

Get involved in a neighbourhood watch scheme – or help to set up one. Your local police will give you details.

- **Discounts**

Some insurers allow a discount from the cost of home contents insurance if you fit specified security measures, like safes and window locks. Ask your insurance company or insurance adviser for details.

INSURANCE

FACT: One in four people do not insure the contents of their properties.

> **FACT:** A recent consumer home insurance report states that if you make three or more claims, or claim over £2,000 a year, you are likely to be blacklisted by the average home insurance company. Insurers deny this, but admit that in areas of high crime or where flooding is virtually a certainty, premiums are likely to be higher or cover harder to get. The flip side? Areas prone to flooding are usually a low burglary risk. Perhaps it's harder to hide the family silver down a pair of waders…

Insurance is a critical part of any house purchase, and it is **up to you to insure the property** from the moment of exchange of contracts. Your mortgage lender cannot insist that you insure the building through them and you can often find a more competitive quote elsewhere. The cheapest way to do this is **via the Internet** – and companies like www.directline.co.uk offer very competitive prices.

See also:

> www.1stquote.co.uk
> www.insurancewide.co.uk
> www.screentrade.co.uk

Brought a priceless Van Gogh – or even a super new camera? Make sure that you have not exceeded your contents cover. You'll get a more competitive quote if you go through an insurance broker than doing a ring round the insurance companies.

Is your burglar alarm a nuisance? You can find insurers that will **insure you without an alarm**, but only if the contents of your house is under a certain threshold (around £45,000 in 2001). Insurers will offer you more competitive premiums if you have one, as well as window locks on all downstairs windows and a safe which is secured to the floor.

For information on insurance contact:

> The Association of British Insurers
> 51 Gresham Street
> London EC2V 7HQ
> Tel: 020 7600 3333
> email: info@abi.org.uk
> www.abi.org.uk

SQUATTERS AND TRESPASSERS (OR IT'S MINE!)

Squatters' rights – or wherever I lay my hat

The rights of squatters entitle them to have the title of the land transferred into their name if they have occupied it for 12 years. In other words, land can become rightfully yours if you have occupied it for long enough. If you have also had *use* of a piece of land without interruption and have not paid rent on it for 12 years, you are entitled to own it too. (This is what local authorities refer to as 'forgotten land'.) The secret of successful squatting, if you think you have a potential claim, is not to acknowledge the owner's title to the land *at any time*. Don't get carried away with gratitude, and say 'thanks for letting me use it'!

It does have to be 'adverse' possession – this means that you cannot take possession of the property if you have a lease or a licence (tenants who let under a tenancy agreement – whether oral or written – can therefore never get squatter's rights to premises).

Squatting with less than ten years' use of the land? **Anyone can enter a premises and take up residence**, but you will be trespassing and the rightful owner of the property would be entitled to a court order against you to have you evicted. Try www.lawsolutions.co.uk for free advice on your legal rights, including land ownership.

If you are the unfortunate landowner, however, and a squatter is claiming their right to the land after 12 years, it is imperative that you get them to acknowledge *your* legal title to the land before taking legal action to remove them.

Forgive us our trespassers

Anyone who comes on to your land without permission is trespassing. For some people, like the postman, there is an **implied permission.** If someone comes on to your land without permission, you can ask them nicely to go but, if they won't, you are allowed by law to use sufficient force (a push perhaps) to get them off. Do that to someone on the street, and it's a criminal offence of assault. If *you* are trespassing, it's not a criminal offence (so don't believe signs that say 'Trespassers will be prosecuted'). However, it is a civil offence for which you could be sued, but only if the landowner can prove tangible damage as a result of your visit.

DISPUTES WITH NEIGHBOURS

An Englishman's home is indeed his castle, and an enormous number of disputes arise between neighbours, be they about boundaries, trees, noise or rubbish disposal. If talking to your neighbour has failed, and before you seek expensive legal advice, **use the services of a mediator**. This is often free and offered by a registered charity. In either case, make sure you have evidence – witnesses, photographs, times and dates written down – which will help you in your case.

Fence offence: if there is no record and nobody can remember who put the fence up for example, look at the support posts. Generally, the fence belongs to the person who has the supports on their side. If you're still not sure, have a look at the deeds of the property. If there are small 'T's marked on the boundaries, this often means that the fence belongs to the person on whose side the 'T' is found (but check the definition of the 'T' against the deeds).

Keep it down! Noisy neighbours are a pain, especially at night. The Noise Act of 1996 states that night time is considered to be between 11pm and 7am, during which period the accepted decibel level is 35dB. So officially if you snore, sneeze (52dB) or flush the lavatory (50dB) between these hours you are breaking the law. But it's a very 'simplistic' Act according to one expert, and very few local authorities have adopted it. It's the background noise that is important and this obviously varies. The Environmental Health Officer measures it and then compares it to the neighbour's noise you are complaining about. He/she will consider lots of factors – volume, when it happens and how often, and whether or not malice is involved – and may issue an Abatement Notice. If breached, your neighbours may then be prosecuted, but each circumstance is very subjective. Be persistent.

You can often get away with a noisy party: the bass-line thud of music is usually mid to low frequency and within the accepted decibel level. Planning a one-off bash? Warn (or invite) the neighbours to keep them sweet. But if you are a serial party animal, you may eventually be prosecuted for **Statutory Nuisance** under the Environmental Health Act, even if the noise is within the accepted levels.

If a developer is building close to your boundary wall, seek the advice of a surveyor experienced in **party wall disputes**. His fees are usually payable by the developer, and so are those of the solicitor you instruct to formulate an agreement. When you are the one building a wall close to a neighbour's building, you have to serve notice if it is within 3m (10 ft). So make sure it is 3.5m (11.5 ft) away.

The **'right to light':** this is another thorny issue, and is usually quoted when a neighbour puts up a wall or your garden becomes overshadowed by a neighbour's trees. If you have had a particular level of light uninterrupted for 20 years or more, you are entitled to keep a reasonable level for normal purposes, but that amount might not be the same as you had in the past. **Think not how much you have lost, but how much you have now.** You can ask for a right to light in your house or your greenhouse, but not in the garden itself. If it's in shadow from a tree, that's tough (though if the tree isn't protected by a preservation order, you are entitled to cut branches that overhang your boundary).

If a tree is causing damage to a pavement and belongs to the council, get them to remove it. Write stiff letters: at worst, try to bring a court action against the council to remove the tree.

UTILITIES

Utility companies have made monstrous profits since privatisation. Don't let them have more of your money. With a few simple precautions, you can save yourself hundreds of pounds:
- 25 per cent of a house's heat is lost through the roof. You could save up to

£70 a year by insulating your loft. The loft insulation should be at least 15cm (6in) deep.

- 40 per cent of your home's heating can be lost through windows and doors. By closing curtains just before dusk (making sure they are tucked behind radiators) you could save up to £15 a year.
- By lowering the temperature of your thermostat by just 1°C you can reduce your heating bill by as much as 10 per cent. An ideal temperature for sitting rooms, dining rooms and bathrooms is 21°C while around 18°C is better in a bedroom or kitchen.
- Foil behind radiators reflects heat back into the room.
- Use the 40°C setting on the washing machine.
- Showering instead of bathing saves water and money (around £15 a year).
- If you need to heat a small amount of water, use the kettle rather than boiling water in a saucepan.
- Around 20 per cent of the energy used in your home goes to heating water. If you turn the water thermostat down to about 60°C, you won't notice the difference in temperature but you will see the difference in your bills – a saving of around £15 a year.
- Off-peak tariffs like Economy 7 save money. Time your tumble dryer, dishwasher and washing machine to function early in the morning or late at night. Electricity is around 30 per cent cheaper at these times.
- Don't burn the midnight oil; turn lights off when you leave a room. Lighting makes up around 10–15 per cent of your electricity bill.

Had a **power cut for more than 24 hours** and it wasn't your fault or the weather's? You are entitled to compensation from your electricity provider. This increases for each additional 12 hours you are without electrical power.

An electricity provider must give you at least five working days' notice before interrupting your electricity supply. If it doesn't, demand compensation.

If British Telecom made an appointment to put in or mend a line and didn't turn up, you are entitled to money off your next bill as compensation. The same applies to the gas supplier, who must give you 24 hours' notice of cancellation.

If you have a septic tank, the cost of sewage disposal should be deducted from your water rates.

About to be cut off? You can't be disconnected for an unpaid electricity bill if the reading was estimated. Technically, the meter hasn't been read, therefore there is no precise sum due. Electricity supply cannot be cut off without warning. If you are having financial difficulties, the electricity company has to offer you a payment plan that will suit you, rather than cut you off. If no agreement can be reached, you can't be disconnected until 20 days after the date of the first bill.

Can you live without utilities? Yes, if you have solar-powered or wind-generated electricity, have a well and a septic tank on your property (not too close together!), and you run your heating from an oil or coal supply. The phone may be a more difficult problem to overcome, though you could rely on a mobile rather than land-line service.

TV LICENCES

It is **virtually impossible to beat the system** when it comes to TV licences. If you use a television set or other television apparatus (such as a TV-enabled computer), the law requires you to be covered by a valid TV licence. As of 1 April 2001, a colour television licence costs £109 annually, and a licence for a black and white set costs £34.50 per year.

The system is based on addresses not detector vans. **The assumption is made that everyone has a TV**, so your only excuse when they knock at the door is that you have no television, and it won't wash to argue that you only watch the commercial stations. Even the BBC chairman has a TV licence – or he should have! – and a separate licence is required for every separately occupied place.

For students and those living in halls of residence, you need to have a separate licence if you use a television set or other television apparatus in your own room. In the cases of shared accommodation, if you have all signed a joint tenancy agreement with your landlord, this is generally treated as an indication that it is one shared place and, therefore, the licence that covers the living room will also cover any televisions in the bedrooms. However, if you have signed individual agreements with your landlord, it is considered that there are separately occupied areas – therefore you will require licences for any additional televisions used in your own rooms.

From 1 November 2000, **anyone aged 75 years** or over was entitled to a free TV licence for their primary place of residence. This includes eligible people living with a younger relative. This is not an exemption from the TV licensing requirements. You will still need a valid TV licence even though the fee is being paid by the Government and not yourself. **You cannot get a free licence for a second home**, only for your primary residence.

From 1 April 2000, **if you are registered blind**, you were able to receive a 50 per cent discount on your TV licence.

Weird and wonderful housing laws

Local authorities in Belhaven, North Carolina, impose a sewer service charge of '$2 per month, per stool' – recently revised to read 'per toilet'.

If you are a tenant living in Rumford, Maine, you are forbidden from biting your landlord.

Need a quickie divorce? In Pennsylvania, a man is innocent of desertion if his wife rents a room to a boarder and crowds him out of the house.

Homeowners in Marin County, California, give up their right to privacy because they must admit, with a warrant or not, a county health inspector to their home during business hours.

Snoring a problem? Don't live in Dunn, North Carolina, where it is against the law to snore and disturb one's neighbours.

In Lake Charles, Louisiana, you will be fined for leaving a rain puddle on your front lawn for more than 12 hours.

USEFUL ADDRESSES

The Association of British Insurers
51 Gresham Street
London EC2V 7HQ
Tel: 020 7600 3333
Email: phil.ward@abi.org.uk
www.abi.org.uk

The British Association of Removers
3 Churchill Court
58 Station Road
North Harrow
Middlesex HA2 7SA
Tel: 020 8861 3331
Email: musers@bar.co.uk

British Rail Property Board
1 Eversholt Street
London NW1 2DD
Tel: 020 7214 9898

CORGI (Council for Registered Gas Installers)
4 Elmwood
Chineham Business Park
Crockford Lane
Basingstoke
Hants RG24 8WG
Tel: 01256 708133

The Electrical Contractors' Association
ESCA House
34 Palace Court
London W2 4HY
Tel: 020 7229 1266
Email: electricalcontractors@eca.co.uk
www.eca.co.uk

English Heritage
Customer Services Department
PO Box 569
Swindon SN2 2YP
Tel: 0870 333 1181
www.english-heritage.org.uk

Federation of Master Builders
14 Great James Street
London WC1N 3DP
Tel: 020 7242 7583
Email: brent/@fmb.org.uk
www.fmb.org.uk

Federation of Overseas Property Developers, Agents and Consultants
3rd Floor
95 Aldwych
London WC2B 4JF
Tel: 020 8941 5588

Gas Consumers' Council
Abford House
15 Wilton Road
London SW1V 1LT
Tel: 020 7931 0977

Guild of Removers and Storers
22a High Street
Chesham
Bucks HP5 1EP
Tel: 01494 792279

Institute of Electrical Engineers
Savoy Place
London WC2R 0BL
Tel: 020 7240 1871

Institute of Plumbing
64 Station Lane
Hornchurch
Essex RM12 6NB
Tel: 01708 472791
Email: info@plumbers.org.uk
www.plumbers.org.uk

Institute of Structural Engineers
11 Upper Belgrave Street
London SW1X 8BH
Tel: 020 7235 4535

Local Energy Advice Centres
Tel: 0800 512012

Legal Services Ombudsman
22 Oxford Court
Oxford Street
Manchester M2 3WQ
Tel: 0161 236 9532

National Approval Council for Security Systems (NACOSS)
Queensgate House
14 Cookham Road
Maidenhead
Berkshire SL6 8AJ
Tel: 01628 637512
www.nacoss.org

National Association of Estate Agents
Arbon House
21 Jury Street
Warwick
Warwickshire CV34 4EH
Tel: 01926 496800
Email: nae@dial.pipex.com
www.propertylive.co.uk

National Association of Plumbing
14 & 15 Ensign House
Ensign Business Centre
Westwood Way
Coventry CV4 8JA
Tel: 02476 470626
www.licensedplumber.co.uk

National House Building Council (NHBC)
Buildmark House
Chiltem Avenue
Amersham
Bucks HP6 5AP
Tel: 01494 434477
www.nhbc.co.uk

National Inspection Council for Electrical Installation Contracting
Vintage House
37 Albert Embankment
London SE1 7UJ
Tel: 020 7735 1322
www.NICEIC.org.uk

Office of Electricity Regulation (OFFER)
Hagley House
83–85 Hagley Road
Edgbaston
Birmingham B16 8QG
Tel: 0121 456 2100

Office of Gas Supply (OFGAS)
Stockley House
130 Wilton Road
London SW1V 1LQ
Tel 020 7828 0898

Office of Water Services (OFWAT)
Centre City Tower
7 Hill Street
Birmingham B5 4UA
Tel: 0121 625 1300

Office of the Ombudsman for Corporate Estate Agents
Beckett House
4 Bridge Street
Salisbury SP1 2LX
Tel: 01722 333306

Royal Institute of British Architects (RIBA)
66 Portland Place
London W1N 4AD
Tel: 020 7580 5533
www.riba.org.uk

Royal Institution of Chartered Surveyors (RICS)
12 Great George Street
London SW1P 3AD
Tel: 020 7222 7000
Email: info@rics.org.uk
www.rics.org.uk

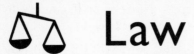 # Law

'Laws are like sausages. You should never watch them being made.' *Comte be Mirabeau*

Keep our noses clean and hopefully the only contact we will have with the law is to ask a policeman the time. But it's not easy to escape the great machine that is the British legal system at some point in our lives – whether it's because you are called up for jury service, are buying a house, getting married (or divorced) or, most importantly, making a will. Here's how to be ahead of the game.

JURY SERVICE

'A jury consists of twelve persons chosen to decide who has the better lawyer.' *Robert Lee Frost (1874–1963)*

Who has to do it?

It's part of your duty as a good citizen to do jury service if you are called and you qualify if you are between 18 and 70, your name is on the register of electors and you have lived in the UK for a period of at least 5 years since you were 13. But jury service can be intrusive, time-consuming (the average stint is ten days) and can prove to be an expensive altruistic duty (especially if you are self-employed). Nor is it often as exciting as episodes of *Kavanagh QC* would have us believe. So if you are called, double-check that you qualify and, if it would affect your life detrimentally, find out if you can be excused.

Reasons for not qualifying

There are many professions which disqualify people from sitting on a jury and most are connected with the judiciary. Even short-hand writers in court or forensic scientists are exempt. You might also consider taking holy orders, becoming a minister in a religious denomination or to make absolutely sure, become a nun or a monk.

You are also exempt if you:
- are currently on bail in criminal proceedings
- have ever been sentenced to life imprisonment, or to imprisonment or youth custody for five years or more
- have been detained at Her Majesty's or the Secretary of State for Northern Ireland's Pleasure
- have in the last ten years been in prison, youth custody or detention

- have a suspended sentence or done community service or been placed on probation within the last five years.

Neither do you qualify if **you have been hospitalised** with a mental disorder or have to get treatment regularly for a mental disorder, or if you are in guardianship under section 37 of the Mental Health Act, 1983.

If you do not fit into any of the above categories, you may still avoid jury service if:
- you are over 65 years old
- you have done jury service within the last two years
- you are a Peer or Peeress who might be summoned to the House of Lords
- you are an MP, officer of the Lords or Commons, or MEP
- you are a dentist, nurse, doctor, vet, midwife, or pharmacist
- you are a member of the armed forces.

Failing all this, you will have to **fall on the mercy of the judge** and argue that jury service is 'inconvenient' and that you have 'special problems which make it difficult' for you to do jury service. This can include personal hardship or conscientious objection, being a sole practitioner, or in some sort of profession that involves emergency call out.

Excuses to try (some of which have worked):
- I work for myself and my children will starve if I'm off work
- I have a strong moral objection to the British legal system
- I do not trust the police or anything they say
- I'm too busy so will just agree with the majority and not bother listening to the evidence
- I am a registered anarchist
- I am the new Messiah.

But the courts are rightly keen to get a good cross-section of people sitting on juries, and might argue that if your business can survive while you go on holiday for a fortnight, it will survive you sitting on a jury for 10 days.

So what about loss of earnings?

Employers are not obliged to pay when an employee attends for jury service. **If you are not going to be paid** while you are serving as a juror, your employer must fill in the 'certificate of loss of earnings', which arrives in the 'confirmation of service' pack. Your employer must complete the form and put the firm's stamp on the certificate or give you a letter which confirms that the information on the certificate is true. The letter must be on your employer's headed paper and brought on your first day of jury service.

If you are self-employed, you will have to provide the court with some evidence that you will lose earnings – get your accountant to plead your penury for you. If you think you will have to pay to get the evidence, ask advice from the court office first. The court may pay up to a maximum allowance for loss of earnings which is as follows (2001):

- in the first ten days of jury service, up to, and including four hours is £25.34 a day
- on the eleventh day of jury service and following days this will increase to a maximum of £50.67 a day
- in the first ten days of jury service, more than four hours is £50.67 a day
- on the eleventh day of jury service and following days this will increase to a maximum of £101.67 a day.

Because it is not always possible for the allowances for loss of earnings to cover the actual loss that has been incurred, you can claim you are suffering 'undue financial hardship' (especially if you are self-employed) by having to carry out the period of jury service. In these cases **you can apply to be excused from jury service** or have the jury service deferred to a time that is more convenient. 'The courts will do what they can to accommodate such requests,' says the Lord Chancellor's office, 'though it must be remembered that jury service is a public duty and circumstances might sometimes mean that excusal or deferral is not possible.'

'We have a criminal jury system which is superior to any in the world and its efficiency is only marred by the difficulty in finding twelve men every day who don't know anything and can't read.' *Mark Twain (1835–1910) speech on Americans and the English, London 1872*

FACT: In Oregon, USA, it is illegal to require a dead person to serve on a jury.

LAWYERS

'A lawyer is someone who profits by your experience.' *Anon*

Somehow lawyers will make money out of you. Just make sure it's the bare minimum. **Sometimes the initial interview is free** which is a nifty way to get advice without paying for it. Most solicitors' firms offer a free 30-minute interview on many points of law. The Citizens Advice Bureau has a list of names and contacts. A solicitor should give you a copy of his or her terms of business known as a letter of appointment or client care letter, and you are obliged to agree to this before work starts.

Working the system

Lawyers tend to charge by the hour so make sure you establish a ceiling amount, and check you know what other charges will be included, such as search fees or barristers' fees. Ask for a schedule of when you will have to pay, and get the bills sent regularly so you don't get a nasty shock at the end. Keep a copy of all correspondence too and ask that you are copied any letters that go out on your behalf.

Check that a qualified solicitor did your work, unless you were advised to the contrary. The Court of Appeal has ruled that the firm cannot recover the fee of any work done by any other adviser if you specifically asked for a solicitor – which means you won't have to pay.

You can't go to a barrister direct; a solicitor has to make the introductions, and you will have to rely on their judgement. However, you can complain about your barrister, though it should come as no surprise to hear that the legal profession is notoriously hard to sue!

Barristers are specialists in a particular area of the law, and you may find that their time is cheaper than a solicitor's, so don't automatically reject the idea of taking your query to a barrister through your solicitor.

Free legal representation?

'Three golden rules for lawyers:
Get the money up front.
Make no promises.
Get the money up front.'
US Anon

Despite the old jokes, it is possible to employ the services of a lawyer without having to pay. Your first stop should be the **Citizens Advice Bureau** which offers free legal advice (from qualified lawyers) and will be able to tell you whether a claim or legal action is worth pursuing. They will also tell you whether or not you qualify for Public Funding, formerly known as Legal Aid. Try too the growing number of legal Internet sites, many of which provide information, though not advice, free, but the information may answer your particular query. Try:

www.compactlaw.co.uk
www.firstlaw.co.uk
www.freelawyer.co.uk
www.lawgym.com
www.legaladvicefree.co.uk
www.legal-advice-online.co.uk
www.lawontheweb.co.uk.

Once you are briefing a solicitor or barrister, negotiate a **'conditional fee agreement'**, known as **'no win no fee'** in the USA. With the increasing abolition of Public Funding (Legal Aid), more and more lawyers are adopting this American system. It becomes in the interest of the lawyer to win your case (the downside being that they may refuse to take your case if they think it is a lost cause and probably unwinnable).

Use the **Small Claims Court**, originally established to help the public obtain compensation without having to use expensive lawyers. 'Small' is actually a misnomer, because the amount you can claim has risen over the years to up to £5,000. (For claims of more than this you are at risk of having to pay your opponent's costs if you don't succeed.) You complete a standard form (available from the courts), and a summons will be sent to the defendant with whom you have the grievance. They can either pay in full or dispute your claim. When proceedings are issued, you complete an N1 form and submit the court fees you must pay. These are not huge (from £27 for a claim up to £200, to £500 for a claim over £50,000, with solicitor's fees on top of that, which are upwards of £25). If you win your case these costs will be refunded. Your case will be heard around a table with just a judge present. Judges are notoriously gentle with lay people, but be careful to behave properly. Abuse, interruptions and overheated emotions will not help you. Visit www.small-claims.co.uk for excellent advice on Small Claims Court procedures.

Bad lawyers? Never!

'Let the lawyers do their job, but the time to fire your lawyer is when he starts telling you how to do yours.' Anon

You do have a claim against your lawyer if you think he has been negligent during legal proceedings. The claim should be by way of legal action. There is, however, what some would describe as a very unfair protection of legal professionals who are thought to have been negligent in Court as they are immune to legal proceedings. Thanks to a recent judgment, however, this immunity is no longer total. Complaints should be lodged to the Office for the Supervision of Solicitors (also known as the Solicitors' Complaints Bureau). You are unlikely to be any better off, but it is possible for the complaint to result in your brief being banned for professional misconduct.

Beat them at their own game by representing yourself in court

This is notoriously hard to do well (remember the saying: 'He who is his own lawyer has a fool for a client'), but certainly worth a bash as it will cost you very little compared with the price of using a solicitor and barrister. In cases of a claim you may have to pay to register it, but if you lose you will have no costs to pay. The people who really beat the system, says one barrister, are the bright people who have done their research. They twist the rules and get away with it far more than lawyers can. Again, judges are notoriously kind to people who represent themselves. Don't antagonise the judge though – just slip in the odd 'error' (like 'revealing' inadmissible evidence) and be wide-eyed with naivety.

Your lawyer is charging you too much?

Solicitors' expenses are a bit of an unknown quantity, and an early estimate may not be the same as the final bill you receive, because it will depend how much work was involved in the case. If you are unhappy about the final bill from your solicitor, you can always get a breakdown of the bill (a legal requirement for solicitors), and then write to the senior partner of the firm, and explain why you think the costs were not **'fair and reasonable'**. If the firm will not renegotiate it, don't pay it. If it doesn't exceed £50,000 or involve court proceedings, you can appeal to the **Office for the Supervision of Solicitors** (OSS)

(01926 822007/8), a department of The Law Society, which deals with cases of inadequate professional service and professional misconduct. But remember: if you have already paid your bill, you are disqualified from contesting it through the OSS.

In situations where cases have involved court proceedings (*contentious* is the technical term), you can have your bill **'assessed'**. This means going to court and having the solicitor justify the charges to a judge. Be warned though: if the bill is reduced by less than 20 per cent, you are liable to pay your own costs and those of the solicitor as well. If you live in Scotland, contact the Law Society of Scotland for advice (see the end of the chapter for the address).

No joy from the OSS? You can approach the **Legal Services Ombudsman**, who offers a free service (0161 236 9532).

MATRIMONIAL AND FAMILY LAW

'I was married by a judge. I should have asked for a jury.'
Groucho Marx (1895–1977)

All marriage ceremonies must take place between 8am and 6pm. **To be wed at any other time** you need to be Jewish or a Quaker, with ceremonies authorised by a registrar general's licence.

Who you can't marry

A man cannot marry:
- his mother, sister or daughter
- his grandmother
- his grand-daughter
- his aunt
- his niece
- his step-daughter
- his step-mother or step-grandmother
- the daughter of a son or a daughter of a former wife
- or his ex-mother-in-law's son's ex-wife!

A woman cannot marry:
- her father, brother or son
- her grandfather
- her grandson
- her uncle
- her nephew
- her step-son
- her step-father or step-grandfather
- the son of the son or daughter of a former husband
- or her ex-father-in-law's daughter's ex-husband.

But the good news is – you can marry your first cousin! But there may be a problem with the gene pool.

English law is very strict in the cases of **sex change**. You can only get married if both parties were a different sex at birth. This law applies even if one of you has undergone gender modification surgery. The solution would be to persuade a sympathetic clergyman to bless a 'union' though it would not be a legal one – this also applies to gay couples wanting to tie the knot. The British legal system does not recognise homosexual marriage … yet. Find yourself a gay priest who will bless your union.

Who can you marry then?

Step-relatives can marry provided they are at least 21 years of age, but it can be complicated. The younger of the couple must at no time before the age of 18 have lived in the same household as the older person. Neither must they have been treated as a child of the older person's family. In other words you cannot marry a step relative with whom you grew up.

A man can marry his sister-in-law and a woman can marry her brother-in-law provided they are both at least 21 years of age and the family memberships involved in creating the **in-law relationships** are both dead. For example, if a man wants to marry his daughter-in-law, both his son and his wife must be dead. In England and Wales, marriages like this aren't allowed with the calling of banns, but can take place in church.

You can get **married as many times as you like**, but have one spouse at a time; you must prove that your previous marriage ended as a result of bereavement or divorce. That means giving the registrar either a copy of your decree absolute or the death certificate of your former spouse. In February 2001, the Church of England announced that it would let divorced couples remarry in church, though this is not popular with some sections of the clergy and may be at the discretion of your local vicar.

At the moment, **pre-nuptial agreements** have no legal standing in the UK because divorce courts have the last word in the division of matrimonial property. This doesn't mean you can't draw up an agreement between yourself and your intended however, and it might be a good idea in the case of second marriages when you are wiser by experience. Make sure an agreement is watertight – have it drawn up by a solicitor.

The rules for unmarried couples are different to their married counterparts and **legally binding contracts** are enforceable as long as the couple remain unmarried. A partner has no recognition in law, so if you do not intend to marry but want your partner to benefit from your will, make sure you make one.

When you get re-married, you should **change your will**. Marriage automatically revokes any previous will, so if you die your new spouse will be left in a difficult position.

Any confidences between husband and wife are respected by law. If you are asked to testify against your spouse, you cannot be forced to … unless you want to.

Changing names

A woman is not obliged by law to change her maiden name to that of her husband. If she does take her husband's name, the marriage certificate is the necessary document to have. Fancy being double barrelled by combining both your surnames? You can do so by a Change of Name Deed, which is far cheaper than by deed poll. Contact your solicitor who can submit your deed poll application for you or do it online at www.weddingguide.co.uk/ weddingstore/deedpoll/DeedPoll.html. Equally, a man can take his wife's maiden name; he should change his name by Change of Name Deed. To start using your new name, write to all the companies and organisations that you deal with and let them know that from a certain date you wish to be known by your new name.

In fact, anyone over the age of 16 can change their name to any name they choose. So, if Fluffy Kitten or Jumping Jack Flash appeals, there's nothing in law to stop you using that name. **It's only an offence if you change your name for fraudulent purposes** – don't do it to try and beat the system. There are no restrictions on how often you change your name (who won the FA Cup this year?). This is called 'changing your name by usage'.

As before, inform everyone that you wish to be known by your new name. In this instance, however, there will be several documents that you can't get changed: for example, your passport, property deeds, income tax, national insurance, bank and building society accounts. To get these records and documents changed, you need to change your name by Change of Name Deed or by deed poll (you'll need to be at least 18 years old). There will be **some documents that retain your original name:** your birth certificate, any previous marriage certificates or decree absolute certificates.

As a British woman, you can keep your **citizenship after marrying** or, depending on the law of the other country involved, claim dual nationality. Some countries require you to give up your own citizenship in order to claim that of your spouse.

Family law point No. 1: there aren't many reasons why a marriage can be annulled. Unless you can prove that the marriage was never consummated or that your spouse had a sexually transmitted disease at the time of the wedding and did not tell you.

Family law point No. 2: a homosexual affair does not count as adultery in legal terms so …

Changed your mind?

Since 1971, the law says that an agreement between two persons to marry does not form a legally enforceable contract. If the engagement is called off, **does the girl have to return the ring?** The law says it's an absolute gift so the recipient is free to throw it in the river if they wish. However, you can protect your sparkling investment by putting it in writing that it was a conditional gift (to be returned if the engagement is broken), then you can legally demand its return. Very romantic.

It may seem cruel, but if you give someone a **wedding gift** and the wedding is called off, you are entitled to claim the gift back from the unhappy couple.

When **the reception or honeymoon is cancelled**, then the normal laws of contract apply to cancellation fees. In other words, the person or persons (usually the bride's parents) who made the booking are responsible, even if it was on behalf of someone else. They will have to pay the penalties mentioned in the original contract. However, as a parent out of pocket, there is nothing to stop you asking for recompense from one or both of the (previously) engaged couple whose decision led to the cancellation.

Getting divorced

'The difference between divorce and legal separation is that legal separation gives a husband time to hide his money.' *Johnny Carson, US television presenter*

The sole ground for divorce is the irretrievable breakdown of the marriage, but the court cannot make a finding of **irretrievable breakdown** unless it is satisfied that one of the following has taken place:
• adultery
• unreasonable behaviour
• desertion
• two years' separation (if the respondent consents to divorce)
• five years' separation (if they don't).

You can only file for divorce if you've been married for at least a year. The marriage has to be seen as having 'broken down irretrievably'. This is a catch-all phrase where nobody is seen as being at fault or solely responsible for the breakdown.

When divorce becomes inevitable, **you will need to be hard-headed**. Find an independent financial adviser to assess your financial needs, so you can beat any system that will penalise you.

Shop around for a solicitor who specialises in matrimonial law or who is a member of the Law Society Family Law Panel; you want to find someone you feel confident with. Your current solicitor may have been brilliant when it came to pushing through the sale of your house, but they won't necessarily be able to get you the best divorce. Someone who specialises in divorce is likely to be quicker than their counterparts who deal with medical negligence or civil rights, for example, and when they're charging by the hour, you don't want them wasting time (and your money!)

Solicitors make expensive marriage guidance counsellors. Don't be tempted to treat your solicitor as your close personal friend or as a counsellor. If you must **find a shoulder to cry on** or have a moan about things, use a friend. Solicitors are there to do a specific job for you and their time is money.

A solicitor who is a member of the SFLA (**Solicitor's Family Law Association**) will have a conciliatory approach to your divorce (i.e. a fair settlement) rather than expensive litigation and, if both husband and wife can be persuaded to agree to an undefended case, you'll beat the system by getting your divorce more quickly, cheaply and simply.

Public Funding (formerly known as Legal Aid) is not always free. If you recover money or property in the divorce proceedings, you will have to repay your costs. Public Funding is only free if the dispute is non-financial (for example, violence is the problem). Sometimes you may have to pay monthly contributions depending on the individual's income and capital.

Consider going for mediation when it comes to **financial or children issues** in your divorce. It will keep costs down and it's better to reach an agreement to preserve a relationship in the family, especially if there are children involved.

How We Beat The System

Susie from Birmingham has recently divorced. She says:
- When you are married know where your money is. Keep a tab on joint accounts and know all the account numbers.
- Don't let your solicitor act as your marriage guidance counsellor. They can waste your time and charge you more for asking you emotionally leading questions which have nothing to do with the points of the divorce.
- You are vulnerable but don't be taken for a ride. Write down what it is you want to ask your solicitor so you don't forget during your meeting and, if you are not feeling confident, take someone with you who can be dispassionate.
- Get the process of divorce clear from the start: ask your solicitor what will happen when, and ask about time-scales. Unless you are a serial divorcer, you will be ignorant of the process and the legal profession can keep you that way.
- You are at a disadvantage if you make the first communication in any consideration during divorce proceedings. It gives the other side time to consider their response.
- But where children are involved, be the first one to make the demands. It gives you the upper hand.

Home ownership is a knotty problem when it comes to breaking up. Unless a pre-nuptial agreement says otherwise, section 37 of the Matrimonial Proceedings and Property Act, 1970 says that either partner making a substantial contribution to improving the property may have acquired a beneficial interest in it, to the extent of the contribution made. Use the Married Women's Property Act of 1882 or the Matrimonial Causes Act, 1973 to apply for a court order giving equitable distribution of the property. And beware, for at present a pre-nuptial agreement may not necessarily be binding.

Beat problems in the future: apply for a clean break through the courts or financial claims against the other party will remain open indefinitely. If one half of the 'former' couple won the National Lottery, for example, a claim could be made by their ex.

You can get a court order to **exclude your violent partner** from your home even if your name doesn't appear on the title deeds or rent book.

> **FACT:** Civil annulments are obtained by about 150 couples each year. In one case a 68-year-old woman won a nullity decree on the basis that her 78-year-old arthritic husband did not fulfil her expectations of a sex life. (*The Times*, August 1999)

Dear departed

If you have made a will and then you get divorced, your will won't be revoked **but your ex-spouse will 'disappear' from the will** as if they had died. They can't act as executor or benefit from your will. You can always remember them by making them a beneficiary of a new will. Leave them your Barry Manilow records perhaps?

ADOPTION AND SURROGACY

Adoption has become more and more difficult due to the social acceptance of abortion and the more tolerant attitude towards single parenthood. Private adoption is illegal in this country and to adopt, you must be at least 21. Many agencies set an upper age limit (around 35 for a woman, 40 for a man), but this is not the law so you are within your rights to apply over this age.

To qualify:
- you don't have to be rich, but you must be able to afford a child
- there will be medical examination and you will be registered with your local social services department
- there will be regular assessment visits by social workers
- you need a clean police record
- you must also complete a home study course.

As well as local social services and social work departments, you could try one of the **voluntary adoption agencies** in your area. Try www.baaf. org.uk/info/vaa.htm.

You have a better chance of adopting a child if you are prepared to adopt an older child, not a baby. These children often come from very disturbed backgrounds and need very special families to adopt them.

Having trouble adopting in this country? Consider adopting a child from abroad: contact your local social services, the Department of Health, the Home Office and the embassy of the country where you intend to go for the child. Try www.adoptionsearch.com.

If you were adopted and want to trace your parents, The Adopted Children's Register keeps details of the child's sex, date of birth and new name as well as the adopter's names, occupations and date and place of the adoption order. It will not give the natural mother or father's name and address. The Register is kept at the Office of National Statistics, but you must be over 18.

You can also find out details from **The Adoption Contact Register** of parents and other relatives (blood or marriage) of an adopted child who want to supply their details. It's a voluntary act so you won't find information on every single family who gave up a child for adoption. Information will only be passed on if both parties want it.

Surrogacy arrangements are a very grey area in law and are unenforceable in the courts. Should a surrogate mother decide to keep the baby, a couple have no redress. This applies even if the baby is genetically theirs. The couple also have no means of recovering any 'expenses' they may have paid out.

It is illegal to advertise for a surrogate mother and to pay a surrogate a fee, but as a surrogate mother you can claim 'reasonable' expenses which are allowed. According to British Medical Association guidelines, these could be between £7,000 and £10,000.

Beat the chance of problems: once the child is born the intended father and the surrogate mother should enter into a Parent Responsibility Agreement. This gives them equal rights over the child. After six weeks the intended parents can apply for a Parental Order which will give them full and permanent parental rights over the child.

The system says that intended mothers who are in employment, face discrimination as **employment law does not recognise their entitlement to maternity leave** or maternity pay if the 'mother' was never pregnant. Make sure you have enough holiday time stored up, or take unpaid leave. Upon adoption, both parents are entitled to unpaid parental leave.

For further information and to find a surrogate mother, explore the Internet with sites such as www.surrogacy.org.uk and www.surrogacy.com.

PERSONAL INJURY AND COMPENSATION

Physical injury

A claim for personal injury (mental or physical) has to be lodged within three years of the event or the date when you realised you had a significant injury. This is easy enough to calculate in the event of say, a car crash, but tricky with an infection or result of exposure to a dangerous substance (like asbestos). **Get ahead of the game** by keeping a record of all details and events. The local authority is responsible for the safety of highways (and this includes pavements), so if you are injured tripping over a paving stone, get immediate evidence: take a photograph of the offending stone as soon as possible. Take pictures too of your injuries, and reports on any subsequent visits to the hospital or doctor. Local authorities do have a statutory defence if they can show that they have taken 'reasonable care' in keeping the highways safe.

FACT: A third party is only liable for someone's injury, mental or physical, if they ought reasonably to have foreseen that what they did or did not do was likely to expose them to risk of injury.

FACT: Around 85 per cent of people who are eligible to claim compensation after an accident don't. Could you be one of them? The Law Society has a free telephone advice line for people who have had an accident. You get a free 30-minute interview and the details of a specialist solicitor. Call Freephone 0500 192939.

FACT: A huge 98 per cent of all personal injury cases are settled out of court, and 50 per cent of cases settle without proceedings ever having started.

But the laws surrounding personal injury are very hard to beat – because so many people have tried to beat them! There are many examples of claimants being videoed whilst in pursuit of their claim to make sure that debilitating injuries do not magically disappear when away from the eyes of the court. (One private detective was sent by a solicitor to pose as a guest at the bed and breakfast establishment run by the wife of a man claiming to have been injured at work. Whilst the claimant was serving breakfast he inadvertently revealed to his 'guest' that the weather was so nice he was off to play golf...) Be cautious about your behaviour whilst in pursuit of your claim, and afterwards too. But beware as your conduct may be fraudulent.

Mental injury

Mental injury, by its very nature, is harder to prove or indeed disprove, and many people have effectively faked mental conditions. In order to bring a claim for mental injury, you have to establish:
• an identifiable psychological condition
• it is associated with an event or sequence of events
• it was reasonably foreseeable that you were open to risk.

The tragedy at Hillsborough Football Stadium in 1989, in which 96 people died, is a case in point. Many people claimed mental injury after watching the scenes on TV. The number of claimants was eventually whittled down to those who had a relative involved in the event, and to those who were close enough in time and space for it to affect them as TV viewers.

Those you sue at your peril

Certain professions are notoriously hard to win compensation from. These include:

- the medical profession. (You have to prove that no responsible body of medical opinion would have behaved the way your doctor did. The only way to pursue a claim is to get a detailed second opinion from a competent expert.)
- the legal profession. (Only a brave or insane person takes on the professionals at their own game.)
- the Army. (The argument being that an element of danger comes with the territory.)
- the Home Office. (Particularly if you are a prisoner.)

How We Beat The System

Suing the system successfully

A man was using the facilities in a public lavatory and enjoying a smoke at the same time. He flicked the cigarette butt into the bowl between his legs and inadvertently ignited the cleaning fluid around the rim of the toilet bowl. With a badly burned behind, he was carried on a stretcher by ambulance men, who, on hearing the woeful tale of how the injury occurred, hooted with laughter and dropped the stretcher. The poor man broke his leg, but successfully sued the local authority responsible for the public conveniences, and the ambulance service for negligence.

CHANGING THE LAW

'Reform? Reform? Why, aren't things bad enough already?' Lord Justice Astbury (1866–1939)

The most effective way to beat any system is to change it. It's a dramatic step to take, but if you feel strongly about something, you can lobby to **change the law**. (It worked for the Suffragettes.) Positive, constructive action is more appealing to the public than negative, 'we want to ban it' action.

It is everyone's right to freedom of speech, so **use the press and media** to get your message across. Put together a well thought out argument, backed up by facts and figures, and try to present the information in a fresh way. New angles are more likely to get press coverage.

Put together a pressure group, with the support of as many influential people as possible, and link up with other groups who are of a similar mind. A co-operative or coalition is more effective than a lone protester. Speak to other successful pressure groups to get ideas on how to proceed. Visit www.electoralcommission.gov.uk/ for information on lobbying Parliament.

Don't resort to violence. The Poll Tax riots may have been effective, but they were also very destructive.

Everyone has the right to **contact their MP** on any issue. You can either write to your MP at the House of Commons, or go to see him or her at a local constituency session or at the House of Commons; fill in a green card and ask the doorkeeper to try and track down your MP for you. You might think you are beating your head against a brick wall, but you may find your MP is sympathetic (especially at re-election time) and a certain number of Private Members' Bills get a reading in the life of each Parliament.

For advice on making a difference, visit www.citizensconnection.net, which offers advice on getting a campaign started, and making it succeed.

LITIGATION

'It is ignorance of the law rather than knowledge of it that leads to litigation.' *Cicero (106–43 BC)*

The only way to beat expensive litigation is **to keep any sort of action out of court**. Either push for a settlement, whatever your claim, or, if someone is making a claim against you, offer to settle before court proceedings ensue.

So how do you keep information out of court? You're involved in a lengthy bout of correspondence over some grievance. You make an offer to settle the grievance. But, if the offer is rejected and the case goes to court, you don't want the fact that you made the offer to be revealed. Writing **'without prejudice'** at the top of your correspondence in which you make the offer means it cannot be used in court.

Be really cheeky and send two letters – one marked 'without prejudice' that mentions the offer and an unmarked one that doesn't mention the offer, but does pursue the argument. That way, you get the best of both worlds.

Taking someone to court may make you feel a whole lot better, but it is fairly pointless if they won't be able to pay when you win. **If you lose, you'll have to pay the defendant's costs as well as your own.** Lawyers can advise you as to your chances of winning the case, and you can also go to the Small Claims Court (see page 115), where you are unlikely to be liable for any costs (other than the court fee) after your claim has been issued, even if you lose.

A fax can be a legal document, but you must follow it up with a hard copy sent though the post. **Emails** are a bit of a grey area. The same rules on confidentiality would apply if it was intended to be a 'without prejudice' communication. The problem concerns the date emails were sent, as they carry no postmark, however, so long as you save the content of emails, and they remain on your server, they will carry a note of the date they were sent. There is no guarantee that they were opened by the recipient however, and emails can be faked.

I haven't got a bean

If you are owed (or indeed if you owe) more than £750 and it is not a secured loan (like a mortgage), you can **petition for bankruptcy** as the creditor or the debtor.

If it is you who owes the money, you don't pay up and the court believes that you can't, you will be declared bankrupt. There is three weeks from a statutory demand (for repayment of the debt) during which you can pay. Bankruptcy is automatically discharged after three years, after which you are not responsible for the original bankruptcy debts, so **it can be worth your while to declare yourself bankrupt**. Bankruptcy can sometimes be discharged after two years if not too serious.

If your builder's made a mess, but you **can't get compensation** because he says he's bankrupt, you can join the queue behind the bank and the Inland Revenue with claims on his assets. Or you can beat the bankruptcy trap by paying for work with a credit card (not always possible with builders). If you have a bad feeling about a builder (besides not employing him in the first place), buy an insurance-backed guarantee that protects you against this situation, or only use a builder who is a member of a trade association.

How We Beat The System

Successful acquittal – it's all down to technicalities

All fledgling lawyers are taught about the case of Collins, a decorator, who, whilst walking home late one night from the pub, noticed the open bedroom window of the daughter of the house where he had recently done some decorating work. Removing his clothes, he climbed a ladder up to the window. The girl, groggy with sleep, assumed the visitor was her boyfriend and invited him in. Sexual intercourse ensued. He was acquitted of rape and burglary because there was some doubt as to whether he had actually had his foot on the window-sill before she invited him in …

WILLS

'What you leave at your death, let it be without controversy; else the lawyers will be your heirs.' *Selleck Osborn (1782–1826), US journalist and poet*

FACT: Two-thirds of people don't have a will when they die. (*The Law Society, 2001*)

Whilst we spend our lives trying to beat systems, **it is not until we die that we have any real power** to do so. Your will is exactly that – it states the way you would like your death to be handled and what you would like done with everything you have left behind. So long as you are of sound mind, it is perfectly within your rights to be buried to the accompaniment of a brass band and dressed in a tutu if that is your final wish.

Intestacy is a headache for all those you leave behind. The most effective way to beat the system (in this case the lawyers and the Inland Revenue) is to ensure you make that final will and testament. Without one, your spouse will only receive a legacy of £125,000 plus a life interest in half of the balance. Your children will receive the other half, plus the remaining half under the life interest when the surviving spouse dies. If you are without dependants or family, then your estate simply goes to the State.

Who can make your will?

Use a solicitor to draw up your will, and there is some legal redress if they do it wrong – they can be sued later for compensation. Banks and building societies will also draw up wills, but they often insist on being the executor as well, for which they charge. Rather than paying a solicitor or bank to draw up the document, **use a charity's will-making service**. Oxfam and Help the Aged both offer such services. In return, they hope you'll leave them a legacy.

There are firms of will writers, so you don't have to have a solicitor to write one for you, but the critical word is *write*. This goes right back to the Wills Act of 1837. **Wills must be written** (i.e. not taped or videoed), and signed by the person who made it at the end, and the signature must be witnessed by two independent witnesses present at the same time. So even if your dying wishes are scrawled on the back of a fag packet (you can actually write your will on anything), keep it brief because two more people need to sign there too. You can even snub the system: one will-maker made out his will on the back of a letter from a creditor.

Once you've got a will ...

There is still no central register of wills and no requirement to lodge a will. So once you have made a will, lodge it with your solicitor and keep a copy yourself. And remember to tell your executor(s) that you have a will.

FACT: It costs under £100 to make a will.

'If it wasn't for wills, lawyers would have to go to work at an essential employment. There is only one way you can beat a lawyer in a death case. That is to die with nothing. Then you can't get a lawyer within ten miles of your house.' *William Penn Adair, 1925*

Odd wills

A man left his widow one farthing, with directions that it be forwarded to her in an unstamped envelope ...

... and another bequeathed his wife 'one pair of my trousers, as a symbol of what she wanted to wear in my lifetime, but did not.'

'To my wife I leave her lover, and the knowledge that I was not the fool she thought me; to my son I leave the pleasure of earning a living. For 20 years he thought the pleasure was mine. He was mistaken.' (*1934*)

Another man bequeathed £1,000 to his widow, declaring that it would have been £10,000 had she let him read his evening newspaper in peace. (*1903*)

A Viennese millionaire directed in his will that an electric light be installed in his vault and another in his coffin. He failed to provide for extra bulbs.

DEALING WITH THE POLICE

An Englishman's house is his castle, and the police normally need a warrant to enter your property, unless, for example, they are trying to stop someone being hurt. To search your house when you are not there, they must leave a copy of the search warrant behind, and leave it secure if they had to break in. Ask for a receipt if the police take anything away from your home.

Being arrested is an experience few of us want to have, and the police is not a system for the faint hearted to try and beat. **You are in fact under no legal obligation to 'help the police with their enquiries'**, and they can't make you go with them to the police station without arresting you (see below).

You also don't have to give the police your name and details, but it's probably a good idea to do so. You can, however, take down their details (a police officer's number will be on his or her uniform) and ask which police station they are from. You can ask them why you are being questioned and **you must receive a good reason**.

It's a fair cop

If you are arrested and taken to a police station, you are under police control and therefore have to do what they say. Don't fight the situation. Being rude, struggling or resisting could only land you in more trouble. But you have rights and don't be afraid to state them. There's a set procedure that you will have to go through: an interview, a possible search and maybe some time in a cell. If you are asked or forced to do something that you know violates your rights, insist that your protest is written down for the record.

Your rights

- You have the right to notify someone of your arrest. Depending on the offence, the police may or may not be prepared to allow you to make a phone call yourself. The person you notify should be a lawyer or else a friend or relative who can contact one for you immediately. If you can't get hold of anybody, ask the police to get you the duty lawyer who is on call.
- You do not have to talk to the police until you've been advised by a solicitor. The solicitor is meant to arrive at the police station within 45 minutes of being told that the client is to be interviewed. In the meantime, you don't have to 'have a chat' with the police, however often they may suggest it. You might end up saying something that incriminates you. If you really are under pressure to talk, you have the right to talk to a solicitor over the phone.
- The police can force you to have your photograph taken without your written consent once you have been charged.
- You can be strip searched providing the police have 'reasonable grounds' to believe one to be necessary. You can only be strip searched by officers of the

same sex as you; no one of the opposite sex should be present. You can't refuse to be strip searched. The best advice is not to create problems if a strip search is carried out, but then to look into the question of whether you might have a claim for assault on the basis that there were not reasonable grounds for carrying it out.

- There are two kinds of search: intimate and non-intimate. A non-intimate search involves taking off all your clothes and being given a visual check. Intimate searches involve internal checks. An officer of superintendent rank or higher has to authorise an intimate search in writing. You should ask to see this authorisation first.

- Often repeating your rights calmly and with authority can get the police to back off until your solicitor arrives.

On the spot searches

Beat trouble later: if you are being searched in public, you should not be asked to remove more than your coat or jacket and gloves. If you are out of sight (in a police van, for example) you can be strip searched as long as it is conducted in the manner described above. You do not have to be arrested before searches like this are carried out. After the search, you either have to be arrested or let go. The police have to keep a **record of the search**, who carried it out and why. You are entitled to ask for a copy of that record for up to a year after the event.

Have you been injured?

If you sustain injuries whilst being arrested or while you are at the police station, go to a doctor as soon as possible. Get photos taken, either with negatives that bear the date or hold up the day's newspaper as proof of when your injuries occurred.

If you have a **complaint against the police** because of a wrongful arrest, you should make it before you leave the police station. However, usually the police will not take details of the complaint there and then, but will ask you to go away and come back. If you didn't make a complaint then, you can go to any police station and ask a senior officer to take your statement. Check when you'll get a written response. And if you're not satisfied with that response, talk to your solicitor about whether you have a case for compensation.

Weird and wonderful laws

Weep in the witness box in a Los Angeles courtroom and you could be found guilty of misconduct.

There is no statutory requirement in Indianapolis that a juror be sane.

Children in Illinois can sue their mothers for negligence during the time whilst the child was in the womb. A similar case is pending in the UK.

Husbands in England can be prosecuted for raping their wives, although if proven the sentence is often less severe than if the rape was perpetrated by someone else. Wives cannot be prosecuted for raping their husbands.

If a Greek man is caught kissing a woman in public, even if she is his wife, he can face the death penalty.

Enter a marriage as a dare in Delaware and you have the right to have it annulled.

In Kentucky it is illegal to marry the same man four times.

In Michigan, a man owns his wife's clothes.

USEFUL ADDRESSES

Association of Personal Injury Lawyers
33 Pilcher Gate
Nottingham NG1 1QE
Tel: 01159 580585

Commission for Racial Equality
Elliot House
10–12 Allington Street
London SW1E 5EH
Tel: 020 7828 7022

Equal Opportunities Commission
Overseas House
Quay Street
Manchester M3 3HN
Tel: 0161 833 9244

House of Commons Information Office
Tel: 020 7219 4272
www.parliament.uk/

House of Lords Information Office
Tel: 020 7219 3107

Law Society of England & Wales
Law Society House
113 Chancery Lane
London WC2A 1PL
Tel: 020 7242 1222

Law Society of Northern Ireland
Law Society House
98 Victoria Street
Belfast BT1 3JZ
Tel: 028 9023 1614

Law Society of Scotland
26 Drumsheugh Gardens
Edinburgh EH3 7YR
Tel: 0131 226 7411

Legal Services Commission
(formerly known as the Legal Aid Board)
85 Gray's Inn Road
London WC1X 8AA
Tel: 020 7813 1000

Legal Services Ombudsman
22 Oxford Court
Oxford Street
Manchester M2 3WG
Tel: 0161 236 9532

Local Government Ombudsman
21 Queen Anne's Gate
London SW1H 9BU
Tel: 020 7915 3210

National Consumer Council
20 Grosvenor Gardens
London SW1W 0DH
Tel: 020 7730 3469

Office for the Supervision of Solicitors
(also known as the Solicitors' Complaints
    Bureau)
Victoria Court
8 Dormer Place
Leamington Spa CV32 5AE
Tel: 01926 822007/8

Office of National Statistics
Segensworth Road
Titchfield
Fareham
Hants PO15 5RR
Tel: 01329 813758

Police Complaints Authority
10 Great George Street
London SW1P 3AE
Tel: 020 7273 6450

Scottish Legal Services Ombudsman
2 Greenside Lane
Edinburgh EH1 3AH
Tel: 0131 556 5574

Solicitors' Family Law Association
PO Box 302
Orpington
Kent BR6 8QX
Tel: 01689 850227

Leisure

'Because you see the main thing today is – shopping…
Today you're unhappy? Can't figure it out? What is the
salvation? Go shopping.' *Arthur Miller*

In Britain, we work longer hours than anywhere else in Europe – between 1971 and 1996 our total free time increased by a measly 5 per cent, yet our spending on leisure has never been higher – £6.98 billion in 1998. Leisure accounts for a higher proportion of our household spending than anything else. So how come we're spending so much in so little time? Pay more, get less? It just doesn't add up. Come on, you owe it to yourself to beat the system.

FACT: The average household is spending a record-breaking £62.50 a week on leisure, £57 a week on housing, £55 a week on food and £53 per week on motoring.

FACT: 57 per cent of the population sometimes work on a Saturday.

FACT: Compared with the US, British consumers are paying more for just about everything (apart from healthcare!). We pay over 50 per cent more for furniture and carpets; over 50 per cent more for hotels and eating out; over 30 per cent more for sporting goods; over 25 per cent more for cars and motorbikes; and over 20 per cent more for electrical goods.

SHOPPING

Finding real bargains takes dedication – but it's possible. Shopping as a competitive sport can be invigorating – aerobic, even. But don't get carried away. A cool head and a razor sharp credit card are what you need to succeed.

When you go shopping, you're entering into a legal contract with the seller every time you buy something. The contract offers protection to both you and the seller. For example, you may be entitled to a full refund of the price you paid if there is something wrong with what you bought, but if you simply decide you don't like the colour, the seller can refuse to refund your money.

Under the Sale and Supply of Goods Act, 1994:
- Goods must be of **satisfactory quality** – and this applies to both new and second-hand goods bought from a trader (but not from a private individual).
- The goods should be durable, safe and have acceptable appearance, taking into account their price, nature, any description applied to them and any other relevant circumstances.

- If goods are very cheap you can't expect top quality, but whatever the price they shouldn't be faulty.
- Sale goods that aren't marked as sub-standard should also be fit for their normal purpose.

Under the Sale of Goods Act, 1979:
- Goods must be **fit for any particular purpose made known** either expressly or by implication, to the seller – this applies to new and second-hand goods bought from a trader (but not from a private individual).
- Goods must be **as described** – this applies to new and second-hand goods bought from a trader or a private individual.
- If any part of the agreement between the seller and the customer has been broken (including breaking the basic statutory rights) this is called **breach of contract**, and the customer will probably be entitled to their money back (a refund).

The Acts give you **six years from the time you buy** something to make a claim. But these rights don't extend to an immediate refund for all that time. You only have a relatively short period to get a full refund, after which it is assumed that you have 'accepted' the item.

If you **buy something in a sale**, you still have all your normal rights.

Don't be drawn in by a **'closing down' sale** – shops can have as many closing down sales as they like without ever having to close.

Even shop prices are simply an **'invitation to tender'**. You are free to make a lower offer for anything. (And the shop assistant is free to make you feel like a prize idiot.)

If you see something obviously **wrongly priced** in a shop, the shop is not in fact obliged to sell you that item at the lower price, as long as it was a genuine mistake.

Break something in a shop where there is a notice saying **'all breakages must be paid for'**? You may not have to pay if you can prove that the shelves were poorly stacked, or the item was sticking out, or if there were other circum-stances whereby it was not your negligence that caused the breakage.

Anyone can **refuse to serve a customer** as long as they are not discriminating unfairly.

If you're **hot on recycling** you are legally entitled to hand extra packaging (such as boxes or bags) back to the shop when you've bought something.

Haggling – for pleasure and profit

There's nothing to stop you haggling – apart from your British reserve, of course. But if it saves you money, surely it's worth a try?

High street chains, where things have a clearly labelled price, are unlikely to accept a lower offer, but **smaller shops and market stalls may be more receptive**, and it is always worth a go for services like building work.

Electrical stores and furniture stores are the most likely to offer deals, according to the Consumers' Association, and independents are a better bet than chains. If you are buying more than one item, you can often get money off, or free delivery and installation at the very least.

Visit the store at **a quiet time**, rather than a busy Saturday afternoon when the weekend staff are on.

If the salesperson says they don't have authority to negotiate, **ask to see the manager**.

Have three prices in your head before you start when you haggle:
* the most you are prepared to pay
* an average price which is acceptable
* a price which you will be over the moon about if you can achieve.

Challenge yourself to achieve the lowest price, but if you can't get the goods at your top price, just walk away.

Always act surprised (disagreeably) when the sales person tells you the price, then just shut up and let them try to justify the price. More often than not, they'll add a few extras in without you even having to ask.

Don't go first in naming a price. Let the seller go first and then work down from there.

Resist buying products in your own home. **Door-to-door salespeople** are adept at getting you tied up in knots and agreeing to an outrageously high price. Never agree to buy at the first meeting. Take a few days to consider, and don't be pressured by never-to-be-repeated offers. If you insist you will still obtain the same discount a few days later.

You was robbed!

Being misled about prices can be a criminal offence. If a trader claims '£99 reduced from £200' – and it never was £200, that is misleading and they can be prosecuted for it. It's also considered misleading if a trader fails to show any hidden extras or say when a price is conditional (on another purchase, for example). The local Trading Standards Officers are your knights in shining white armour in cases like these.

Clothes shopping

Even if a mail-order catalogue is too expensive for you, there's no harm being **on the mailing list**. The end of season sales are often fantastic, but you have to be quick off the mark when it comes to ordering, as the stock levels may be extremely low.

Catalogues with big mailing lists usually send out their catalogues in **alphabetical order**. When the sales catalogues go out, this could mean that Mrs Aardvark will get hers before Mrs Zebra – and if stocks are low, Mrs Zebra may never get a look in. Request another catalogue to your address, but give a surname beginning with A or even Aa.

Get fabulous fashion items from **designer outlet stores**. Even when there's no sale, the stock (which is usually end of lines) can be discounted by as much as 60 or 70 per cent. Add on an extra 10 to 30 per cent during their sale time and you're laughing.

If you're a teeny size 8–10, we hate you, but you can buy samples from clothing manufacturers and designers at hugely reduced price.

If you're feeling brave, **try an Internet swap shop**. You simply register with details of what you want to swap, then wait for interested parties to get in touch.

> www.webswappers.com
> www.webwedding.co.uk (where you can pick up a second-hand wedding dress)
> www.swapitshop.co.uk

Buy a copy of *The Good Deal Directory*, aptly subtitled 'The Bargain Hunter's Bible'. It contains listings, by region, of discount outlets, factory shops and dress agencies throughout the country, with categories including clothes, household and giftwear, electrical equipment, furniture and soft furnishings, and food and leisure. Published by the author, the brilliant Noelle Walsh, it is available from book shops or direct from The Good Deal Directory, PO Box 4, Lechlade, Gloucestershire, GL7 3YB (01367 860016), www.gooddealdirectory.co.uk.

Factory outlets

Factory outlet villages, like Bicester, are a dream come true for bargain hunters, but if you know a few tricks you can do even better.
- Try to go on a weekday when things are quiet – **80 per cent of factory village shopping customers visit on a weekend**.
- Although they rarely advertise this, most factory villages slash prices still further at the same times as the traditional high street sale times – January and June/July.
- The best buys overall are the more expensive items, so go up a brand from what you would normally buy.
- Turnover is usually very fast. So if you like something, buy it; you are unlikely to find it again.
- Make a note of any measurements (family members as well as curtain sizes) so that you are ready to snap up bargains without having to check.
- Call first (particularly if you are coming from a long way away) to check on availability of specific items and on opening times.

- Just because it was a long drive – you don't have to buy something to make it worthwhile.
- When buying discounted goods, you have the same rights under the Sale and Supply of Goods Act, 1994, the Sale of Goods Act, 1979 and the Consumer Protection Act, 1987 as you would in ordinary shops.
- Check if an item is a second. You'll usually find a label on the garment stating why this is so. Although your statutory rights are in place at factory shops, you can't return a second because of a fault indicated at the outset.
- Clothes tend not to look as good as they do in conventional stores – they're often less artfully presented and racks are often crowded. Don't be put off – have a rummage and you could come up with a real find.

Weddings on the cheap

Getting married can put a serious dent in your finances, but it doesn't have to be that way! Try these ideas for cutting costs.

- Get hitched in Scotland! No seriously, a basic church wedding there will cost around £35, almost half the price of a register office job in England and Wales, once you include the notice fee, the attendance of the registrar and the certificate.
- Another advantage of getting married in Scotland is that, once you've got the bride and groom, the minister and two witnesses, you can do it anywhere – even in a park. Take a picnic and cut down on catering costs!
- Try getting married on Friday. You'll get fewer people turning up for a start, and venues, photographers and caterers are all cheaper.
- When hiring your venue, don't say it's for a wedding as that can bump the fee up immediately.
- Clothes rental shops often sell gowns, wedding and bridesmaid dresses, dress suits and hats once they've been rented out a few times.

Comfort stops

Anyone will tell you, it's impossible to give shopping the care and attention it merits if you're dying to go to the loo. Despite the fact that women take around twice as long as men when emptying their bladders, there are rarely more women's loos in shops than mens. There is a British Standard which recommends that any store with a sales area of over 1,000 sq m (10,760 sq ft) should provide lavatories for its customers. However, it is only a recommendation. Shops can't make money if there's a loo where a clothes rail could be, and many don't.

Restaurants, however, must provide lavatories for their customers, so shops with cafés will always have facilities for desperate shoppers.

The counterfeiting of all goods, including business software, music, video and computer games, costs UK companies between £4 billion and £6.2 billion annually, and it's illegal to sell counterfeit goods. It's not, however, an offence to buy or wear counterfeit goods. Just as well, really, as it's reckoned that 10 per cent of the clothing we now wear is fake. And rivalling Hong Kong as a source of counterfeit goods, let's hear it for our very own Leicester! But if you don't want to dodge the Trading Standards Officers, you can buy fakes – sorry, replicas – on the net. Try www.anyknockoffs.com, and www.replicashop.com for a wide range of designer-inspired goods at tempting prices.

Unwelcome visitors

You are sent unsolicited goods and an invoice. Don't pay, but hang on to the goods. You could contact the sender and tell them you didn't order them and suggest they come and pick them up. If they don't, the goods are yours after 30 days. Equally, you don't have to do anything. If the goods are still with you after six months, you can keep them. However, if they ask for them back and offer to pay the postage within that period, you can't refuse, neither can you stop them picking the goods up.

Fed up with junk mail dropping through your door every morning? Contact the Mailing Preference Service asking them to get your name removed from mailing lists. The service was set up by the direct mail industry and is free. It can take up to three months for the junk mail to stop arriving:

> The Mailing Preference Services
> Freepost 22
> London W1E 7EZ
> Tel: 0345 034599

If you're being **pestered by telephone sales people**, you can cut down on the number of calls, although you'll probably never stop them altogether. Register with the Telephone Preference Service (TPS) by contacting:

> The Telephone Preference Service Ltd
> 5th Floor
> Haymarket House
> 1 Oxenden Street
> London SW1Y 4EE
> Tel: 0845 070 0707

Due credit

If you're **refused credit by a shop**, you can ask for the name of the Credit Reference Agency that the shop uses. You have 28 days to ask for the information after you've been refused credit. They must give you the information within seven days of you asking for it; it's a criminal offence for them to refuse.

You can contact the **Credit Reference Agency** and ask for details of your file; you will have to pay a small sum of money for this. It's worth checking because the records could be incorrect, out of date or incomplete.

If you buy using credit, you get **extra rights** to protect you. This applies if the goods cost more than £100. The credit card or finance company is equally liable for any claim you have against a trader; you might be able to claim from them rather than the trader. This doesn't apply to debit cards or a charge card (where you have to pay in full within a few weeks of receiving the account).

Sometimes, credit is given **only if the loan can be secured against your home**. A secured loan like this gives security to the lender, not to you. That means if you fail to keep up the repayments, the lender can sell your home to cover their loss. This option isn't available if you rent. The good side of it is that you often get lower rates of interest but the downside is that you could lose your home if things go wrong.

Wary of warranties

Extended warranties are a form of guarantee but they can be extremely expensive. You're usually offered one when buying goods such as washing machines and TVs. But these items often break down in the first 12 months of using them ... when they're still covered by the original manufacturer's guarantee, or after five years, when the warranty will usually have expired. Repair costs may be cheaper in the long run than buying an extended warranty. Think about it before you get one.

If a **business goes bust**, taking your deposit with it, you almost certainly won't get your money back. You're the last in a long line of creditors. However, if the goods have been clearly marked as yours, not the trader's, and put to one side they then belong to you.

If you **pay your deposit using your credit card** and it's for more than £100, you have some protection. You could claim from the credit card company.

Deliveries

FACT: A staggering 56 million working days are lost every year waiting for the delivery man to arrive. Frustratingly they quite often don't even turn up, wasting our time and money.

Goods don't have to be **delivered within a set period of time**. The Sale of Goods Act, 1979 says that a retailer must deliver to you 'within a reasonable time'. If date of delivery is important, you should put it in writing when making the contract. If the delivery is then delayed, you can cancel the contract and receive a full refund. If it then costs you more to get the same goods elsewhere, you can claim the extra cost from the original retailer.

In some cases, the **date of delivery is not specified** but implied – Christmas, for example. If goods arrive late, you can cancel the contract and get a refund plus any extra costs.

You are often required **to sign for a delivery note**. Read it carefully. If it says that by signing you are acknowledging that the goods have been delivered in good order, you could be signing away your right to reject them later. Make sure you write 'unexamined' on the delivery note before you sign.

Goods are sometimes damaged in transit. Many mail-order companies that belong to trade associations will agree to replace damaged goods free of charge. If the supplier can't prove that the goods left their premises in good condition, you may well have a claim. If the items were obviously damaged while in transit, you can claim against the carrier. Compensation is awarded on a sliding scale and it may not cover the actual cost of the item. The Sale of Goods Act, 1979 states that once goods are handed over to the carrier by the supplier they become the property of the buyer who should bear the risk of accidental loss or damage in transit. However, the Act also says that the supplier should make sure that the goods are covered by adequate insurance while in transit. If the goods turn up damaged and the supplier hasn't got any insurance protection, you can refuse to accept the goods and ask for your money back.

How We Beat The System

Therese O'Dell, frustrated by a series of failed attempts to have her washing machine mended held a repairman hostage for three hours until the manufacturers promised to replace it. Here's what happened: The machine broke down within its 12-month guarantee period so she contacted the customer helpline. Engineers failed to keep two appointments, then an engineer eventually arrived three weeks after her first call and told her that he had to order spare parts before he could repair it. When that spare part arrived, the machine broke down during its first wash. Another engineer turned up a week later, and said that another spare part would be needed, but that it would take another week. That's when Mrs O'Dell launched her protest. She told the engineer that he was not leaving until she had a working washing machine, and allowed him to call head office to explain. A few minutes later, a representative of the manufacturers called the woman and promised to deliver a replacement within 24 hours and, for the first time in the whole sorry saga, they kept their word!

Buyer beware

When you're buying from a private seller, you have fewer rights than if you were buying from a shop or business. You can only claim if the goods don't match the description you were given, the seller was guilty of misrepresentation or if the goods didn't belong to them in the first place. Take someone with you when you're buying privately; they can act as a witness if necessary.

Some traders pretend to be private sellers to take advantage of the fact that the buyer has fewer rights. This is illegal and you can contact your local Trading Standards Department if you suspect something fishy is going on. Warning signals to look out for if you think the private seller is, in fact, a trader:
• there are lots of small ads in the local paper with the same phone number

- the seller insists on coming to your house
- they insist on cash and refuse to give a receipt
- they won't give their address.

Many happy returns

Goods bought from a trader must fit their description, be of merchantable quality and fit for their purpose (Sale of Goods Act, 1979). If they're not, return them.

Stores may say they **don't give refunds**. But they can't dodge their responsibilities. If what you've bought is faulty, not as described or unfit for purpose, they are obliged to give you a monetary refund, or at least pay for the goods to be repaired.

You don't need a receipt for a refund – simply **proof of purchase**. If the store has CCTV cameras which have recorded you buying something, then this is sufficient, as is a credit card receipt, or the witness of someone else such as the person who dealt with your purchase.

You have the **same rights when you buy sale goods** as at any other time.

Beware of traders who display notices that say 'no refunds on sale goods'. These are illegal and local authorities can prosecute the trader.

You've bought a pair of boots, taken them home and then decided that you don't want them. There's nothing wrong with them; you suddenly realise that fake snakeskin cowboy boots are just not you. Legally, a **shop doesn't have to exchange them** or give you a credit note. However, many shops have a goodwill return and refund policy; they want to keep you coming back, not turn you away. So it's always worth asking (nicely!).

While we're on the subject of shoes, there is something called the **Footwear Code of Practice**. Although it sounds like a shoe fetishist's dream, it's actually a code that the majority of reputable shoe shops abide by. Say you have a problem with some shoes you bought and the shop you are dealing with won't give you your money back, a credit note or replace the shoes. Yet you feel you have a valid complaint about the shoes. If the shop is covered by the code, you can ask for the shoes to be sent to the Footwear Testing Centre for an independent opinion. You and the shop fill in a form giving each side of the story. The shoes are sent away and a week later you get the result. The shop has to abide by whatever the report says. There is a charge of which you pay one third and the shop pays the rest (including the postage). If the Centre finds that you have a valid case, you will receive a refund, compensation or replacement and your costs will be refunded.

If you buy a product that is marked as **'shop soiled'** or 'faulty' you can't then return it, complaining that it's damaged. However, if it then turns out to be unsafe, you do have a case.

Never let a shopkeeper get out of giving you a refund for a faulty good because **'it's the manufacturer's fault'**. Your contract is with the shopkeeper, not the manufacturer.

Full and complete instructions should come with goods. If they are inadequate this can make a product unsatisfactory. Under the Sale of Goods Act, 1979, products must be of satisfactory quality.

Don't be fobbed off by arguments about **time limits**. Your rights to complain for a breach of contract or negligence last for six years (five in Scotland). Even if you lose the right to reject faulty goods, you could still claim compensation.

Some traders try and wriggle out of their responsibilities by putting **exclusion clauses** in their contracts (for example, refusing to accept liability for any loss or damage). If an exclusion clause is unfair, it can't be used against you because it's legally void. Try muttering 'Trading Standards' and 'Citizens Advice' – it may be enough to make them back down.
www.tradingstandards.gov.uk
www.nacab.org.uk

'Special purchase' often means that the goods have been bought in just for the sales and so may not be of the usual standard. However, they still should be of satisfactory quality (that is, free from hidden defects) and as described.

A sales contract is between the shop and the purchaser so how do you **return a gift**? Be nice – most shops will offer to exchange your gift; they want your goodwill.

If you are given a **credit not**e, check whether it's only valid for a limited period.

You're not legally obliged to **return faulty goods** at your own expense.

Guarantees are useful in that they give you extra rights. They can't replace or remove your statutory rights. Guarantees have to be clear, unambiguous and available for you to see before you buy the goods or service. Some items have a manufacturer's registration card to return to the manufacturer, make sure you or the seller fills it in; if you don't, you may not be able to claim anything.

Keep a file of receipts, whatever the value of the product you have bought. **Receipts are essential proof of purchase** if you need to return a product for whatever reason.

If you buy faulty goods you should return them to the shop, with the receipt and you will be entitled to some or all of your money back.

Decided you don't like it after all? You will only be able to change it, have a credit note or refund if this was **agreed at the time of the sale** with the seller. Check before you buy if you aren't sure.

Beware when buying goods on extended credit. If you want to cancel the agreement, for example, because you can no longer afford the goods, you will only be able to change your mind about keeping them if:
- the goods were bought at your home and the order is cancelled within a short period; or
- the seller agrees to cancel the sale. Some sellers do this, others may provide a credit note instead of a cash refund; or

- the agreement contains cancellation clauses. These will set out whether and when cancellation is allowed and may also set out any charges payable on cancellation.

You may be able to claim compensation if you told the seller you needed goods delivered by a certain date and they were **not delivered on time**. If no date was given, then you must give the seller a date by which you expect the goods to be delivered before taking any further action.

If you receive an invoice or letter asking for payment for goods which were not ordered, either ignore it or report the matter to the local Trading Standards Office as the sender may have committed a criminal offence. Try writing to the sender to complain too.

Buying second-hand? You cannot expect second-hand goods to be in the same condition as if they were new, unless the seller says that this is the case. The basic statutory rights apply to second-hand goods bought from a seller: the goods must be of satisfactory quality and must match their description, but take into account the price and the age of the goods when assessing the quality. If the seller has already pointed out stains, chips, cracks etc., you cannot complain about defects afterwards.

It is a good idea to take someone along when buying second-hand goods especially if they are expensive. The other person can take notes of what the seller says about the condition of the goods. This is particularly useful in private sales, where not all the basic statutory rights apply.

MAKING A COMPLAINT

If you want to complain, write to the top person in the business. It will get handed down to the right person eventually but they may well prioritise it, as it has been referred to them by their superior. Also look on the Internet at www.bbc.co.uk/watchdog.

If you need to make **a complaint by telephone**, stand up when you make the call. Psychologists say that this gives you a greater sense of authority. Swallow before you speak – it will give you an authoritative pause. And make your complaint effectively; don't let yourself be sidetracked. Stay calm and polite. Remember to record the date, time and their name as well as what was discussed. Companies often record telephone conversations themselves but need to know the details before they can verify what has been said.

If you are making a **complaint face to face**, try and relax. If you're tense, it will show. Take a few deep breaths, relax your shoulders and face muscles as you breathe out.

Complain to the right person. There's no point in shouting at the person who picks up the phone or answers the door. It just wastes energy and you're not talking to the person who has the authority to make decisions. Track down the manager, customer services manager or managing director.

Give the trader a chance to make things right once you've complained. **Know what it is you want** them to do to make things better – money back, compensation, replacement goods, a letter of apology or their head on a platter.

Follow up your complaint in writing if you can't resolve things immediately. This is known as **the 'letter before action'**. Address it to a named individual so it ends up on someone's desk, rather than being passed from pillar to post. Add any references or numbers that might be relevant.

Give the company a **deadline for their response** to your complaint and take a note of every response you get, particularly verbal ones. If your first letter or first phone call is not answered properly within a couple of weeks, send them another letter but this time by recorded delivery. Tell them that you will be taking legal action if they do not respond.

When writing a **complaints letter**, stick to the point. You may feel better producing a long, angry letter which gets things off your chest but it won't help you in the long run. If you must, write a mad rant first (but don't send it) then write the real letter. State the facts clearly. Don't get personal. If you have to send documents to back up your argument, send copies. Always keep the originals. Keep copies of your letters and use recorded delivery, then no one can say that they didn't receive your complaint.

If you are complaining about faulty goods, quote the **Sale of Goods Act, 1979** (as amended) or the **Supply of Goods and Services Act, 1982** if you've received inadequate service. It shows you know your rights. You may not know the actual Acts back to front and word for word but it's unlikely that the person you're complaining to does either. And they don't know that you're not a legal eagle, do they?

If you're complaining about being **overcharged**, get quotations from other companies to compare costs.

Don't be tempted to withhold payment if you have a credit agreement. If you stop paying, it can affect your chances of getting credit in the future. If you carry on paying, it won't undermine any claim you have against the lender for unsatisfactory service by a supplier.

You can always take your complaint to a **head office**. Or call upon the local Trading Standards Office or trade association. If you need to bring in the heavy guns, consider going to consumer organisations or TV and radio consumer programmes. There's nothing like a bit of adverse publicity to make companies back down.

Back up complaints with **evidence**. Receipts, bills, contracts, statements from witnesses, photographs, expert evidence ... whatever it takes.

As a result of your complaint, you may be sent a cheque in **'full and final settlement'** of your claim. If you're happy with that, fine. However, you may feel that the amount isn't enough. **Don't cash it; send it back.** If you cash it, you have accepted it and won't be able to claim any more. If in doubt, send it back.

Recognise a fair offer when it appears. Sometimes, it's not worth holding out for the impossible.

If you are late or fail to turn up to meet someone who is supplying you with a service, like a hairdresser or dentist, they can **charge you for the appointment**. That's why they often take your number when you book. But this works both ways. If you've taken time off work to wait for someone to arrive and they don't arrive or turn up late, you can charge them a reasonable sum for your time. The best way to do this is to knock it off their final bill.

The **Government's Consumer Gateway** site at www.consumer.gov.uk gives information on sites linked to shopping rights. You can get online advice about buying safely on the Internet from the Office of Fair Trading website – www.oft.gov.uk.

NOT-SO-SUPERMARKETS

FACT: If you shop when you are hungry, you'll spend between 17 and 20 per cent more on your groceries.

FACT: Take your kids shopping and you'll add an average of 30 per cent to your grocery bill.

Ever popped in to the supermarket for some milk and bread and come out wondering how you managed to spend 50 quid? Well here's the reason – and **how to avoid the traps** the supermarkets set.

When you first enter the store, you'll almost certainly come across flowers, magazines, fruit and the bakery. That's it – you're in sensory overload. You'll linger to admire the lovely stuff on offer. You've already been put in a much more pleasant state of mind by the associations triggered by these high-profit departments. Can you feel that blood pressure dropping?

Staple items are placed at the **four corners of the store**. It's not Feng Shui – it's to make sure you have to walk all round the store, even if you just wanted the basics. You'll have to spend longer there and you're more likely to succumb to an impulse buy – or ten.

Like lab rats, we're used to our little route through the store. The layout is planned so you'll go up and down the aisles, zigzagging your way to the end. You'll find most people go the same route, and that higher priced items will be placed on your right, where shoppers tend to make their selection, so lower priced items will be on the left, to move them faster. **Strike a blow for freedom!** Do your shopping backwards. Instead of starting where the supermarket planners want you to start – the produce department, start at the other end of the store. You won't be as likely to buy impulse items that are not on your list, because supermarket planners position 'specials' to face the flow of traffic. Shopping in this way can save 10 to 12 per cent on your usual grocery bill.

In the cereal section, the 'healthier' cereals – branflakes, muesli, oats and so on are usually on the top shelf. Bargain cereals and bulk or bagged cereals are generally placed on the bottom shelf. At a child's eye level, are all the sugary cereals with little give-away models (usually 101 to collect). Right opposite, or at least nearby, are the sweets – it's a mother's nightmare area.

At adult's eye level, products are all higher priced. Suppliers even pay to have their goods displayed in this **coveted position**, so keep looking up and down.

Massive **end-of-aisle displays**, large window signs and a cluttered look create a bargain-basement look that is often not borne out by low prices.

Comparison shop within the store. The same product may be differently priced – deli products are usually dearer for the same item than pre-packaged. Having it plonked into a little tub before your eyes makes you think it's somehow fresher, when the reverse may be true.

Less than 6 per cent of shoppers ever **redeem rebates or mail-in offers**. But they're a great incentive to buy a product or to purchase multiple packages to comply with the offer. Before you put the products in your trolley, decide that you really will redeem the offer.

Shopping more frequently, paradoxically, means that you **spend less** because you focus on fewer meals rather than panicking and trying to cater for the whole week. This way you can also go directly to what you want rather than shopping through the whole store. Remember to use a basket so you can go through the express checkout.

Finally, to get out fast, **avoid shopping at peak times**, of course, but go when the shop is moderately busy so that you can be sure there will be a full staff on duty.

How We Beat The System

Student life

Sally Shaw lives near a large campus university in the Midlands, and regularly uses the shops there. 'The prices are so much lower', she enthuses. 'And although they don't have a huge range of choice, it's worth the visit for the savings I make on staples, snack foods and fruit.'

Check your dates

'Use by' is used on perishables, such as dairy produce, cakes, sandwiches and ready meals. The food should be safe to eat or cook up to midnight on the stated date. It is an offence for produce to be sold after the 'use-by' date.

'Best before' appears on cans, cereals, preserves and eggs, indicating when quality and taste may start to deteriorate, though some foods can stay edible for a long time after. The food can be sold, so long as it hasn't gone off.

'**Display until**' and '**sell by**', which are often found on fruit and vegetables, aren't legally binding and are more for the shopkeeper's benefit.

Chicken or egg?

Food labelling, like the truth, is seldom pure and never simple. But the Food Standards Agency is trying to make things clearer. Take eggs, for example. The term **'Farm Fresh'** means absolutely nothing at all, although more than 35 per cent of shoppers believe that eggs described as 'Farm Fresh' come from free-range hens. In fact, the term is commonly used on produce from factory farms, as are the terms **'Country Fresh'** and simply **'Fresh'**. Following campaigns by consumer and animal rights groups, some retailers are now labelling battery eggs more clearly as 'Eggs From Caged Hens'.

According to the law, **'Free Range'** eggs should be produced by hens that have continuous daytime access to open-air runs. The organisation Compassion in World Farming recommends that 'Free Range' is still the best choice for eggs but warns that the term does not have any legal meaning when applied to products other than eggs and poultry.

Food described as **Natural** must be made of naturally produced ingredients – nothing sterilised, pasteurised, frozen or concentrated.

Pure describes food that contains no additives and is free from contamination from other food.

Make the most of coupons

It takes a bit of organisation, but you can cut your shopping bills to a considerable extent by making full use of the coupons available in newspapers, in supermarket promotional magazines, on products and in mail-outs. But remember, it's only a bargain if you were going to buy it in the first place.

- Look for coupons everywhere. Have your scissors in hand when you read the paper. Check store entrances for free newspapers and flyers for coupons.
- Keep your coupons organised, by product type, expiration date, alphabetical order – or all of the above, if you're a complete obsessive.
- Make a shopping list before you go shopping and put a little star next to the products you have coupons for.
- Make the most of your coupons. Swap them with friends, workmates, family and neighbours.
- Some coupons are only available by calling the manufacturers. The numbers to call are generally freephone numbers, and sometimes they have an option for requesting free samples. Go for it.
- Snap up rebates, freebies or vouchers for cheaper petrol with minimum store purchases, but only if you're going to use them.
- Forget brand loyalty. Be willing to switch brands to take advantage of lower prices and/or coupon offers.
- You can often get **coupons for free things** by calling the company (freephone numbers on the box), and either telling them how much you like or

dislike their product. This goes for fast-food chains and other types of stores too. They want to know what people think so phone up with any comment, good or bad and wait for the coupon.

- Write off for **free samples and information from companies launching new products**. You soon get the knack of spotting the promotional packs, and once you're on the mailing list, you may go on getting samples as new brands emerge. There are websites that specialise in finding free stuff and gathering all the information together for you to browse. In exchange for a little information about yourself, and your email address you can request samples of cosmetics, drinks, pet foods, health products – ooh, lots of things. US free sites have much better offers than the UK sites, so stick to sites like the ones below, or you'll be green with envy:

www.2001freebies.co.uk
www.allforfree.co.uk
www.freeukstuff.co.uk

SOMETHING FOR (NEXT TO) NOTHING

For knockdown prices on **clothing, electrical goods, office equipment, tools, sports equipment and bicycles**, go to auctions of lost property and seized goods – held by organisations such as the Police, London Transport, the Airports Authority and Customs and Excise. R F Greasby Ltd (Public Auctioneers) run regular auctions where the bargains are as mind boggling as the range of items for sale. If you want to bid, you have to leave a £50 deposit, which is refunded or discounted as appropriate. The sales are held every second Tuesday at 211 Longley Road, Tooting (call 020 8672 2972 for details).

Unclaimed goods from Customs and Excise, lost property from airports and goods lost in transit are sold at auctions every other Wednesday at Lloyds International Auction Galleries, 118 Putney Bridge Road, London SW15 2QN. Admission is by catalogue, price £2.00.

There are also sales of **goods left at dry cleaners all over the UK**, at a warehouse in Retford Road, Handsworth, Sheffield, where at previous sales, everything has been sold for £5. Yes, that's £5 for a wedding dress, a Persian rug or a pair of curtains. Officially, the items become the property of the dry cleaning company after a year, so unless you want your favourite suit to go the same way, go and pick up your cleaning *now*.

You can buy **ex-MOD office and domestic furniture**, and even office equipment from a series of huge hangars on an RAF site in Gloucestershire. There are crazy bargains to be had, and the stock changes all the time, so you have to go and view. For further details, call 01452 720735.

Visit big **trade exhibitions on the last day**. As they dismantle the stands, exhibitors will often sell off their stock cheap, rather than have to drag it to their vans and lug it home.

Something for nothing? If you take up an offer which is for a 'free-trial period' of a certain number of days you are legally bound to pay for it if you don't return it within the set period. Make sure you contact the company that has offered the free trial, and tell them you don't want to continue. Sometimes they'll offer to continue it, free of charge, as a way of trying to get you to become a paying customer.

FINDERS KEEPERS

When can you call another person's goods your own? How can you turn a lucky find to your advantage – without breaking the law?

Explore the possibilities. The goods could be:
• uncollected or abandoned
• stolen
• or lost.

Uncollected goods could include goods left for repair and never collected, property left behind by a home owner or tenant, builders' equipment left on site, sports equipment left after a match.

If you want to sell goods of this type, you must try to trace the original owner, perhaps by placing adverts in local papers (keep a note of the steps you took to trace the owner). If you can't track down the owner, the goods are yours to sell. If you do find them, give the owner reasonable time to collect the goods – at least three months. If the original owner does not collect the goods within the time given, you can only sell the goods after you have sent the owner two formal notices. If the owner does not collect the goods by the date given in the notice, then you can sell them. If the goods are a car, you have to fill in a form (B62) for change of possession, available from post offices, before you can sell the car (see the Motoring chapter). Once you have recouped your expenses, you must give the owner the money from the sale, if you can contact them. If not, after six years the owner has no further claim over the money.

Stolen goods remain the legal property of the rightful owner. Courts can order stolen goods to be returned, or compensation to be paid to the rightful owner. If you have bought stolen goods, even if you didn't realise they were stolen, you generally won't get legal right of ownership, but you could try to claim compensation from the seller.

Lost goods are yours to keep provided:
• you didn't find them while trespassing or on your employer's property
• you take reasonable action to find the owner
• the goods are not uncollected, stolen or treasure
• they are not attached to premises owned by someone else, such as a station, sports club, public transport or a shop.

If you take lost goods to a police station and they are unclaimed, the police will contact you after six weeks, and they are officially yours. The police will keep them for longer if they think they can trace the owner, or if they form part of an investigation. Once the property has been returned to the finder by the police, the original owner cannot usually then claim the goods.

TREASURE

You're digging up potatoes when you stumble across a hoard of treasure. Well, it could happen!

Treasure is the property of the Crown, so you must report your find to your local coroner within 14 days. If you don't, it's a criminal offence. It may take several months for the coroner to decide if what you've found is strictly speaking treasure. Basically, though, it's treasure if it fulfils one of these criteria:
- 300 years old or more
- an object other than a coin, of which at least 10 per cent in weight is gold or silver
- a coin, found with at least one other, of which at least 10 per cent in weight is gold or silver
- a coin of which less than 10 per cent in weight is gold or silver, but which was found with at least nine other coins
- a single coin or another object that is found with other objects that are treasure.

If the treasure is not important enough to be kept in a **museum**, you can sell it yourself, but if part or all of the treasure is kept for a museum, you'll be paid a sum equal to the market value as a reward. So get digging!

If you go looking for treasure with a **metal detector**, you must:
- get the landowner's permission before searching on private land
- report any historical finds to the landowner
- get permission from English Heritage, in Wales, the Secretary of State for the Environment, and in Scotland, Historic Scotland before you can use a metal detector on a listed ancient monument or other protected site. You can be fined for doing so without permission.

Useful addresses for treasure-seekers

Federation of Independent Detectorists
Detector Lodge
44 Heol Dulais
Birchgrove
Swansea SA7 9LT
Tel: 01635 522578

English Heritage
Fortress House
23 Savile Row
London W1X 1AB

Tel: 020 7973 3000
www.english-heritage.org.uk

Secretary of State for Wales
Cathays Park
Cardiff CF1 3NQ
Tel: 029 2082 5111

Historic Scotland
Longmore House
Salisbury Place
Edinburgh EH9 1SH
Tel: 0131 668 8999

Beachcombers beware

Property found in the sea or on the seashore could be from a ship and is known technically as 'wreck'. Wreck cannot be treasure because it will not have been buried with the intention to recover it, but all wreck must be reported to:

The Receiver of Wreck
Bay 105
Spring Place
105 Commercial Road
Southampton
Hampshire SO15 1EG
Tel: 023 8032 9474
Fax: 023 8032 9477

AUCTIONS

Attend auctions to get the feel of what happens, particularly of the saleroom where you are likely to buy. No two auctions are quite the same.

Some auctions are **admittance by catalogue only**, and that can be expensive but the catalogue is a useful reference, particularly if you make a note of the successful bids.

Read adverts in papers notifying auctions carefully. They may specify details such as **'no reserves'**.

Subscribe to the *Antiques Trade Gazette* – it has a diary of fairs and auctions, and lots of other interesting information. Write to 115 Shaftsbury Avenue, London WC2H 8AD.

Read catalogues to understand the terminology. Pay particular attention to the **'terms and conditions of sale'** that should be printed in the catalogue. These are the rules of the particular auction house. Read any **'glossary of terms'** as these give further explanation of what the catalogue description actually means, particularly for pictures, e.g. artist's name printed in full, or 'style of ...', 'circle of ...', or even 'after...'. All mean very different things.

Check what any **symbols** mean against a lot number. These can vary between auction houses. In Phillips, an * against a lot number means that VAT is payable on the hammer price for that lot – and 17.5 per cent is a significant extra charge! Check what percentage is payable as **buyers' premium**, if any, at a given saleroom and remember that VAT is payable on the premium.

Don't feel embarrassed to ask questions of the auction staff. They are there to help.

If you can't make the whole auction, ask about how many lots per hour will be sold, and work out when the lot you're interested in will come up, but don't cut it too fine.

Find out in advance what you need to do about payment (cheques accepted, credit cards etc.?) and find out what the arrangements are for clearing (taking away) purchases.

When you know which sale you want to attend, you must view the sale carefully and examine each lot that might be of interest. Remember, the catalogue description may not make any mention of damage and it is your responsibility to satisfy yourself as to actual condition. Feel free to turn things upside down, pull out the drawers etc. A good saleroom will be happy to give unbiased advice on pieces, but if you're intending to spend a lot of money or hope to start a collection, you'd be well advised to take a dealer with you.

Don't turn up at the last minute for viewing – they sometimes close the doors early because it can take a while to get people out. It is very disappointing if you've come a long way and you can't even get in. And if you have to come a long way, it's worth phoning the day before to make sure that the sale is going ahead as planned and that any lots that you are interested in are still included.

Catalogues usually make things look better than they really are. If you can't view, most auctions houses will provide a **written condition report** to make things clearer.

Buyers' premium is sometimes on a sliding scale – more expensive items may attract a lower level of buyers' premium than cheaper items. The catalogue will contain details like this.

Houses vary, but some consistently give **low catalogue estimates**. Don't assume you'll be able to buy the items at anywhere near that price.

If there's another auction in the locality on the same day, you may pick up **bargains**, because the competition will be halved.

Aim to strike up a useful friendship with a porter or other member of staff who could bid for you if you can't or would rather not be there in person. They may even be able to give you a clue as to reserve prices. Remember to show your appreciation.

Set the maximum amount you want to bid (remembering buyers' premium and any other charges).

Arrive in good time at the sale before your lot is coming up. You will probably be asked to register (give your name and address and show some form of identification) and be given a **bidding number** to show to the auctioneer when you buy a lot. (This may be called a **'paddle' number** – a strange word, but was first used in the USA where the system started!)

If you're known at an auction house, particularly at local sales, you might want to be inconspicuous. Personal feelings can come into play and rivals may enter the bidding just to push the price up. By standing at the back, you can see the whole room and see who's doing what.

If you can't be at the auction, you can leave a bid but make sure you write clearly. Some houses accept email bids, but make sure you leave a bid well in advance. On the day of the sale, it could well be overlooked in the rush of other things that have to be done. If you are making a **phone bid**, you generally fill in a form and the auction house will give you an idea of when your lot will come up so you can stay by the phone and wait for their call. Again, give plenty of notice.

Play it cool when your lot comes up. Allow bidding to proceed in the room. The auctioneer should take bids alternately from two people; then when one drops out, look for any further bidders.

If you want to bid, make a **clear signal** to the auctioneer. A raised eyebrow or flick of a finger may be sufficient for the seasoned professional but not for the beginner.

Once you start bidding, **do not exceed your maximum** in the heat of the moment. Once the hammer falls, you have entered a legally binding contract and will have to pay up.

If you're bidding in a **foreign currency**, make sure what exchange rate is to be used and any extra charges that might be incurred for conversion.

If your bid is successful, note the price you paid and show your bidding number to the auctioneer. Make sure your number is recorded correctly. Then follow instructions about payment and clearance. You will not make a good start to your relationship with the saleroom if you pay late or do not clear your purchase promptly.

It happens in comedy films, but not in real life. If you sneeze or scratch your head, you will not end up with an unwanted purchase. A good auctioneer will always ask you if you are bidding if they are in any doubt. However, it is not a good idea to wave to a friend across the saleroom.

Buyer beware – not all salerooms have a good reputation, sadly. The beginner should try to get personal recommendation from an existing buyer before starting.

Internet auctions

There are few places you can get as comprehensively ripped-off as an Internet auction site. With a staggering 1.5 million auctions transactions going on every day, this comes as no surprise. Fraudsters hide behind email addresses, fake log-in names, PO boxes, bouncing cheques and the fact that all transactions take place sight unseen; the photographs featured may not even be of the item for sale. Yet the majority of Internet auction users do get what they paid for and get paid for what they sell, and can revel in unprecedented access to a huge global market – make sure you are one of the satisfied majority.

Person-to-person auctions are not covered by the Sale of Goods Act, so there is little redress in law, but if you pay by credit card, UK purchases of over £100 and under £30,000 are covered under the Consumer Credit Act. If there's a problem resulting in goods arriving damaged or failing to arrive at all, you can claim a refund from your card issuer.

Safety in numbers

Letsbuyit.com is an ingenious idea for a website. It brings consumers together to pool power, on the assumption that buying in bulk leads to lower unit price. The idea is that members request products and services on the site, and letsbuyit.com finds a suitable wholesaler and negotiates a discount for them. The more people tag on to the sale, the cheaper it gets for everyone. Delivery is free on all items. Definitely worth a look. www.letsbuyit.com

---

COMPETITIONS

If you can be bothered (and some people can), there are lots of prizes out there just waiting for someone to win them. There is no doubt that the best results are achieved by people who dedicate themselves to the cause, body and soul, but … you have to be in to win … it could be you … and so on. If you decide that comping is for you, then go about it scientifically. Get one of those magazines, use a website and just blitz them, but be prepared to win lots of things you don't want (they could come in handy as gifts) or be selective and win less. It's up to you, but the downside is you'll get yourself on lots of tiresome mailing lists.

> www.youcanwin.co.uk/competitions/competitions.htm
> www.comps.org
> www.loquax.co.uk
> www.compnet.pwp.blueyonder.co.uk

With competitions on products in the shops, even though the package says (usually in very small type) that you don't have to buy the product to enter, you still feel your chances must be better if you do. Don't go buying things you don't want just for a better chance of winning. Regulations are very strict and companies are not allowed to show a preference towards purchasers.

CLUBS, PUBS AND OTHER FUN

'The brutal truth is that good-looking people get into clubs and ugly people get turned away.' *David Taylor, manager of Soho members' bar Abigail's Party*

> **FACT:** 25 per cent of couples meet in pubs.

Where angels fear to tread

Why just read about it in the magazines – you could be there too. If you're absolutely determined to get into the clubs and parties where the rich and beautiful go to be seen, you'll have to make a bit of an effort – and be prepared for the ignominy of not making it from time to time. But just imagine if you do manage to get in…

Want to get into a club but don't reckon you'll make it past the doorman? **Do your homework** and you'll have no problem. Ring up and find out the capacity of the club and their policies. Then tell them you are from Universal Studios or similar and that you are investigating the club as a venue for an after-show party. Ask if you can come along one night to see the club in full swing.

Call up a club and say you want to write and complain about something. **Ask for the manager's name.** Then when you go along that evening, mention the name at the door and it should get you in.

The insider's tip is if you are stopped at the door, say you work as a doorman at another venue, and not only will they let you in, but they'll let you in free. Of course you have to look the part!

If you end up having to pay, at many clubs, it's cheaper before 11 pm, when entry will often be free and drinks will be at reduced prices. Some venues offer **free admission for female guests** on certain nights.

If you are a woman, claim to work for a fashion PR company. Call ahead and ask to be put **on the guest list**. Say you'll be coming early and don't expect to stay long – clubs like attractive women coming early in the evening as it draws men into the club.

Due to the right of freedom of association, you need only two members to start a **'national association'** of something and you don't need to pay any fees or register anywhere. Start one and make yourself the Chairperson or President. You can use it to get invited to launches and blag free samples of products which you can then 'endorse'. It's a great CV enhancer, too.

Where possible, use a fax first, then follow that up with a phone call two or three days later. If possible, use headed paper – an average PC should be capable of making a believable logo. The point here is to **make it look official**.

Be inventive: simply saying that you are a DJ's mate won't get you very far, but don't go too far over the top. Who's going to believe you if you claim to be CEO of MTV? Try to think of something a bit more plausible.

Overall, you want **the club to think they're going to benefit** from you being at their event, so hint at the coverage you can give them, or the likelihood of your wanting to rent the whole club for an event of your own.

Get some cards made up and take them with you on the night. Whenever you meet someone who could invite you to another event, make sure you **exchange cards** with them. Follow up the contact with a call, and you could find yourself getting invited all over the place.

Be polite: any sign of arrogance and you will blow your cover. Most PRs are chatty, direct, breezy and very confident in their manner. Work on perfecting your telephone manner.

Make your initial contact early: for a big event, start about two or three weeks ahead so you can get your name on the list before the rush.

How We Beat The System

Clare was in Paris and really wanted to get into a hot new exhibition on the opening day, so she rang up the press number and claimed to be a journalist on an English paper. They gave her a press pass and she got in free – and filled up on canapés too. The only sticky moment came when a Frenchman she'd been talking to said he'd mentioned her to another English journalist there, who wanted to meet her. Now whenever she goes abroad, she volunteers to write an article for free if a newspaper can get her a press pass for events in advance. It normally works. She also makes sure she has her British Library ticket to hand at all times. A quick flash seems to impress!

Whenever Paul goes abroad, he checks out the cultural events that are going to be on, then phones round the newspapers offering to write a feature or review, if they'll arrange a press pass for him. Once he's there, he'll take in every show, go to every reception and network like mad. His address book is looking very impressive these days, and he's getting more and more work – and free theatre tickets.

Tom can get into anywhere and anything free. He's got into top events by pretending to be an after-dinner hypnotist act, and pop concerts as a paramedic. His handsome appearance, suave manners and irresistible charm means even when he is caught, he is normally allowed to stay! On holiday he heads for the very best hotel for a free breakfast and free use of the pool – he claims that if you can look confident enough, you never get questioned, and the old trick of walking into a place as if you own it always does the trick. His number one tip? 'Wherever you go, take a dinner suit. If there is a party or a function going on and you arrive dressed the part, nine times out of ten you will get let in and never questioned.'

System beaters – please be warned that this is illegal and amounts to a criminal offence.

EATING OUT

'Never eat more than you can lift.' *Miss Piggy*

It's official – there is no such thing as a free lunch, but don't let that put you off manoeuvring for the best deal. Eating out is now a national sport – in 1999 we spent £20.6bn on eating out. If we're spending that kind of money, we want the best!

Lost your shirt? Cloakrooms often have signs telling people they are leaving items at their own risk. The sign is invalid – if they require you to leave your possession, then they are responsible for any loss or damage if they were not taking reasonable care.

Don't be the first to be served from the bar. If the bar area is cold overnight, the drop in air pressure can cause the first couple of measures given to be short. Be a gentleman and let someone else order first.

If you book a table at a restaurant and when you arrive there is no space, you can claim both your travel expenses for getting there and back, and for the disappointment and inconvenience suffered. **The Supply of Goods and Services Act, 1982** is what you want to quote here.

If you book a table then don't turn up or arrive late, the restaurant can claim reasonable compensation from you. In order for their claim to be successful, the restaurant will have to show that it made every effort to reduce its loss (by refilling the table, for example). A **'reasonable amount'** would be the cost of a typical meal. This is why they often ask for a phone number when you book.

Some restaurants are sending out faxed booking forms which ask for credit card details when you book a table. You are under no obligation to give them this information. However, your booking could well be refused if you don't.

If you're going for a meal, pretend that you are inspecting a hotel or restaurant for a wedding reception. You'll be given extra-special treatment.

Drink the house wine. A restaurant will not make themselves look bad by having a bad house wine.

Great restaurants in office areas (like the City of London) are packed out at lunchtime, but **often have space at night**. You can get a table there when restaurants around theatres and concert halls would be booked out. Call at around 5pm to be on the safe side, or try a restaurant booking service, like www.5pm.co.uk or www.toptable.co.uk.

Lunch is one of the great underrated bargains in restaurants. You can often enjoy the same menu for a fraction of the cost by shifting your meal out from dinner time to lunchtime. **Fixed price menus** are an even better deal.

All restaurants must **display prices on a menu** at or near the entrance so customers can see them before they sit down. These prices must include VAT and the menu should show any service, cover or minimum charges. If this information is not displayed, you should contact the local Trading Standards Officer (www.tradingstandards.gov.uk or you can get the number from the local council offices). But if you book a table without knowing the prices and decide to leave because the restaurant is too expensive, even if you had not ordered, the restaurant could sue you for loss of profit.

A waiter spills soup on your favourite pair of trousers. If you can prove that the waiter was negligent by failing to take reasonable care while serving you, you are entitled to **claim full compensation** from the restaurant for the cleaning bill, or even a new pair. Get evidence from witnesses.

GM foods? Since September 1999, restaurants are legally obliged to tell you if any dishes contain genetically modified soya or maize.

Restaurants should prepare and serve food **with reasonable skill and care**. If a meal isn't up to scratch for some reason, you can complain. If, after complaining, the matter is not put right, you are entitled to deduct a reasonable sum from your bill (say, the cost of the dish in question). You have to pay for the food and drink that you did consume. Or you can pay the bill under protest. Write **'under protest'** on the back of the cheque and then follow the matter up by writing to the restaurant afterwards. Keep a copy of your letter. If you pay under protest, you keep the option open to claim your money back later.

The Supply of Goods and Services Act, 1982 states that any food and drink ordered should be as described. So home-made soup should be just that... not come out of a packet. If the restaurant is misleading customers by not serving food as described on the menu, this is a breach of the Trade Descriptions Act, 1968. Contact the Trading Standards department at the local council offices.

Why is it that wine waiters are often really snooty? There's always that moment of panic when they ask you to taste the wine... what if it's off? **How can you tell?** Should you expect another bottle of wine? The wine is most definitely off if it smells musty and a bit fungal. If there's a burning sensation when you sniff it, there's too much sulphur. And if the wine has a sort of muddy colour and very little smell, then it's oxidised. You can ask for a fresh bottle. Bits of cork floating in your glass doesn't mean the wine is 'corked', neither do fine clear crystals at the bottom of the bottle or round the rim.

If your bottle of wine is brought to you already opened, watch out! There have been stories of restaurants mixing dregs of other bottles together and serving them to unsuspecting customers. It's far better practice to **open the bottle at the table**. If it's a bottle of red that needs to breathe, it should be opened at your table at the start of meal and left on the table until you are ready to drink.

Is there a drunk person sitting at the table next to you in the pub? Would you rather they weren't? If so, the publican is **legally obliged to tell a drunk to leave** the premises. If they do not, they are causing a criminal offence.

If a restaurant says **'10 per cent added for service'**, you are perfectly entitled to knock that 10 per cent off your bill. Not only is there no obligation to pay service charges, but restaurants that do this may not even be passing the money on to the waiter. If the service was good, knock the 10 per cent off the bill and give the money directly to the waiter.

If **service is not included**, it's up to you whether you leave a tip, how much and how you pay it (with the bill or by leaving cash on the table).

A restaurant bill is made up of a price for the food and drink and a charge for the service. If one is acceptable but the other not, you can deduct a reasonable sum from your bill. Leave your name and address with the restaurant. It will be up to them to claim against you if they don't agree with your deduction.

If you're not happy with the **quality of service**, let the restaurant know. Always give them the opportunity to put things right.

Ever had the feeling that the restaurant wants you to hurry up and finish your meal? If you aren't made aware that there was a **time limit** on your meal *before* you sat down, you can claim about poor service. Don't pay the full service charge at the end of the meal … or knock it off altogether.

When you're **paying by credit card**, check that the total box is not left blank. A dodgy restaurant can fill it in afterwards and add extra to it. You agreed to pay what was shown on the bill; you didn't authorise any extra payments. Therefore, if you do notice that you've paid more than you expected when your credit card bill arrives, you should write to the restaurant straight away and enclose a copy of the credit slip. The restaurant is legally obliged to reimburse you with the extra. Let your credit card company know as well. They can reimburse you and get the extra back from the restaurant,

A stroke some restaurants pull is to **leave the total box empty** even when service is included. They are relying on you adding on another extra 10–15 per cent to the total including service.

How We Beat The System

Potato and fuse-wire salad

Ed Barnes found a piece of coiled up fuse wire in his potato salad in a restaurant in Covent Garden. The price of his meal was refunded, of course. He could have reported the matter to the local Environmental Health Department, as selling food with a 'foreign body' in it can be an offence under the Food Safety Act.

He told the story to a friend who started carrying a piece of fuse-wire around with him when he went to restaurants, and surreptitiously adding it to his meal – but only once he'd eaten most of it. It worked a few times, but he was recently told that no tables were available in a restaurant that was half empty. He had never been there before, and now he wonders if the word is out on his little fuse-wire trick, and fears he may never eat in this town again!

Restaurant guides

Some restaurant guides are more equal than others. The world-famous Michelin guide is strictly independent. The company pays its own way, and the inspectors write what they choose and all work undercover, so no one even knows they are there. But others charge for the inspection, yearly membership and inclusion on their website.

An inspector calls?

If you feel like having some fun, see if you can make the staff think you're a restaurant critic or hotel inspector. Now, it's well known that restaurant reviewers, especially those who write for the Sunday supplements, are shy, retiring and mild-mannered folk so you won't want to come over as arrogant, rude, petulant or domineering – will you? Still, you may want to try one of these tips and see if you can take the waiters in. You may notice they suddenly become extra attentive!

- Hotel inspectors often eat alone.
- Pretend you have trouble remembering the name you booked under – as if it's one you made up. You are incognito, after all.
- If you're with friends, make sure everyone tries something different, and try everyone's food.
- Don't have a notebook on the table next to your plate – too obvious.
- Ask the wine waiter for recommendations to go with each course, but don't necessarily take them. Just raise your eyebrows.
- Pretend to make notes discreetly under the table.
- Don't order simple dishes, like smoked salmon or a simple salad – go for complex dishes and specials.
- Don't finish everything on your plate, but try everything.
- Pay cash, but go through the bill carefully.

SPORTING LIFE

Whether you take part, watch it, listen to it or just think you may get around to it one day, sport can be a costly hobby. But there are ways of getting it on the cheap.

Never join a gym at New Year – it's the **peak time**, and it's crowded as well as expensive. By March, most of the slackers will have given up and gone back to channel-hopping as their favoured exercise. By then, the gym will be almost empty, but the best bargains are in July, when the six-month memberships have run out and the gym is on the lookout for new members.

Sports clubs often have deals for **cheap tickets** for sporting fixtures and cut price equipment, even (in the case of rugby and football clubs) cheap bars!

Winning ways at Wimbledon

Wimbledon is a prime example of a premier sporting event where tickets are, on the face of it, like gold dust. But don't despair, this and all the other major sporting fixtures can be approached by stealth too.

Wimbledon runs a **mail lottery** for one pair of tickets per applicant for one day of play. You are limited to one application per household. To increase your chances, use names and addresses of friends and family, provided that they are not entering. Send a self-addressed, stamped envelope, no later than 31 December, to:

> All England Lawn Tennis & Croquet Club
> PO Box 98
> Wimbledon
> London SW19 5AE

The draw takes place in February.

You can also stand in line for **daily tickets**, although you will have to queue the night before for a good chance of getting seats.

Tickets become available for **resale in the afternoon**, as ticket holders leave early. Holders of tickets for show courts who leave before close of play are asked to put their tickets in the red ticket boxes provided around the grounds. They are sold on a first-come, first-served basis to people inside the grounds. You can get terrific seats this way, and the proceeds go to charity. Prices are £5 before 5pm and £3 after 5pm. With first week ground admission costing £7 after 5pm, you could see a centre court match for as little as £10.

For info on Wimbledon, log on to www.wimbledon.com.

Another way to get into Wimbledon is to get on the staff there. During the Championships many **temporary staff** are employed, although they won't all get to see the matches. These are just a few of the types of job available, and there will be similar positions to be filled at any sporting events or festivals.

Ballboys and girls come from local schools in the boroughs of Merton and Wandsworth.

Strawberries and cream, anyone? The official caterer is FMC Ltd, Church Road, Wimbledon, London SW19 5AE. They are looking for managers, chefs, porters, food service assistants, silver service, plate waiting and bar staff. Applicants must be at least 18 years of age and have either a National Insurance number or the relevant work permit documents if coming from abroad. For an application form, contact the Personnel Department on 020 8947 7430.

Computer literate and keen on tennis? IBM supplies IT for Wimbledon, and looks for temporary workers to help collect scores and match statistics. County players upwards of 18 years of age can apply.

'Guess who I had in the back of my cab?' You too could be saying this if you're taken on as a driver by Gemini II International Ltd. Players and officials have to get to the club on time, and if you're 25 or over, with a minimum of four years' driving, a clean licence and a good sense of direction, apply to:

Hill Place House
55a High Street
Wimbledon Village
London SW19 5BA

Security for the championships is provided by:

Securicor Guarding Ltd
Tollington Park House
5 Tollington Place
London N4 3QS

Ever present at events, shows, exhibitions and performances are the **St John Ambulance volunteers**. Now it may seem a bit extreme to get yourself trained as a first aider to get into matches and concerts, and you do have to wear that uniform, but really everyone should know something about first aid and the events they cover range from the London Marathon, the London to Brighton Bike Ride, Cricket at Lords, the Grand Prix at Silverstone, the Epsom Derby, Royal Ascot, not to mention pop festivals, concerts, West End shows – anywhere there are crowds of people. Try www.sja.org.uk/stjohn/default.asp.

SHOWS, FILMS AND CONCERTS

Even the hottest shows occasionally have **cancellations**. Turn up on the off chance and make yourself known to the box office. Be charming and polite and wear something distinctive so they'll remember you and be able to pick you out easily as you lurk in the foyer, hoping for a return.

Half-price tickets for most musicals and plays on the day of the show only are available from the **half-price ticket booth** in Leicester Square. It's usually not possible to buy tickets for the top-rated shows, but for ones that have been on for some time, it's definitely worth a go. Turn up in person to buy tickets. There is a smaller outlet run by a ticket agency inside the Criterion Theatre at Piccadilly Circus which sells half-price tickets for a limited number of shows.

Some theatres and concert halls have a policy of holding back just a few tickets for the morning of the show, but you'll have to turn up at the box office in person. **Returns** are unlikely to be available until just before the show, but get to the box office early and put your name down. Give them your mobile phone number if there's a big crowd or loiter nearby so they can see you.

Press nights and previews of new shows offer the opportunity to get cheap, or sometimes even free, tickets. If it's a children's show, they'll want to pack the house with kids to get the right noise levels and reactions for the actors (and reviewers) so you may not get in unless you bring a gaggle of kids. Look at theatre schedules to see when they preview and contact the box office.

Hat Trick Productions (www.hat-trick.co.uk) record the majority of their shows before a live studio audience. Tickets are always free and the shows are recorded at The London Studios, about five minutes from Waterloo Station. Check the website for shows currently being recorded or call 020 7287 1598/1599. Other channels have similar arrangements, but some popular shows have long waiting lists.

Getting on to theatre and orchestra **mailing lists** is a good way of getting priority booking, and finding out about when and where rehearsals are happening. You may even be able to get into technical or dress rehearsals for next to nothing. Orchestras sometimes run special 'friends' events with priority ticket booking too.

The **A-list types** who get sent comps for all the new shows and films are often too busy swanning somewhere else. If they don't turn up, the front rows can look distinctly sparse. Ask the ushers if you can take their place in the second half, or just sneak down once the lights go down.

Even if you're told that there are no seats, **it's worth asking about boxes**. They sometimes get forgotten, or the box office staff may assume you don't want them.

Ask about **restricted view seats**. There may be some left that they don't bother to sell and they should be cheap. Keep a look out for (better) empty seats and move during the interval.

Rent videos from grocery stores or the library instead of big video stores – much cheaper.

Matinée performances of films and shows are often much cheaper (and easier to get into).

Front-of-house work in theatres, cinemas and concerts is usually poorly paid, but if you get to see the shows it makes it all worthwhile. Ushers, stewards and programme sellers are all needed but the jobs may be fiercely contested. Many of these posts are recruited by word of mouth, but others may be advertised in regional newspapers. It is always worth a speculative application, making it clear that you can be available and contactable at short notice.

Say you are a student to get a better rate. If they ask for a **student card**, either say you don't have one but show your passport (only if you are under 27) or pretend to look for it and discover that – oops, you must have misplaced it. A **British Library card** looks pretty official and may work (particularly abroad). But do take care, as this amounts to a criminal offence.

Enter at the exit. This can work in museums and art galleries but you may be unceremoniously kicked out or even arrested.

How We Beat The System

An impoverished film student buys a ticket for the first showing at his local multiplex cinema (using his student card, of course), then casually moves to the next auditorium for the next film, and then the next, and so on. He always plans his outings carefully using a copy of the local paper, so he only sees films he quite fancies, and so far has only been chucked out once. He's been lucky, though, as this is a criminal offence.

Star (b)illing

What if you've paid big money to see your favourite actor or opera singer only to find out that the understudy is appearing. Understudies have to step in if the star is ill, but big telly names often have other commitments during the run of the show and will have planned in advance when they can and can't appear. The show's publicity and hoardings may mention the star (and others) by name, but to find out who is performing when you'll have to check the schedule in the box office, although staff there will not be willing to guarantee that a particular person will be performing on a specific date. As a rule of thumb, if the star's name appears above the name of the show on publicity and hoarding, the theatre should tell you in advance if the actor will be missing. If you feel you were misled when you bought your ticket, complain to the management and, in most cases, you will be offered free tickets for a night when your fave rave is appearing.

Weird and wonderful leisure laws

In Australia, bars are required to stable, water and feed the horses of their patrons.

All English males over the age 14 are to carry out two or so hours of longbow practice a week supervised by the local clergy.

In Switzerland, it is an offence to mow your lawn on a Sunday.

In Xenia, Ohio, it is illegal to spit in a salad bowl.

Don't eat garlic less than four hours before going to the theatre in Gary, Indiana – it's illegal.

USEFUL WEBSITES

www.which.net

www.ceg.co.uk – consumers in europe

www.tradingstandards.gov.uk

www.nacab.org.uk – National Association
of Citizens Advice Bureaux

www.gooddealdirectory.com – consumer
website with tips on cheap finds

www.loquax.com – online competitions

www.greasbys.com – London Transport
and lost property auctions

www.lloyds-auction.co.uk – Customs and
Excise and BAA auctions

www.consumer.gov.uk

www.adviceguide.org.uk

USEFUL ADDRESSES

Advertising Standards Authority
Brook House
2 Torrington Place
London WC1 E 7HW
Tel: 020 7580 5555
www.asa.org.uk

Citizens Advice Bureau
Find details in the local phone book or call:
Tel: 020 7833 2181
www.nacab.org.uk

Consumers' Association
2 Marylebone Road
London NW1 4DF
Tel: 020 7486 5544
www.which.net

Direct Marketing Association
Haymarket House
1 Oxendon Street
London SW1Y 4EE
Tel: 020 7321 2525

Direct Selling Association Ltd
29 Floral Street
London WC2E 9DP
Tel: 020 7497 1234

Mail Order Protection Scheme
16 Tooks Court
London EC4A 1LB
Tel: 020 7405 6806

Mailing Preference Services
Freepost 22
London W1E 7EZ
Tel: 0345 034599

The National Consumer Council
20 Grosvenor Gardens
London SW1W 0DH
Tel: 020 7730 3469
www.ncc.org.uk

**The National Newspapers' Mail Order
Protection Scheme**
(Mail Order Secretariat)
16 Tooks Court
London EC4A 1LB
Tel: 020 7405 6806
(national daily newspaper protection
scheme)

The Newspaper Society
74–77 Great Russell Street
London WC1B 3DA
Tel: 020 7636 7014
(regional and local newspaper protection
scheme)

Office of Fair Trading
Fleetbank House
2–6 Salisbury Square
London EC4Y 8JX
Tel: 0345 224499
www.oft.gov.uk

The Telephone Preference Service Ltd
5th Floor
Haymarket House
1 Oxenden Street
London SW1Y 4EE
Tel: 0845 070 0707
Fax: 0845 070 0706

# Motoring

'Take most people, they're crazy about cars. I'd rather have a goddamn horse. A horse is at least human, for God's sake.' *J D Salinger*

The myth of motoring is a seductive one: all high performance, alloy trim, walnut fascia and high-speed stunt driving past flaming sugar plantations before slipping smoothly into a parking space right outside the opera house. The reality of motoring is, sadly, more black vinyl and furry dice.

First you can't pass your test, then you can't afford a car that actually runs, then you can't get insurance without selling your granny, then – when you're finally mobile, it's parking tickets, stationary traffic, speed cameras (if you ever get going that fast) and fuel you can't afford.

If ever a system needed beating, it's this one.

FACT: Traffic delays cost the country around £15 billion a year.

FACT: Car traffic is forecast to increase by 22 per cent by 2010 from the current levels of 321 billion vehicle kilometres (per year) if no action is taken.

FACT: In 1999, the total licensed vehicle stock in Great Britain was estimated to be 28.4 million vehicles. 85 per cent of that were cars.

TESTING TIMES

The driving test – that well-loved white-knuckle ride of passage. The only good thing about it is that everyone's in the same situation – or are they?

Legally, **you can drive when you are 17**. You'll need a provisional licence; get the form from the local post office. You must always have L-plates displayed and be accompanied by a fully licensed driver over 21 years old while you are learning to drive. Make sure the car is insured for a learner driver.

Professional driving instructors must be qualified; they have to display their green **ADI** (approved driving instructor) licence in the windscreen. Trainee instructors have a red licence.

There are two parts to passing your driving test. The first is the driving **theory test** which you have to pass before you can sit, or even apply for, the **practical**

driving test. Out of 600 possible questions on the theory test, you have to answer 35 multiple-choice questions.

It's a good idea to take the practical driving test in **a car that you know**. You must show your provisional licence as well as photo ID to the examiner before you start. Arrive in good time. The test will take around 30 minutes.

If you want a driving test quickly, you could claim to be in the armed forces or Voluntary Service Overseas (VSO) and about to go back overseas. Alternatively, you could ring to see if there are any cancellations.

You can apply to take your test in any **Driving Test Centre**. Pass rates for the 335 permanent Driving Test Centres in the UK vary widely. In recent years, the centre with the highest overall pass rate has been Carmarthen in South Wales, with 69.8 per cent while the Scilly Isles had the lowest with only *one* recorded pass in the whole year! Mind you, with a population of just over 2,000, maybe that's not so surprising.

Don't shoot the messenger! Female candidates taking the **theory** driving test have a better pass rate than males, but male candidates have a better pass rate than females on the **practical** test.

If it's raining when you take your test, make sure you take your wet coat off before entering the test car – you'll fog up the windows.

Adjust your rear-view mirror slightly, so you have to make a **visible head movement** to look in it. This makes it clear to the examiner that you are using your mirror while taking the test.

Ten most common reasons for failing a driving test:
- failure to act properly at road junctions
- reversing round a corner incorrectly
- failure to make proper use of steering
- problems with parking
- failure to make proper use of gears
- failure to make effective use of the mirrors
- driving too slowly
- failure to act properly when turning right
- causing delay by not pulling out promptly at junctions
- failure to move away correctly from stationary positions.

Driving test cheats

Completely illegal, of course, but according to the *Bolton Evening News*, a number of people are attempting to cheat their way through the written driving test by getting someone else to take the exam on their behalf.

To take the exam, you need an ID certificate, signed by a public figure, such as a JP, a doctor or your driving instructor stating that the photograph is authentic, but candidates could add someone else's photograph and fake the name of an invented driving school and instructor. Invigilators have no way of checking the information on the certificate and, provided it looks authentic, anyone could be taking the exam under a false name. If discovered, however, they could be charged with fraud.

The DSA have made photographic ID compulsory for both written and driving tests, and approved documents include passports, photo-bearing credit cards and trade union memberships, but if no other ID is available, the DSA permits the typed certificate and signed picture. A provisional licence, which has no photograph, also has to be produced so test officials can check the candidate's signature, but if the signature is forged, the cheats can slip through.

Licences

To drive any motor vehicle on any road in the United Kingdom, you *must* hold a current driving licence. This may be one of the following:
- a full UK driving licence
- a UK provisional driving licence, for learner drivers accompanied by a qualified driver with a minimum of three years' experience and who is over 21 years of age. The fact that you are a learner must also be clearly shown on the front and back of the vehicle in the form of L-plates, obtainable from most garages and motorist shops.
- an international driving licence or a full driving licence from abroad. Holders of licences issued in EU countries can use these in the UK for as long as they remain valid. Licences issued by other countries can only be used for the first 12 months of your stay in the UK, after which you must apply to take a driving test through the Department of Transport *before* the 12 months expires.
- If your licence was issued by one of the following countries, you can exchange it for a UK licence without taking a driving test, although there is a charge for this:
    All EU countries
    Australia
    Barbados
    British Virgin Islands
    Canada
    Cyprus (Republic)
    Gibraltar
    Hong Kong
    Japan
    Kenya
    Malta
    New Zealand
    Singapore
    South Africa
    Switzerland
    Zimbabwe

Less testing tests

If you can't hack the driving test in the UK, you could always try another country. Countries with remarkably high pass rates include:

- Greek islands, specifically Symi, near Rhodes, where all that is required is for the candidate to drive 500 metres (550 yards) along a straight road, turn the car round and drive back
- Nigeria, where tests are often conducted in fields
- Massachusetts, USA, where the brief test includes no manoeuvres or parking and can be over in a matter of minutes
- Honduras, where there is a voluntary written test – but nothing further, and licences cost a mere $7
- Rural New Zealand, where (coincidentally?) there is a dreadful road safety record
- Maryland, USA, where the test is conducted in a car park
- China, where the practical part of the test may be conducted in an automatic, and not necessarily on a public highway, and the answers to the written exam are provided in advance.

How We Beat The System

A long way round – (but think of the air miles)

A young Irishman (who must, for obvious reasons, remain nameless) with a provisional licence went to Tanzania for a spell of voluntary work. There he was given a full Tanzanian licence and drove around freely. He returned to Ireland via Germany where, thanks to historical colonial links, he exchanged his Tanzanian licence for a full German licence. Once back in Ireland, he traded his full German licence for a full Irish licence all without taking a test!

CAR OWNERSHIP AND REGISTRATION

FACT: Italy has 577 cars for every 1,000 inhabitants, more than any other country. The USA has 506, Germany has 505.

FACT: In the past 10 years, the percentage of households owning a car in the UK has increased from 62 to over 72. That means more households own cars than own tumble-driers!

If you sell your car privately, don't part with the registration document until:
- the buyer has paid up
- the DVLA has been notified.

If you hand over the documentation without registering the change and telling the DVLA, you may find yourself liable for someone else's traffic offence.

Car been off the road for a while? You don't need to tax it for that period. Fill in a **Statutory Off Road Notification** (available from the Post Office) and send it to the DVLA.

Caught driving without tax? You'll have to pay the full back duty, even if you were only on the road for a short time. You could also be fined up to £1,000 or five times the annual duty for your vehicle (whichever is the greater).

Forget the grubby note on the windscreen saying **'Tax applied for'**. It's no guarantee that you won't get reported. If you've lost your tax disc, get a form from the Post Office to send off for a duplicate. If your vehicle is genuinely taxed, you won't be prosecuted by the DVLA.

You can't swap a tax disc from one car to the other. This is even worse than displaying nothing at all. You can get a **refund** on your old tax disc from the Post Office and use the money to buy a new one for your new car.

Abandoned vehicle take your fancy? If you notice a vehicle parked in the same spot for a considerable length of time and apparently abandoned, you can apply to have it re-registered in your name (see below).

A car for the price of a stamp?

Over a million cars are now abandoned each year in the UK. This represents a shocking increase of 500 per cent in three years. But why? Because the price of scrap metal has plunged, so has the scrap value of cars. There is little incentive to take an unwanted car to a scrapyard. But there may be a way you could make this work for you.

Jenny Bates noticed a G-reg Vauxhall Nova parked on her street in Wandsworth. Day after day – it never moved. After nine months she rang the DVLA to report it abandoned, and found out that she could apply to register it in her own name. So she filled in a form and the DVLA sent a letter to the owner notifying her that she should write back within two weeks if she wanted to keep the car. She didn't reply – and the car was officially Jenny's! However, it later emerged that the driver had been unable to drive the car for nine months due to injury, and when the letter arrived she was on holiday. She replied to it but was two days late, and had lost her rights to the car. She was no longer considered the registered owner.

BUYING FROM A REGISTERED DEALER

'Dealers just want to shift metal. They have a dealer margin and a "soft money" margin on every price. Make them an offer – you'll be surprised.'
Kevin Duck, www.Car-Now.com

FACT: 140,000 people have imported new cars last year – that's 10 per cent of the new car market. (*Car Importing* magazine)

FACT: On average it costs 21 per cent more to buy a new car in Britain than elsewhere in the EU.

Buying a car, whether new or used, is a major undertaking. After a house, it's the biggest purchase most people ever make. Consumers are more aware than ever of the pitfalls of buying without asking the right questions and exploring all the angles. Here are some you may not know.

Cars seriously **depreciate in value during their first year** so try to find one that's almost a year old. Demonstrator models are good value.

Colour does matter. Reds, silvers and blacks always sell well and can add up to 20 per cent on top of the price.

Don't be swayed by **'special edition'** cars. Often all that means is the odd extra and a few graphics. You can't get discounts and resale is more difficult.

Timing is everything. Try making your car salesperson an offer he or she can't refuse two or three days before the end of the month. Most have monthly targets, and if they aren't close to making theirs, you could find they're anxious to make a sale. If it's been a bad month, you may be able to haggle a bit more and get some extra deals or discounts thrown in. March and September are also good months for getting discounts on cars with the previous registration.

Try asking for around 7–8 per cent discount. Ask the salesperson which models will get the best **manufacturer's bonus** (some manufacturers give the dealer more of an incentive when they sell particular cars). See if you can get any discount on factory-fitted items or on-the-road costs. Remember, if you don't ask, you don't get!

If you buy a car on **hire purchase**, you won't own it until you have completed the payments. If you fail to keep repayments up, the car can be repossessed. Nor will you be able to sell the car on without settling up with the finance company.

If you want to **end your loan**, you can do so. The Customer Credit Act, 1974 will let you end the agreement and return the car to the finance company – but you must have paid at least half of the credit price of the car.

Check out the **residual value** – the rate at which the type of car you're buying depreciates – before you purchase. Depreciation can be the biggest single cost of running a car. It might well be worth splashing out a little more initially if that car will hold its value better for resale. To check this out, visit www.whatcar.com.

Certain marques of car hold their value better than others. Mercedes, for example, have a particularly **good residual value**. For this reason, it's often better to buy an entry-level model from a prestige marque than a luxury model from a lesser marque.

Make buying your new car and trading in your old one **two separate deals**. Tell the dealer you are not trading and negotiate a selling price for the new car. After they agree on the new car selling price, tell them you want to trade in and how much you want. They may accept, they may not, but at least you'll know how low they will really go on the selling price of the new car.

When paying for your new car, avoid charges for a banker's draft by giving a cheque five working days before you pick the car up. You don't compromise your consumer rights.

A 'new' car means a car that has not been previously registered. In fact, a **so-called 'new' car** may have been sitting in a warehouse or on a forecourt for years. Checking the vehicle identification number (VIN) will tell you how old the car actually is.

Don't be taken in by **manufacturers' hype** about the popularity of their cars. Sometimes the figures have been bumped up by including fleet sales, so they will not indicate which cars are most popular with private buyers, whose criteria will be completely different.

If something is amiss with your car from the outset – **be persistent** about complaining. Get any rattles, stereo problems, or even seemingly trivial bodywork faults resolved while the car is still under warranty.

If you buy from dealers who are members of a trade association like the Retail Motor Industry Federation, you will have some legal comeback against them if necessary. Used cars sold by motor traders are subject to the Sale of Goods Act, 1979 which means that the car's condition has to be made clear to the person buying it. However, if you're buying from a private individual, a used car isn't covered by this Act.

Always haggle, even if the dealer has a 'no haggle' sign up. You might be able to negotiate a discount if you are paying by credit. Many dealers earn commission from selling finance deals.

If you are using your old car in a **part-exchange deal**, find out how much it is worth (look at car magazines, local papers, other garages and so on). Ask for a cash price and balance this against the savings you might get using it in a part-exchange deal.

For great deals on **ex-MOD Land Rovers**, click on www.landrover-sales.com, or call 01562 730404.

How We Beat The System

Pensioner Bryn Curwood took on the might of Hyundai – and won. His story is an inspiring example of the power of persistence, pestering – and fluorescent posters!

'Me and the wife had saved up for a brand new teal Hyundai Accent to treat ourselves, as at our time of life you want a bit of luxury! Anyway, after only three months the paint-work was all scuffed and faded round the wheel arches. Being a new car it was still under warranty, but Hyundai refused to repair it, even after we got an independent assessment from the RAC. We were devastated as it was really ruined and we didn't see why we would have to foot the bill for their faults. We had a mountain of paperwork between us and Hyundai customer services. But I wasn't getting anywhere. So we put some ads in the local free papers for anyone wanting information about faulty paintwork on Hyundais. This just got us a warning from Hyundai customer services.

'Well, we were going on holiday, touring round. So we made big signs on bright orange fluorescent card and stuck them in all the back windows of the car. Being disabled I can park where I like, so everywhere we went we left the car parked outside the Hyundai dealerships. People used to crowd around the car to read the notices and even chase us on motorways. It gave us great satisfaction! And to boot, when we got home there was a telephone call asking us to bring the car into the nearest Hyundai garage to be repaired for free – a complete respray. Smashing.'

BUYING FROM AN INDIVIDUAL

FACT: There are 30,000 'cut and shut' cars on Britain's roads.

FACT: There is a one-in-three chance that any car you inspect has had its mileage reading altered.

Buying a used car from an individual has its pros and cons. **For:** it's often the cheapest way of buying a car. **Against:** you have very little legal protection. If you do buy from a private seller, however, remember the longer the last owner had it the better.

Never buy a car without a **log book** and don't take 'no' for an answer.

Some motor traders pretend to deal as individuals because of this reduced legal protection. If you're looking through the local press, see if the same telephone number crops up more than once against different cars. Be wary of ads that have a mobile phone number or specify a time when to call (it might even be a public phone box).When you phone with your enquiry, ask about 'the car'. If the reply is 'which one?' then you can guess that they're a dealer. Don't let the seller bring the car to you or suggest meeting somewhere other than at their home.

Never go and look at a car on your own if you're buying privately. **Take someone with you.** Not only does this give you added security but you also have a witness to whatever the seller is promising you. Arrange to **meet at the seller's house**. Leave the name and address of the place that you are going to with a friend.

You might consider paying for an **independent inspection** by a professional mechanic. AA, RAC and Green Flag all offer this service.

Beware of a car with a warm bonnet. It's a favourite trick to warm the car up before a potential buyer turns up. If a car has a mechanical problem, it usually shows up when you try to start the car. And if it hasn't been raining, be very suspicious of a car that is wet. The seller may have sprayed it with water to **conceal defects** in the paintwork.

If the seller claims that defects in the car are easy/cheap to fix, ask yourself, if it's that easy to fix, why hasn't he or she done it? If the seller claims that the car is still under its extended warranty, ask to see the **service record book**. The car should have been regularly serviced under the terms of the extended warranty.

Before buying a used car, **park it under a neon street light**. It will be much easier to see if parts of the car are painted slightly different shades – thus revealing whether the car has been in a serious accident or, even worse, is a cut and shut.

If you are going to take a car for a **test drive**, make sure you are covered by your own insurance to drive another person's car. Don't just rely on the seller blithely assuring you that you are covered.

When buying, get firm proof of the **car seller's name and address**. If the vehicle turns out to be stolen and has to be returned to the rightful owner, you are entitled to claim your costs from the person who sold you the car, regardless of whether that person knew it was stolen or not.

If the used car you are looking at has especially **shiny paint** on the middle of the front doors – forget it. The patches are where the paint has been protected by signs, showing the car has been a minicab.

If you're buying from a dealer, never pay cash for a deposit on a car. If the deal goes south, you'll never get your cash back, but you can always dispute a credit transaction.

Don't assume that a **digital odometer** is always reliable. Digital types can be rolled back by reprogramming the EEPROM chip.

Look at the **number plate fixings and the plates themselves**. If both plates look as scratched as you would expect from normal wear, but the fixing holes are cleaner and more free of dust than the surrounding body, it could be that the plates have been removed to allow a respray, or have been transferred from another vehicle.

If you suspect that the seller doesn't really live at the house outside which the car is parked, **ask if you can use the loo**. If they won't let you, don't buy the car.

If the car is parked on the road, rather than on the seller's drive, take a look at the drive for **oil stains**.

Poke the tip of your little finger into the gap between the panels and slide it along. You can detect uneven gaps by the depth to which your finger goes in. This could indicate **poor accident repairs**.

Check the finger well behind the passenger door handles. If there are so many fine scratches in the paint that the whole area is duller than the rest of the body, the car has probably been used as a **taxi**.

Pricey repairs. Some repairs are costlier than others – here are some danger signs, even before you start the engine:
- rusty sills, wheel arches and door bottoms
- bubbling or flaking paintwork
- oil leaks or damaged hoses/drive belts under the bonnet
- damaged or worn tyres
- damaged or fraying seat belts
- leaky seals round doors and windows
- faulty electrics – exterior/interior lights, dashboard warning lights not working
- signs of oil or water leaks on ground under car.

Clues that the car may have been in an **accident:**
- car looks lopsided or tilted, either front to back or side to side
- body panels have been repaired
- colour and/or texture of paintwork is patchy
- signs of welding in the boot, door sills or under bonnet.

Bad signs during the test drive:
- unresponsive or squealing brakes
- car pulls to one side when you brake
- unusual noises – don't let the seller switch on the radio
- defective handbrake – try pulling away in second with it on
- shaky steering wheel
- car pulls to one side on road with no camber
- difficult to get car into gear, particularly 3rd down to 2nd
- crunching noises when changing gear
- car slips out of gear when you brake or accelerate
- engine sound varies if clutch depressed when car is in neutral
- smell of petrol or oil inside car
- blue, grey or black smoke from exhaust (leak of water or oil into engine)
- oil filler cap has thick greyish deposit underneath.

Hot wheels!

FACT: Every year over 450,000 accident-damaged vehicles are written off by insurance companies.

FACT: In the UK there could be as many as 28,000 unsafe cars in circulation on the roads each year following inadequate accident repairs.

FACT: Over 30,000 MOT certificates are stolen each year.

FACT: Each year over 3.5 million vehicles are sold using secured loans, many of which are still outstanding when they next change hands.

FACT: Clockers make approximately £100 million each year – 1,600 km (1,000 miles) taken off the clock is about £30 in the seller's pocket.

If you buy a stolen car the police can take it away from you and return it to its rightful owner. Even if you bought the car in good faith, you won't get any compensation. You might be able to sue the seller for your losses but it's unlikely that they'll still be around to be sued. If you bought the car on credit, you may still have to pay off the loan. Spotting a stolen car is definitely not easy. But there are one or two things to look out for:

- look at the vehicle registration document (V5). If the seller hasn't got one, you should be suspicious. A common, and often genuine, excuse is that it's been sent off to the DVLA to be updated. However, if you can't check the car's ownership and identity details, you can't prove it's not stolen.
- is the number plate the same as on the V5? It should be.
- if the car was bought recently and the V5 is with the DVLA, the seller should have a green slip (this applies to cars issued with new V5s introduced in March 1997).
- check the V5 for alterations and spelling mistakes. If you spot one, it means it's a forgery. Genuine V5s have watermarks.
- ask to see some proof of identity from the seller (passport, driving licence, recent household bill). You want to see that the name and address matches the one on the V5.
- check that the vehicle identification number (VIN) which can be found on a metal plate in the engine compartment, stamped on the bodywork under the bonnet and under the driver's seat, is the same as the one on the V5. Also, some cars have the VIN etched on to the windows or lamps.
- ask to see the seller's insurance policy with details of their car
- ask to see the service history.

Look out for the **'cut and shuts'** – two damaged cars welded into one. They are extremely unsafe. Tell-tale signs are repaired body panels, patchy paint work or paint work of different textures, evidence of welding in the engine or boot (look under the carpet in the boot). Also check for stickers concealing altered etching, deliberate scratching to windows, head lights, tail lights and sun roof and evidence that the VIN has been tampered with.

Low mileage is a strong selling point. That's why **clocking** – turning the mileage clock back is such a lucrative but highly illegal business. Again, there are signs to look out for. Despite apparently low mileage:

- heavy wear and tear on the car
- a new steering wheel, new pedal rubbers, and gear stick knob
- mileometer numbers don't quite line up
- mileage on the last MOT certificate is more than or very close to current mileometer reading
- mileage on service documentation doesn't tally with mileometer reading
- mileage when car was last sold doesn't tally with mileometer reading (check with previous owner(s) and ask them).

Look at MOT certificates and service documents; they should all record the car's mileage. Ask what the car was used for (short trips or regular motorway driving). If the V5 lists previous owners, you can ask them.

A car bought on **hire purchase** belongs to the finance company until the payments have all been made. If you buy such a car and there is outstanding finance on it, the lender can take it back. You can sue whoever sold you the car – if you can find them. There are some limited exceptions to this. If you were not aware that the car was subject to an outstanding credit agreement and bought it in good faith, you may be allowed to keep it.

HPI to the rescue

However closely you inspect a car, you won't be able to tell for sure if it's stolen, if it's an insurance right-off, or if it still belongs to a finance company. An organisation called HPI (stands for hire purchase information) holds information on more than 60 million vehicles, and offers a car fraud detection service that can reveal the real facts, no matter what lengths the seller may go to to conceal them. An amazing one in three cars they check is not what it appears to be.

Call the car fraud detection database on 01722 435 525, Monday to Saturday, 8am–8pm, Sunday 10am–5pm. Or check on their Internet service, www.hpi.co.uk, where you can check up to three cars for just £12.50. You must supply the vehicle registration number and the 17-digit VIN number – the system does the rest.

But bear in mind that a stolen car may not make it on to the database for more than 72 hours after it has been stolen – plenty of time for you to be ripped off!

Trash or treasure

If you know what you're doing and are prepared to put in some work, you can pick up a serviceable car for well under the price of a mountain bike. With used car prices lower than ever, if a well-cared-for but oldish car has even a minor prang, it may not be worth getting the bodywork fixed. In scrapyards throughout the land, these faithful old friends are being stripped for parts. If you're lucky enough to find one with a few months to run before its MOT you've got plenty of time to hunt around for spares and fix it up yourself.

BUYING ABROAD

Despite the recent drop in new car prices, British drivers are still paying over 20 per cent more for their cars than drivers in other EU countries. UK prices are the highest pre-tax as well and depreciation rates are higher in Britain too. No wonder British buyers are flooding to the Continent and to Eire. But it pays to be careful who you deal with. Brokers are not always what they seem, and there have been cases of 'brokers' offering their services over the Internet, then vanishing with deposits paid to them by unwary would-be customers. There are plenty of legit specialist brokers and dealers who can take a lot of the strain out of buying from the Continent – but they also take a cut of the saving that could otherwise be yours. It is entirely possible to organise a new car purchase from Europe on your own, cutting out the middle man or importer. Here are a few of the things you need to consider.

First, find your dealer/agent. This will probably be a personal recommendation from someone you know who has dealt with them successfully. Failing that, visit the website of the car manufacturer you're interested in – you should find a list of dealers there. Choose a main dealer, for preference.

Get them to **quote for the model and options you've chosen**, confirming the spec on company notepaper by letter/fax. All the details should be there – RHD (right-hand drive), UK spec headlights, speedo, wipers, handbook and service log, along with the price including option costs. This quote should be tax free (although in Germany you may have to pay VAT and claim it back later). The price you are quoted will be the price you pay the dealer (in Euros). You can check the price you've been quoted by requesting a brochure with a complete price list from the manufacturer's website.

In Belgium **BTW** means VAT and not 'by the way'. In France, it's **TVA** and it runs at 21 per cent. You can request that it isn't included in the quote (unless you're buying from Germany), but you'll have to provide proof that you are a UK resident.

Get **written confirmation of delivery time**. Check with other British clients to make sure they are being realistic.

Supplying a RHD car attracts an **'administration fee'**. Make sure this is included in the quote. It shouldn't be more than a couple of hundred pounds.

You absolutely need a **'Type Approval Certificate'** – proof that the car satisfies UK and EC safety and emissions standards. Without it, you can't register the car in the UK, so make it a condition of purchase. Many buyers have come unstuck with Japanese or US imports in this area.

Sticky deposit? Don't panic – most dealers will ask for about 20 per cent deposit when you place the order. They don't want to get stuck with a RHD if you pull out. Make sure you get a receipt. If you pay by credit card, you are protected if something goes awry with the sale but there will be a commission charge, and probably not at the most advantageous exchange rate. You could pay by Foreign Currency Banker's Draft. Dealers like them because they are rock solid. The cheapest method is a transfer from a UK bank to the dealer's bank.

Your dealer should sort out **transit plates** and **'green card' insurance**. Find out if this is included in the original quote. Don't send your passport to the dealer – this is an unnecessary security risk. You can get proof of UK residence from your local council (provided you're on the electoral register).

If you haven't paid VAT in the country of purchase, you have to pay **17.5 per cent of the purchase value** within 30 days of bringing the car into the UK. You can either pay VAT based on the rate you paid when you changed your money, so make sure you get a receipt from your bank, or at the rate offered by Customs. In addition, you need to pay £25 to your local VRO (vehicle registration office) for registering your car and having a registration number allocated, and you'll have to buy a tax disk, and new number plates.

No need to declare your new car when you drive off the ferry in Britain – though you may be so proud, you'll want to.

How We Beat The System

Lee Waterhouse saved thousands by going it alone:

'I'd heard about importing cars through watching *Top Gear*, so when I wanted a new car I phoned a few UK importers. But I wasn't comfortable with any of them really. So I phoned the importing companies direct – the one for Holland and the one for Belgium. They faxed me a list of their dealers in Holland and Belgium. I got out a map and found out where they were, and then phoned the nearest ones. Belgium was about £2,000 cheaper than Holland, so I ordered one from a dealer there – after getting a written offer by fax. One of my colleagues at work, Cathy, also wanted the same model of car, so we got together and ordered two, therefore getting more money off due to a bulk buy. I arranged to pay by credit card, and then waited until the exchange rate was really favourable. I then 'locked' the rate by agreeing to buy so many Euros at that rate on a certain day. By doing that I saved about £500.

'We waited until the start of September to go and fetch the cars as by then we would have the new registration number. Me and my girlfriend Helen hired a car, and Cathy and her brother also came with us. We left the hire car at Dover, went over on the ferry and drove back in our new cars, with boots full of booze! We did it all in one day, which I wouldn't recommend – next time we'll stay the night.

'By buying over there I saved about £5,500. Helen and I are going on holiday to France this summer, and we're having the car serviced over there when we go. That in itself is saving us £90.'

These websites are an excellent starting point for anyone hoping to drive a bargain:

www.oneswoop.com
www.eurekar.com
www.carseekers.co.uk
www.showroom4cars.com

AUCTIONS

Car auctions are not for the faint hearted. With no test drive, minimal time to examine the vehicle, hard-nosed dealers as your competition, and auctioneers who can sell a vehicle in less than a minute, you could come seriously unstuck.

Yet some three or four thousand cars pass through auction every day, and there are certainly bargains to be had.

Julian Trim, who offers an auction buyer service, sourcing cars for potential buyers then handling the bidding for them, recommends that:
- you **attend an auction** on at least four occasions before you bid
- you should **always take someone with you** who knows the ropes.

Failing that, his company will do it for you. You specify the kind of car you're after, he contacts you several hours before the auction with the spec of what's available, along with a report on the condition and how much work it may need. If you give him the go-ahead and agree a top price, his agent will handle the bidding and you pay the amount on the auction house invoice plus 6 per cent.

Julian Trim and Co (01747 838888)
Douglas Coker Associates (020 8351 7976)

West Oxfordshire Motor Auctions holds sales of ex-police vehicles twice a month. Sadly, the blue flashing lights and all other police paraphernalia will have been removed beforehand, but although the mileage may be on the high side, and the spec a bit basic, you can bet they've been well maintained!

West Oxfordshire Motor Auctions (01993 774413)

SELLING YOUR CAR

Time to get rid of your old banger? I mean, you're reluctantly having to part with your reliable, comfortable, fuel-efficient, treasured, well cared-for car. Better clean out the ashtrays and brush up on your sales patter.

Part exchange is a very straightforward, if not very lucrative way of getting rid of one car and buying another. The upside is you don't have to advertise or spend loads of time dealing with potential customers. The downside is that you could end up with getting less for your old car than if you'd sold it privately. One way to make the best of the situation is to find the lowest retail price for the car you want to buy and the trade price of your current car (use *Parker's Car Price Guide*, available from most newsagents). You want to pay the difference between the two prices which is called the 'price to change'. Haggle with the dealer to get a discount on the 'new' car and once you get the discount bring your part-exchange car into the discussion.

If you're **advertising your car privately** in the newspapers, remember to include information on the make/model, mileage, year, condition, full service history and any extras (like metallic finish, CD player, whether it's convertible or not and so on), price, phone number and when people should call.

For a car worth **up to £3,000**, it's worth putting a postcard in the newsagent's window, advertising in local newspapers or free-sheets – but not much more.

If you are listing your car **in a magazine**, use a whole roll of film to take pictures with your car in different positions against different backgrounds and choose the best one.

Listing your car **on the web** is much more effective than advertising in a newspaper. It's cheaper, runs for longer and reaches far more people. This is worth considering if your car is special enough for people to want to travel for. You could even create your own web page to help sell your car. If you're online anyway, you probably have the capability to create a home page with your ISP (Internet Service Provider). If you already have a website, just add a page and provide a link to it, or advertise it on the index page. You can scan in images of the car and provide information about its condition.

Don't park your car on a road to sell it. It could get vandalised, ticketed, towed or even stolen. **Keep it on your driveway.** This also reassures buyers that you're not a dealer posing as a private seller. If your own neighbourhood doesn't do you justice, you could always try parking the car in front of a better looking place, and selling from there.

Fix up your car before you sell it. Put a good wax job on the car, vacuum the inside, even have it steam cleaned, and gloss up the tyres. **Appearance is everything.** Replace dud bulbs and fuses. The cost is minimal to you, but it gives the buyer an excuse to offer less if it's not sorted. **Make sure your tyres are all properly inflated!**

Take the name, telephone number and, if possible, address of the callers who ring about your car. Make an excuse to end the conversation, then **call them back**. Only then should you tell them your address. When they turn up, note down their registration number. People may ask for details and then come and steal the car.

Add a few accessories to the car to make it even more attractive, like a warning triangle, a steering lock, or furry dice – just kidding!

Avoid being on your own when a buyer comes to view. A couple of able-bodied friends nearby may come in handy. Better safe than sorry.

Keep your **maintenance records** looking neat. Even list the oil changes. Every time your car is serviced, add the receipt to the notebook, then you'll never lose track. This makes a terrific impression, and hardly anyone does it.

Print out a **colour flyer** for possible buyers. This gives you the chance to include detail that you could never afford to put in a newspaper ad. If you've created a web page, just print it out. You can add all sorts of info of the 'one non-smoking owner' variety.

Before the first buyer comes, prepare yourself for the inevitable assault on your asking price by printing out the **market value** for cars of the same model and age from Internet car pricing sites. Always put 10–15 per cent above the price you'll actually settle for. That gives you a margin for haggling and makes the buyer feel they've got a bargain. Practise negotiation with a friend before you do it for real.

If the buyer complains about every scratch, mark or stain on your car, tell them it's normal **wear and tear** for a car of that age and mileage, that's why you're not asking the price of a new car. Every used car has scratches from road debris. That's all accounted for in the depreciated value.

Your car is still worth market value no matter what money the buyer has. Make it clear in the ads that your **asking price is firm and non-negotiable**. Never use terms like 'o.n.o.' – it makes you seem desperate to sell. If a buyer is trying to knock down your price, ask them where they get their figure from, and what research it was based on. They won't have a leg to stand on.

Auction houses usually put between 8–10 per cent plus VAT on the price of a car. Prices are usually quite close to trade price.

If you've got a **convertible**, sell it during the summer. **Four-wheel drives** sell well in winter but avoid selling other cars at this time.

Spring, summer and September are when used-car values go up.

Average mileage is about 10,000 a year. Figures above or below this will affect the price.

Never let buyers **test drive** your car alone, even if they leave their own car behind. For a start, your insurance won't cover damage that occurs from another driver if they are not family. It could even be that the car they leave behind is stolen and they'll disappear with yours. Always go with the car. **Don't hand over the keys** until you are safely in beside the buyer, and strapped in. If you drive first and swap over halfway, take the keys out of the ignition before you change places with the buyer.

Never let the buyer bring another person with him/her for the test drive unless you have similar back up.

Check they have a **valid driver's licence and insurance**. If you let an un-licensed driver behind the wheel, and an accident happens, you could be at fault. If they want to take your car to a mechanic, go with them. But don't drop your price on the say-so of their mechanic – they could be in partnership.

If they say they want the car but don't have the full amount with them, get a 10 per cent **non-refundable deposit** from them. Write them a receipt, saying it's non-refundable. Hang on to the car until you get the full amount and the cheque has cleared.

Get shot of an old banger

What, you mean no one wanted to buy it? Incredible! So what do you do now? Well don't leave it around on the street. If it's registered to you, you'll end up having to move it eventually once the local council gets on to you. These are the best methods to try:

Take it to a scrapyard, if it's still driveable and has at least a bit of MOT left. The local Trading Standards Office can give you a list of registered scrapyards and dismantlers – this is important because they'll follow environmental guidelines. You may not get any money for it, or perhaps just a bit for spares. If you're really unlucky you may have to pay for disposal.

Look in the adverts of your local paper for scrapyards offering to take cars away – but check them out with the local Trading Standards Office. Some unscrupulous operators take your money and then dump the car in the street.

Contact your local council and they may take your car away for nothing, or a relatively modest charge – typically £20–£50 – although there may be a wait for collection. Some councils have been inundated and are unable to take more, but it is more than worth a call. Cars disposed of by the council are usually crushed without any parts being salvaged – if you consider that wasteful, you should try passing the car on to a vehicle dismantler, as described above.

Inform the DVLC when you dispose of your car. You should send the registration document to the DVLC, confirming that you have scrapped it. This is important, because if you don't, and it ends up in unscrupulous hands and is dumped illegally, you could be held responsible.

Abandon all hope?

If a car has clearly been abandoned on your street (and you don't want it yourself – see page 149), you should report it to your local council. This is not likely to get instant results. First, the council has to trace the owner, which takes time, and requires the co-operation of the DVLC. If the registered owner is no longer the owner, it will take even longer.

If the car is abandoned in a dangerous spot or is causing an obstruction, you can contact the police, who can have it removed immediately.

PARKING PROBLEMS

'It doesn't matter to me if it's the Prime Minister or the ordinary man in the street. You can't park here unless it's an emergency.' *Robert Twyman, parking attendant*

FACT: Buying an orange disabled badge on the black market will cost you around £250.

Parking regulations change continually. Many roadside markings (such as red lines drawn on the kerb) are now legally defunct. However, some local authorities don't know about this and not only fail to delete the lines, but continue to dole out fines for parking on them. So, if you are charged with illegal parking, do a bit of research to find out whether or not the road marking was valid.

Even if you are apparently **legally parked** (not on yellow lines or in a restricted area), you can still be fined for causing an obstruction.

You are allowed to stop on a **single yellow line** to load or unload goods or to set down or collect passengers. So, if you see a traffic warden near your car – get someone to come out of the shop with you and claim you were picking them up.

Parking wardens are supposed to observe a vehicle for four or five minutes to determine whether or not you are loading or unloading. If you really have been away for just a minute and find a ticket on your car, you can appeal on grounds you were loading or unloading, which is difficult for the traffic warden to disprove. It helps if you've got some cardboard boxes in the back of the car.

Thinking of disputing a parking fine? About 25 per cent of drivers who tell the council that they are going to the **independent adjudicator** have the fine dropped. Councils have to pay a fee for every case that goes to adjudication. Are these facts in some way related?

Don't, whatever you do, park on the **white zig-zags** either side of pedestrian crossings. As well as a fine, you'll get your licence endorsed.

Yellow zig-zags outside school entrances cannot be enforced unless there are also signs showing the times they are in force. If the signs showing times are present, even stopping on the zig-zags during the specified times is an offence.

Watch out for DPE (decriminalised parking enforcement). When local councils take over parking enforcement from the police, the number of tickets issued usually goes up by about 300 per cent. You've been warned!

Better to park in an area without **'pay and display'** or anything that indicates the time you arrived. That way, the traffic warden has to come by twice to give you a ticket. With 'pay and display' or on a meter, they can give you a ticket straight away.

Wriggle out of that ticket

Stay calm! Once a ticket is issued it is impossible for the traffic warden or parking attendant to cancel it, so it is counter-productive to give him/her a hard time.

Ask why the ticket was issued and explain why you think you should have been allowed to park where you did. Ask the warden/attendant to make a note of your comments in his/her pocket book. **Collect evidence** before you drive away. It is a good idea to carry a disposable camera in the car so that you can make a record of missing or faded lines or misleading signs.

Write to the **issuing body** as soon as possible, with any information to support your case – shortcomings in the lines or signs, mitigating circumstances etc. Whoever the ticket was issued by, they should be **'fair'** and **'timely'** in dealing with aggrieved motorists. If they take months to reply and you respond 'by return' you will be in a strong position should you decide to pursue the matter in court or with an adjudicator.

The issuing authority can cancel a ticket on compassionate grounds, or if there are mitigating circumstances, but if it goes to adjudication it can only be cancelled if the ticket was wrongly issued; for example, if the signs were missing or incorrect, the wrong offence code was put in by the parking attendant, there was an error or discrepancy in the parking order, etc, so don't refer the matter to the adjudicator unless you have a really good case.

If you've parked in a **pay and display** without showing a ticket, you could try and get a ticket from someone else parked nearby at the same time. It's quite dishonest, of course, but a lively trade in used tickets does go on after the traffic wardens have made a swoop.

Make sure all the **details on the ticket are correct**. If they're not, you may have grounds to dispute it (see below).

How We Beat The System

If you get a ticket, check the details carefully. Any slip up by the parking warden could give you grounds for disputing the fine.

Mike Cushman parked his BMW, after 6pm on a Sunday, on a single yellow line in Edgware. When he returned to the car, he had been issued with a parking ticket, but the parking warden had put the make of car down as a Mercedes. He sent off copies of the vehicle registration and tax disc, and the fine was dropped because it could not be proved that the correct vehicle had been ticketed. The (im)moral of this story is that if you have an unusual car, take the badges off it and get a tax disc holder with another manufacturer's name on it. If you get a ticket there's a possibility that the parking attendant will put the wrong make on the form and you won't have to pay.

For more information on parking and the law, visit www.parkingticket.co.uk.

SPEEDING FINES

If you exceed the speed limit, you risk getting caught, either by a police officer or by one of the ever increasing battery of technologically advanced speed detection devices. Here's how to try and avoid this sad state of affairs.

Look as far ahead as you can, and **check your mirrors** regularly. This is not only a good way to spot speed traps early, it is also good practice in safe driving.

If you're the only car visible, don't exceed the limit by too much, especially at night when traffic is light, and police cars are hard to spot. If you are caught speeding, there is no one else you can blame.

If there is someone ahead going even faster than you, don't be tempted to over-take. **Let him or her go first and find the speed traps!** Keep a look-out behind, though.

If there are other cars around, try not to be the one going fastest, and don't draw attention to yourself by **changing lanes** all the time. That kind of driving really stands out on cameras.

Motorway bridges are a favourite location for **hand-held speed traps**. Look out for a car parked on the bridge, or officers underneath the bridge, or cars on the sliproad.

Remember police cars are often **unmarked**. Don't dismiss everything that doesn't have a blue light on top. Look out for extra antennas (for their radio), and anything suspiciously clean in the winter. Police motorcyclists tend to have white helmets.

Beware of cars that come up behind you at night, then sit on your tail. Slow down a bit – nothing obvious – and keep your hands at ten to two. If they stay behind, get ready to be pulled over.

Watch out for **cars parked on the hard shoulder**. There could be a hand-held trap nearby.

Some cars just yell **'Arrest me!'** Known high-performance cars, go-faster stripes and boy-racer types all draw unwanted attention. A nice dull people-mover is probably your best bet for persuading the constabulary that you're a respectable type of person. Bright colours, particularly red, attract attention. Light, pastel colours have a tendency to blend with the environment and dark colours such as black and navy not only blend in, they look positively serious. **Tinted windows** look shifty and give out the wrong message to the police.

If you think you've been clocked on a **radar trap**, and a police vehicle pulls out, probably with the intention of stopping you, all is not lost. Provided the officer isn't right on your tail with a positive ID, you may still be able to evade being stopped by pulling off at the next turning (you'd better hope it's soon), main-taining an inconspicuous speed and trying to merge in with other traffic. This only works if you have a nice dull car (see above).

Word perfect?

If you are being reported for speeding, the police officer must say the following: '…you will be reported for consideration of the question of prosecuting you for exceeding the speed limit.'

It must either be given verbally or in writing at the time, or in writing within 14 days.

After this Notice of Intended Prosecution (NIP), the officer should then caution you by saying, 'You do not have to say anything, but it may harm your defence if you do not mention when questioned, something you later rely on in Court. Anything you do say may be given in evidence.'

Under section 1 of the Road Traffic Offenders Act, 1988, it states, 'A person **shall not be convicted of an offence** to which this section applies, (speeding, dangerous driving, careless driving, failing to conform to traffic lights, failing to conform to stop signs, continuous white lines in the middle of the road and other mandatory road signs) unless the Notice of Intended Prosecution was given.'

So if you can distract the officer so he or she doesn't actually say these words, you should get off. If you're booked for speeding or any other offence, if possible, switch on a tape recorder or dictaphone so that you have a record of what the officer says. But some police forces do have the NIP printed on forms so they don't have to go through the spiel.

Well, officer…

What happens if you're caught speeding? In most areas, the guidelines that police officers are given are:

- a verbal caution is given if you're up to 10 mph over the limit
- between 10 and 25 mph over the limit, an endorsable fixed penalty can be given
- over 25 mph the driver should be reported and summoned to court.

In reality, the police are given an element of discretion in these matters; for instance, it's not unusual for the law to be enforced on motorways only if the speed is over 85 mph. Whatever the situation, you're not going to make it any better by getting stroppy. The way you behave with the police may make the difference between a hefty fine and points on your licence, and a verbal warning. So don't try to be a smart arse.

As soon as you notice the police and have realised what's going on, **pull over smartly and safely**, using mirrors and indicators. No matter what they think you've done, it will at least demonstrate a basic understanding of road sense. **Shut off the engine!** This is the most important first step. Shutting off the engine removes any suspicion the officer may have that you might try to run him or her over or run away. Plus, you are going to be stopped for at least five to ten minutes, so shutting off the engine saves fuel.

Call it prejudice, but people who take care of their cars look like they're responsible drivers. A dented car is one that has been involved in accidents before. Make sure that your glove box is fairly clean so that you don't have to search for your registration documents. Realise that those terribly witty stickers may also give an impression.

When the officer comes to your window, remain seated, roll down the window and have both hands on the steering wheel. Remove your sun-glasses if you have them on. The idea is to **look like a model citizen**. If you have tinted windows, get passengers to roll theirs down too.

If you've committed an offence, the first officer to speak to you should caution you before saying anything else. If you're not cautioned immediately, they're stopping you for something else.

Once you've been cautioned, **be very careful what you say**. You're on the record and anything you say after that point could be brought up should the case go to court.

If you think you might just get off with a caution, **keep talking**. It humanises the situation. If you're absolutely sure that you've not done anything wrong, or that the officer can't prove that you've done anything wrong, say so. Don't be aggressive, just straightforward.

If you're going to try **the bladder excuse**, make sure it's the first thing you say as the officer approaches. It has to look urgent. Ask them to follow you to the nearest public loo. Appear co-operative but desperate. It might just work for a range of offences, included speeding, shooting the lights and illegal turns.

Don't be tricked into incriminating yourself. If the officer says 'Did you know that you were doing 95 back there, and I had to really speed up to catch you?' don't reply 'Officer, I was going probably no faster than 85.' **Just stick with something bland**, like 'Officer, I believe you were mistaken and I am sure I wasn't going that fast.'

Even if you have your licence with you, say that you don't. It's up to the discretion of the officer whether to issue a producer (i.e. telling you to take your licence to an appointed police station). You can't be issued with a fixed penalty notice until an officer has seen your driving licence. You will usually be given a provisional fixed penalty, to be confirmed by another officer at the station when the licence is produced. If no producer is issued and the officer has not seen the licence, he can't give a fixed penalty at all. If you do have your licence on you, then you'll get a regular fixed penalty notice.

It might be worth asking the officer a question at this point. If you can **distract him or her** so they don't sign the fixed penalty notice, then it won't be valid.

The best excuse for going through a red traffic light…if you **sneeze** while driving at 40 mph, you travel 80 yards or so with your eyes shut – enough not to know that the lights have changed. Mind you, the police are wise to this so maybe it's best not to try it on!

You are more likely to get let off by a **normal officer** (black hat, black uniform) than by a **traffic officer** (white hat, green overcoat). It's a traffic cop's vocation in life to catch you, the normal cop probably does not want the added paperwork.

Before you start arguing – police officers are legally accredited with being **speed experts**. The speedos in their patrol cars provide sufficient back-up to prove an offence in court. They don't even have to be accompanied because the speedo corroborates their estimation that you were over the speed limit.

But traffic police cars have much more accurate speedos than ordinary police cars, and they are calibrated more frequently. If you are stopped by a non-traffic officer, and told that he or she followed you and you were speeding, try asking when his or her speedo was last calibrated. If you were only a little over the limit, you may be let off.

Some patrol cars have **VASCAR** (Vehicle Average Speed Computer and Recorder) units which can be linked to video cameras. They can give a target vehicle's average speed over a given distance, so they've got you bang to rights. It's much safer to stick to the speed limit!

Cameras, however, are often set at a lower speed than a policeman would set. Be careful in areas like London where cameras are set at the speed limit plus 10 per cent plus 2 mph; that means that they'd be set at 35 mph in a 30 mph area, If in doubt, visit the website www.ukgatsos.com for information on the **location of speed traps**, and for the opportunity to 'grass up a gatso' yourself. The site www.speed-trap.co.uk provides a wealth of information on how different types of speed trap work.

Try to find out when **police duty shifts** change. If you're stopped about half an hour before the shift ends, you may get lucky because the officers will want to get off duty. One way to find out is to get the names of a few local officers, then call the police station to speak to them. If they're there, hang up fast unless you can think of an excuse for calling, but if they're not, ask when they'll be back.

FACT: Men account for 92% of all convictions for driving offences, and 98% of convictions for dangerous driving.

There is no need for you to have committed an offence for the police to stop you and administer a breath test. Any vehicle can be stopped if it's being driven on a road or other public place. The smell of alcohol, staggering away from your car, even a phone call complaining that you had been drinking and driving … all are sufficient grounds to **demand a breath test**.

A breath test is only an indication of the alcohol you have consumed. If your reading is under 50, you are entitled to a urine or blood test, but the police decide which.

If new drivers get six or more **penalty points** on their licence within two years of passing their test, they will have to take the theory and practical driving tests again.

How We Beat The System

Identical twins were snapped speeding in their father's car by a radar trap, but they managed to escape a fine because police didn't know which one to accuse. The 19-year-old women students from the University of Hildesheim, Germany, each said the other was at the wheel.

It was a dark and stormy night, when a police officer knocked on Chris Swann's door and said a tree had blown across the road, and would he mind moving his car round on to the drive so vehicles could get past? Chris moved the car but while doing so got stopped by another police car and breathalysed – and he was over the limit. It went to court, but given the circumstances he got off.

A woman was stopped for speeding. When the policeman came to the car, he saw she was pregnant. She claimed she was having contractions and driving herself to the hospital. He let her off, but in fact she was only six months pregnant and nowhere near having the baby.

But...

A driver in the USA was stopped for speeding in the early hours. He claimed to be a vampire and said he had to get back to his coffin before sunrise.

If you're going to fight it...

Not many people do – they simply accept it, get the points and pay the fine. The worst thing that can happen is that you will be convicted of your original offence. You can, in theory, get a heavier fine and more points in court, but unless you were doing silly speeds, it's unlikely.

Never surrender your licence at the roadside, you will get a chance to take it to a police station. Surrendering your licence at the roadside is the same as admitting that you're guilty.

If you were caught on a **radar gun**, ask to have a look at it and check that it displays the speed that you were stopped for. If possible, get the make, model and serial number of the radar gun.

Ask the officer to demonstrate that the radar gun is calibrated (he will probably not do this, if not, assume it is not calibrated and use it as evidence).

If you were caught on a **LIDAR (Light Detection and Ranging) gun**, again ask to check that the gun displays the speed that you were stopped for. If possible, get the make, model and serial number of the unit.

Note the positioning of the unit in relation to the sun or any other bright red or white light. LIDAR uses infrared light, and does not work as well when aimed into infrared light sources like the sun or high-beam headlights. Ask when the unit was last calibrated.

Note the **positions of other cars**. You may be able to claim that the officer metered someone else, but stopped you (particularly lorries, since radar is good at locking into a larger object).

If you were **caught on a camera**, the police *must* send you a notice of intended prosecution within 14 days. If they do not, the case is a non-starter.

If you take pictures to support your case, don't use a digital camera. **Digital images are not admissable.** Make sure your pictures show the whole area, including any road signs. It is also very important that your pictures are clear.

If the prosecution asks for an adjournment because the officer can't appear on the trial date which was set, do not agree. You should claim that you had to make special arrangements – a day off work or child care – but be prepared to prove it. If the adjournment is denied, the **charges should be dropped** since you can't have a case without the officer's presence.

Check in with the prosecutor and usher and make sure you are **on the case list**, and that they know you have appeared for trial. This is just to get it on record that you have appeared and to give the prosecutor a chance to drop the case or bargain over the plea.

Look out for the officer who stopped you. If he or she doesn't appear, the charges should be dropped. This is why it's helpful to take a photo, note their name or write an accurate description of him or her at the scene.

Make the right impression – clean, neat haircut, close shave, suit and tie, will make you more plausible (unless you're a woman – in which case they'll make you look weird – but you get the idea). Be polite to the judge and officers of the courts.

Ask about the **radar or LIDAR equipment**. If the officer refused to demonstrate the calibration at the time, ask why and demand to know if the unit was truly calibrated. You're aiming to imply that it could have been inaccurate.

Use your photos and notes, ask the officer questions about the day to establish whether he really remembers the incident and you. If he doesn't seem to, ask him directly whether he really remembers what happened that day.

Speeding is an **absolute offence** and it is no defence to argue that the speeding did not cause any danger. If danger was caused then it is likely that the more serious charges of careless or dangerous driving may also be brought.

Banned! Incredibly, there are some insurance companies that will offer you cover in the event of your losing your licence. Isle of Man Assurance offer an insurance plan that will cover the cost of 'alternative' transport should you end up losing your licence. Now far be it from us to endorse something we've never tried, but this does seem like a fairly unique policy. If you want information about it, try the websites www.st-christopher.com and www.ioma.co.uk. For motorcyclists, the Motorcycle Action Group offers similar coverage. Try the website, www.mag.weaverweb.co.uk, or call 0845 300 2211.

Points that don't win prizes

Up-to-date information on endorsements can be found on the DVLA website on www.dvla.gov.uk/drivers/endorem.htm, but below is a short summary:

Three points
- driving with uncorrected defective eyesight
- exceeding a speed limit (dealt with by a fixed penalty) i.e. £40 fine payable within 28 days
- failure to obey sign exhibited by school crossing patrol
- contravention of pedestrian crossing regulations
- contravention of traffic regulations on special roads (e.g. motorways)
- contravention of certain construction and use regulations (e.g. dangerous condition, defective breaks, steering or tyres)
- leaving a vehicle in a dangerous position and stopping within the confines of a pelican/zebra crossing
- failure to give information.

Three–six points
- learner motorcyclist with a passenger
- driving otherwise than in accordance with a licence (e.g. under age, unsupervised in car, no L-plates)
- exceeding a speed limit (summons).

Three–nine points
- careless or inconsiderate driving.

Three–eleven points
- dangerous driving (disqualify for 12 months minimum, unless special reason and order extended re-test; custodial sentence may apply).

Four points
- refusing roadside breath test.

Five–ten points
- failing to stop after an accident (discretionary disqualification)
- failing to report an accident to the police (discretionary disqualification).

Six points
- driving while disqualified by order of court (discretionary disqualification).

Six–eight points
- using, or causing or permitting use of, motor vehicle uninsured and unsecured against third party risks (discretionary disqualification).

Ten points
- being in charge of a motor vehicle when unfit through drink or drugs (discretionary disqualification; custodial sentence may apply)
- driving with excess alcohol (mandatory disqualification of at least one year unless special reasons can be shown. A second conviction within ten years carries a mandatory disqualification of at least 3 years.)
- failing to provide specimen for analysis in 'in charge' cases (discretionary disqualification; custodial sentence may apply).

Twelve points
- If your licence is endorsed with twelve points within three years, you are liable to a mandatory disqualification of at least six months unless exceptional hardships can be shown.

DRIVING SAFELY – AND LEGALLY

You don't have to wear a seat belt if:
- you're reversing
- you have a doctor's note stating you have a medical reason for not wearing one
- you are in the process of carrying out door-to-door deliveries
- you drive a vehicle in excess of 3,500kg m.g.w. (maximum gross weight)
- there is no seat belt fitted in your vehicle (sometimes the case with vintage cars).

The middle-seated passenger in the back of a car doesn't need to wear a seat belt if there isn't one available. The two-point belt or lap belt is not legally recognised as a seat belt.

You can leave a car on the **hard shoulder** of a motorway for two hours maximum. The police will then contact a breakdown service to take your vehicle away but you will be liable for the full cost of the call-out.

If you have to use the **emergency phone box** on the motorway, use the arrows on the marker posts to find the nearest one to you. You don't need money to make a call on these phones. You will automatically be put through to police control.

If you **break down on the motorway**, stand on the embankment while you wait for help. If a strange car pulls up while you're waiting, get back into your car and lock the door.

Don't immediately believe someone who signals that there is something wrong with your car. It could be a ruse to get you **out of the safety of your car**. If someone has indicated there is a problem, drive to the nearest garage or police station and then check it out.

If you've broken down and think you might be able to sort things out yourself ... but aren't too sure, give the AA or RAC a call. They will give **free mechanical advice** over the phone to members.

Road rage is sadly a fact of life now.
- Avoid confrontation and don't respond to the other driver's aggression.
- Don't make eye contact.
- If you are not moving and someone is hassling you, use your mobile phone or take their registration number down and make it obvious what you're doing.
- If you're being followed, drive to a busy place, like a garage forecourt, a pub car park, a police, fire or ambulance station.
- If you are forced to stop, lock the doors and keep the engine running.
- If you are approached, put your hazard lights on and sound the horn continuously.
- If you've got a mobile, call the police.

The number plate debate

Number plates have very precise measurements and requirements. Just because you can buy number plates with italic figures or with altered spacing to form names doesn't mean that they are legal (and anyway they look really naff). The shops will cover themselves by having a small sign stating that these plates are not for highway use – i.e. they are illegal for use on the roads. If you have an illegal number plate, you could get a maximum fine of £1,000 and have the registration marks withdrawn without compensation.

INSURANCE

The Road Traffic Act requires all motorists to be insured against their liability for injuries to others, including passengers, and for damage to other people's property resulting from the use of a vehicle on the road. It's an offence to drive your car or allow other people to drive it without insurance.

FACT: The UK has one of the highest uninsured driving populations in Western Europe. Around one in 20 motorists is believed to be driving without insurance.

FACT: The average premium is currently around £500.

FACT: Driving without a policy of insurance is a serious offence. The penalties that can be imposed include disqualification, penalty points up to a maximum of eight and a fine of up to £5,000. Yet the average fine for driving without insurance is £200 – less than half the average yearly premium.

FACT: The number of convictions for uninsured driving in England and Wales alone in 1999 was almost 300,000.

There are three types of insurance:
- comprehensive: which includes damage to the insured car, third-party liability which covers the cost of repairing the other car, legal costs for defence, repairs, personal accident cover, medical expenses and personal effects
- third party, fire and theft: will cover repairs on the other car, loss or damage due to theft and legal requirements to other people
- third party only: the compulsory minimum, it only includes cover for damage to the other car, its driver and any legal costs.

The younger you are, the greater the cubic capacity of the car's engine, the less driving experience you've got … all mean a **higher cost to insure**.

Where you live is also a factor in how much you pay for your insurance. Claims are more frequent in urban areas so people in cities tend to pay more than their country cousins.

A 'no claims discount' is a reward to a policy holder who has a record of claim-free insurance. You can transfer your 'no claims discount' from company to company. It's worth it. Discounts can be worth as much as 30 per cent for the first year, 10 per cent annually up to 60 per cent with some companies. You can protect your no claims discount. If your insurer is able to make a full recovery from the other party (or is only prevented from doing so by the knock-for-knock agreement – see page 197) your no claims discount may not be affected.

You can make savings on your motor insurance by:
- limiting the number of drivers
- paying voluntary excess on each claim made
- putting the car in a garage overnight
- limiting the mileage covered in a year
- passing your Advanced Driver's Test
- insuring all your vehicles with one company to take advantage of multi-car discounts
- asking about multi-line discounts if you are also buying other lines of insurance
- knowing the value of your vehicles – drop the collision and comprehensive coverage on older vehicles you can afford to replace
- checking before changing cars since rates on cars of equal value can vary
- asking about discounts for air bags, anti-theft devices, anti-lock brakes and similar equipment
- asking about discounts for drivers over 40 or 50, if applicable
- buying only coverage you do not already have from some other source
- making an older, less valuable vehicle the primary transportation for younger drivers in your household
- joining a car club. If you have a classic car like a Jaguar, owners' clubs can arrange cheaper insurance. Seek out a specialist insurer. Firms that focus on insuring particular models can come up with bargain quotes.
- keeping the car for private use only, to and from work and so on. Using it for your work will bump up what you pay.

- asking your union or professional group (such as the CSMA, Civil Servants Motoring Association, 01273 744744, www.csma.ukcom) whether they run car insurance schemes.

Motor insurance companies have agreed that if your passengers contribute towards the running costs of your car, your **insurance cover won't be affected**, providing you are giving lifts in a vehicle that seats eight passengers or fewer. The agreement doesn't apply if you make a profit from the payments received or if carrying passengers is your business.

If you take your **car abroad**, your UK motor policy will automatically provide you with the minimum cover required by law in other EC countries. But this doesn't normally include theft or damage to the car and you may not be completely covered in your liability to other people. Contact your insurers if you are contemplating taking your car abroad.

A drink-driving conviction bumps your premium up at least 100 per cent. If you are hurt and were not wearing a seat belt, you will get reduced compensation.

If you have an accident, let your insurers know, even if you are not intending to make a claim. Send them a letter, marking it **'for information only'**. Informing your insurers is a condition of your policy so make sure you do it.

If you are unlucky enough to be in an accident with someone who isn't insured, contact the **Motor Insurers Bureau**. They have a fund which could compensate you.

Motor Insurers Bureau
152 Silbury Boulevard
Central Milton Keynes MK9 2SY
Tel: 01908 830001

If your policy covers damage to your car, go to a **reputable garage** and let your insurers know what's happening. They may require you to take the car to a garage recommended by them so go there if possible. You will need to get an estimate for any work that needs doing and get this sent off to the insurance company. They will check the estimate and agree to repairs subject to a satisfactory claim form.

Your insurance company may have a list of **approved repairers**, and will only allow you to have a courtesy car if you use someone from their list. Problem is, they tend not to publish the lists – wonder why?

If you've got an excess on your policy, you will have to pay it (direct to the garage) regardless of whose fault the accident was.

If you don't have comprehensive cover for your car, and you want to claim against a third party, you will have to let the other driver know (in writing) that you intend to claim from him or her. You must tell the driver that you hold him or her responsible and ask the driver to let his or her insurers know. If you have his or her insurance company's details, write to them yourself. Let your own insurers know that you are claiming against the third party.

If the other driver hasn't told his insurance company about the accident, they won't be able to deal with your claim.

It's usually quicker to claim from your insurers rather than the third party – but you can only do this if you've got comprehensive insurance. If your insurers have a **'knock-for-knock'** agreement with the third party's insurers, this means that they agree to each pay for their own policyholder's losses, regardless of who is to blame. 'Knock-for-knock' speeds everything up and reduces costs.

An insurance company usually declares a car a **write-off** when the cost of repairs is more than three-quarters of the value of the car. In such cases, the insurance company will pay you the full value of the car before the accident and sell the wreckage for scrap.

Insurance companies use *Glass's Guide* to work out the prices of second-hand cars. There is a similar guide, called *Parker's*, which is available to the general public from newsagents. If you disagree with an insurance company's estimate of your car's value, you will need to prove to them that it is worth more. Take statements from car dealers and get copies of advertisements of similar cars. If you are a member of the RAC or AA, you could enlist their help. The Institute of Automotive Engineer Assessors can give you the names of value assessors in your area (see the end of the chapter for their address).

If your car is stolen, tell the police straight away and then let your insurance company know. You will probably have to wait quite a long time to see if your car is recovered. If the thieves leave the car behind but take your property from the car, the procedure is the same. Let the police, then your insurers know. Comprehensive cover sometimes gives you protection against loss or damage to rugs, clothing and personal belongings in the car up to a stated amount. Check your policy for the details.

The highest risk professions for car insurance are actors and pub landlords. The lowest are civil servants and teachers.

When renewing your insurance, never accept the quote your current company gives you. They have set guidelines for quoting renewals. Tell them you have got a **better quote elsewhere** and then you'll get a personal assessment of your renewal – and a cheaper quote.

CAR SECURITY

> **FACT:** Over 100,000 bicycles are stolen each year. (1993 *Trading Standards*)
>
> **FACT:** Most car crime happens on a Monday.
>
> **FACT:** A quarter of car crime happens in car parks.
>
> **FACT:** One in five car-owning households is likely to experience car crime during a year.
>
> **FACT:** One-third of all reported stolen cars – around 150,000 each year – are never recovered.

Don't leave anything on view in the car. If you have to leave something behind, try to hide it … but not under the seat – it's the first place they'll look. Put your handbag, briefcase or wallet on the floor, never on the front passenger seat. Car jacking (grabbing property out of the car when it's at a standstill) is sadly on the increase.

When stopping at **traffic lights**, always leave enough room between you and the car in front so that you can pull out quickly if you need to.

Make sure your vehicle is **well maintained**.

Be sure you have at least **enough fuel** for your journey, and **plan** your route.

Join a **motoring organisation**. Carry a **mobile phone**, in case of emergencies but keep it out of sight. Make sure the battery is well charged and programme essential numbers (including that of the motoring organisation) into the memory to save time.

If you place **valuable items in the boot**, be aware that you may be vulnerable when retrieving them, particularly if you have reversed into a parking bay.

Try to **avoid parking in unlit areas**. If parking during the day, give some thought to what the surroundings will be like at night.

Reverse into parking spaces. This makes exiting in a hurry much easier. If using a **multi-storey car park**, try to park as close as possible to the attendant's booth.

Keep your doors locked when driving.

Never leave your car unlocked, and always check behind the front seats before you get in. Have your keys ready in your hand when returning to your car, and **mark your car key**, and your front door key, with luminous paint so you can pick them out easily in the dark. If your car has **electronic locking**, don't unlock the doors until you are close to it. This reduces the opportunity for someone else to get in before you do. Also remember that central locking is also central unlocking, so watch out for anyone near your car as you get in.

Women drivers – remove anything that advertises your car as a woman's car – soft toys, tissues, brollies and any window stickers that carry witticisms about men!

If you don't want your car to be stolen, buy a yellow one. Surveys have shown that car thieves are put off by their conspicuousness, and **yellow cars** are the least stolen colour of vehicle.

Be careful when driving a **hire car**. Thieves tend to target them because they are driven by business people (laptops, mobile phones) or tourists (clothes, cameras, money). Most car hire firms now remove incriminating stickers which mark the car out as a hire vehicle but make sure your hire car doesn't stand out in any way.

ACCIDENTS

FACT: Sunday is by far the safest day to drive – simply because there are fewer cars on the roads.

FACT: There are over a million incidents of car crime per year, costing around 3 billion pounds.

FACT: Most accidents happen on a Wednesday.

If you have an accident, get the names and addresses of the other driver or drivers involved. Take their registration number, the make and model of the car. They should give you the name of their insurers and their policy or certificate number. Make a rough sketch of the accident. If someone has been hurt, you will need to show your certificate of insurance. **Get statements, names and addresses** (and licence plate numbers if you can't speak to the drivers) from any witnesses. If the other driver involved in the accident disappears, try to get their licence plate number.

If you have an accident where somebody has been hurt or injured, or the accident is causing congestion or there is a dispute by law, you must stop, and **call the police** (and emergency services if someone is hurt). Give them your name and address (or the name of whoever owns the car). If there's some reason why you can't give your details immediately, you have 24 hours in which to **report the accident at a police station**. You should then also report the incident to your insurance company.

If you're shaken up after an accident, don't give your statement to the police straight away. You may say something which could be used against you by the other driver's insurance company. You can give your details (name and address) but say that you'll **give a statement later**.

You don't have to report all car accidents to the police – it could be a costly mistake if they turn up and find something else amiss! Make sure you give all your details to the other party though.

If there's even **a whiff of alcohol** on the other driver's breath, or if they start getting aggressive, call the police straight away,

Be polite following an accident. Don't admit guilt or apologise if it wasn't your fault – or even if it was.

SERVICING YOUR CAR

Don't get ripped off by **cowboy garages**. Always check the price of parts; you can call your car's manufacturers to find out the Recommended Retail Price. Equally, be suspicious of very cheap parts; you might be being fobbed off with second-hand or faulty parts. Also be careful if the garage doesn't charge you for an initial examination; they might be trying to get their money by charging more for parts or labour.

If the garage says parts need changing, have them give the old ones back to you in the box the new parts came in. That way they can't pretend they changed parts they haven't or put in second-hand ones.

When having an **oil change**, ask what oil they need and provide your own. This will avoid their huge mark-up.

Where it says **'miscellaneous items'** on the bill, ask what they mean. You may find you are being charged for use of tools, or they are asking you to pay for oil they have disposed of.

Always check your **service book has been stamped** – essential when you come to sell the vehicle.

Big-name tyre and brake specialists aren't always the cheapest. Check with the dealership which sells your make of car. They may have parts cheaper.

Make sure the garage working on your car is a member of the **Retail Motor Industry Federation**, or similar body. It will avoid duff repairs or rip-offs. Also use a garage that is a member of a trade association. They will then subscribe to the Motor Industry Code of Practice or the Code of Practice for Vehicle Body Repair.

Many cars **fail their MOTs for minor defects** like faulty lights or blown bulbs. Check the car before submitting it for its test, to save it having to be retested.

Check your oil level and tyre pressure after a service. If these aren't right, mention it to the garage and consider using another garage next time.

Always ask for a **written quotation** if work is going to be done on your car. This legally binds the garage to an agreed fee.

If you have a particular problem that you want the garage to sort out, **put it in writing** first. If the car has gone in for its regular service, find out exactly what that entails and make sure that it's done. If there's anything you don't want doing, agree it with the garage beforehand. However, that could invalidate the car's warranty.

When your car is in the garage, make sure that they have a **contact number** for you. If the agreed price looks like it's going to go up or more work needs to be done on the car, you should be phoned first.

Get an **itemised bill**, listing all the work that was carried out, the parts that have been replaced and how much the labour was.

If you are not happy with the work that the garage has done or you're not happy at the size of the bill, talk to the person in charge straight away. If you can't sort things out there and then, you may well have to pay the bill to get the car back. If this is the case, write the garage a letter along with your payment. Clearly state what your complaint is, say that you are not happy and that payment is made **'without prejudice'**. That last bit is important. It means that the trader can't say in court that you accepted that the repair or work was satisfactory because you paid the bill.

If the garage won't release your car without payment, write **'under protest'** on the back of the cheque and any other paperwork. This means that you still have the right to claim your money back at a later date, such as through the Small Claims Court.

If no price is agreed in advance, you don't have to pay the exorbitant prices a garage may charge for work done on your car. You are only legally obliged to pay what is **'reasonable'**. Don't pay the bill, but phone round other local garages to get an idea of what is 'reasonable' for the work done, and offer that amount.

If the garage has done work on your car that subsequently fails or breaks, they are obliged to replace the parts and redo the work **under warranty**.

Legal responsibility lies with the garage … not with the manufacturer.

Get your car serviced on holiday. Hourly rates for labour in the south of the country can be far higher – for example a Jaguar garage in London charges about £92.82 an hour whereas in Carlisle the charge is more like £58.75. Or go abroad – a Mazda garage in Leamington Spa charges around £130 for a service, whereas in Belgium the cost is £40.

CUTTING COSTS

So you've got the car, your taxed, insured, MOT'd and ready for action. But hang on! How can it possibly be that expensive to fill up?

> **FACT:** A double-decker bus carries the same number of people as 20 fully occupied cars but takes up a seventh of the road space.

Motorway petrol stations are very expensive, so if you're getting short of fuel on the motorway, buy just enough to get you off the motorway so you can fill up somewhere cheaper. For the average car, this will save you pounds.

The AA has taken over a hugely successful website, www.petrolbusters.com, which allows users to find the **cheapest petrol in their area**. Just log in for free and give your postcode.

If you learn to **drive more economically**, you can reduce your fuel consumption significantly (and reduce emissions).

On yer bike! Cutting out some of those short journeys could really help in reducing emissions. Journeys of less than 2 miles (3.2km) use the most fuel and cause the most pollution because the engine is cold and under strain. A huge 58 per cent of car trips are under 5 miles (8km) and 25 per cent are less than 2 miles.

Check your **fuel consumption**, and make sure your car is running as efficiently as possible. If in doubt, get it serviced.

Reducing your speed saves lives and money too. You use 30 per cent more fuel driving at 70 mph than 50 mph.

Drive calmly. Think ahead – and avoid sharp braking and rapid acceleration. It saves fuel, wear and tear on your clutch and on your brakes – oh and your nerves too.

Don't idle. If you've stopped, switch off! Idling also stops the catalytic converter, which is a device that removes pollution in the exhaust, from working properly.

Check your tyres. If they're at the right pressure, you'll drive more smoothly and save fuel. For every 6psi a tyre is under-inflated, fuel consumption can rise by 1 per cent.

Cut down on wind resistance. Remove roof racks and other accessories if you're not using them: a fully loaded roof rack increases consumption by 30 per cent! Other gas guzzlers include wide-open windows, heavy clutter in the boot and air conditioning. Finally, using your air conditioning when you don't need to can cost you 1.5km (1 mile) for every 2 litres (half a gallon) of fuel – turn up your air vents instead.

Drive in **as high a gear as possible**. You'll use a quarter less fuel doing 40 mph in fifth than in third!

Don't get lost. There's no surer way to waste fuel than to spend ages bumbling around aimlessly. Be certain that you have planned the best way to your destination, and think about the time you travel – don't travel in the rush hour, if you can avoid it. Keep a map close at hand and if you're lost – *ask*.

Share your car. You'll save emissions and share the cost. Seven out of ten journeys to work are by car and at school peak travel times nearly one in five cars on town roads are taking children to and from school.

Better off by bus?

According to figures worked out by the Environmental Transport Association (www.eta.co.uk), given the fixed costs of car ownership and motoring, if you travel less than 3,200km (2,000 miles) a year, you would actually be better off selling your car and travelling everywhere by taxi, at a cost of about £1.10 per 1.6km (1 mile). Even if you travel 8,050km (5,000 miles) a year by car, you would still be better selling your car, travelling a third of the miles by taxi, a third by train and the remaining third by bus.

Fuel efficient cars

New cars bought from March 2001 are rated for vehicle excise duty (VED) according to how much they pollute the air with CO_2 (carbon dioxide). New cars are allocated a CO_2 figure (in grammes per kilometre), and this remains fixed for the car's life, unless the car is adapted to use a different type of fuel. Basically, the cleaner the fuel you use, the less VED you pay. Also from March 2001 existing cars with engines up to 1200cc pay a lower rate. For further details see the website www.dvla.gov.uk/newved.htm or call the leaflet line 0845 605 2222

Cars registered before 1 March 2001 will continue to be charged under the existing system (by engine size).

TAXIS

Black cabs have a reputation for being a safe form of transport but you should look out for tell-tale signs that might indicate they're not all that they seem to be. A new law now means that all black cabs have wheelchair access. Rather than convert the old cab, drivers are buying new models…which means that there are a lot of second-hand black cabs on the market. There could be one or two dodgy operators who take advantage of the situation. The only legal requirement is the removal of both the licence plate (issued by the carriage office) and the meter. But the familiar yellow light-up 'hire' sign is built-in and can't be taken away. To check that a black cab is the real McCoy:

- look for the driver's identity badge which should be hanging round their neck
- older style taxis will have been sold off rather than the newer bubble-shaped ones which already have wheelchair access
- check the cab has a number plate with a hologram, registration number and expiry date
- don't get in if the yellow taxi sign is off
- licensed cabbies know where they're going; if your driver gets lost, get out.

Only use taxis registered as **licensed hackney carriages**. These are regulated by strict rules, and can be identified by a licence plate.

When **travelling alone by mini cab**, or if you are the last of a group to be dropped off, always sit in the near-side rear seat. This protects you from the driver and will allow you to get out fast if you need to.

Try to **book a mini cab in advance**. Take precautions, such as asking for the name of the driver and the colour, make and model of the vehicle.

Weird and wonderful motoring laws

In San Francisco, it is illegal to wipe your car with used underwear.

Taxi cabs in Australia are required to carry a bale of hay in the boot.

In Belgium, a driver who needs to turn through oncoming traffic has the right of way unless he slows down or stops.

In Montreal, 'For Sale' signs are not permitted in the windows of moving vehicles.

When driving in Denmark, you must have someone in front of your car with a flag to warn horse-drawn carriages that a motorcar is coming.

In England, it is legal for a man to urinate in public, provided it is on the rear wheel of his motor vehicle and his right hand is on the vehicle.

USEFUL WEBSITES

www.parkingticket.co.uk
www.egroups.co.uk/group/parkingticket
www.detr.gov.uk
www.petrolbusters.com

www.ukgatsos.com
www.doingit4u.co.uk
www.carimporting.co.uk
www.carbusters.com

USEFUL ADDRESSES

Accident Line
The Law Society
Freepost
London WC2A 1BR
Tel: 0500 192 939

Association of British Insurers
51 Gresham Street
London EC2V 7HQ
Tel: 020 7600 3333
email: phil.ward@abi.org.uk
www.abi.org.uk

Automobile Association
Tel: 0990 500600
Technical advice line: 0161 488 7295
Vehicle inspection department: 0345 500610

Customer Complaints Service
Scottish Motor Trade Association
3 Palmerston Place
Edinburgh EH12 5AF
Tel: 0131 225 3643
For complaints about used cars, repairs and
   servicing in Scotland

Driving Instructor's Association
Safety House
Beddington Farm Road
Croydon CR0 4XZ
Tel: 020 8665 5151

DVLA
Swansea
SA6 7JL
Tel: 01792 772151 (drivers); 01792 772134
   (vehicles)

Green Flag
Tel: 01332 393666

Institute of Advanced Motorists
IAM House
359 High Road
Chiswick
London W4 4HS
Tel: 020 8994 4403

**Institute of Automotive Engineer
   Assessors**
Mansell House
22 Bore Street
Lichfield
Staffordshire WS13 6LP
Tel: 01543 251346

Motor Insurers Bureau
152 Silbury Boulevard
Central Milton Keynes MK9 2SY
Tel: 01908 830001

The National Conciliation Service
Retail Motor Industry Federation
9 North Street
Rugby CV21 2AB
Tel: 01788 576465
For complaints about used cars, repairs and
   servicing in England, Wales & Northern
   Ireland

Parking Appeals Service
Tel: 020 7747 4700

RAC
Tel: 0800 550550
Legal service: 0345 300400
Car examinations: 0800 333660

Retail Motor Industry Federation
20 Great Portland Street
London W1N 6AB
Tel: 020 7580 9122

Society of Motor Auctions
Chestnut House
32 North Street
Rugby
Warwickshire CV21 2AH
Tel: 01788 576465

Society of Motor Manufacturers & Traders
(Customer Relations Advisor)
Forbes House
Halkin Street
London SW1X 7DS
Tel: 020 7235 7000
For complaints about cars still under a
   manufacturer's warranty

**The Vehicle Builders and Repairers
   Association**
(The Conciliation Service)
Belmont House
102 Finkle Lane
Gildersome
Leeds LS27 7TW
Tel: 0113 253 8333
For complaints about car body repair

# Travel and Holidays

'To travel hopefully is a better thing than to arrive...'
Robert Louis Stevenson

Since 1975 the number of visits abroad by UK residents has gone up by more than 500 per cent. This means more fun, more sangria and more suntans, but also more delays, more blockades, more holding patterns, more near misses and more frustration. It's enough to make you need a holiday. This is one area where understanding the system will definitely help you – from planning and booking, through the awful scrum at the airport, while you're away, right through to your return journey and beyond. Who knows, you could even find your next holiday relaxing!

FACT: In 2000, British residents made an estimated 53.6 million trips overseas.

FACT: An amazing 38 per cent of secretaries travel abroad at least three times a year, and prefer sunny, long-haul destinations such as Mexico, Barbados and Thailand.

BEATING THE TRAVEL AGENT

When you book a holiday through an agent, you trust them to sell you a holiday that satisfies (and preferably exceeds) your requirements. Improve your chances of having the holiday of a lifetime with these tips:

- Tax should be included in the price of the holiday, but not all companies follow this rule. If the price is substantially cheaper than any others you've found, check the small print.
- It's safer to book holidays that include 'named' accommodation rather than deals that offer 'accommodation on arrival' – especially if you're travelling with kids.
- Ring to confirm your flight the day before departure. It may go right 99 per cent of the time, but if you're at the airport with no flight, you'll be gutted.
- If you're prepared to be flexible, you can often get discounts on your holiday. Midweek and night-time flights are cheapest. School term time (especially June and November) is also a good time to pick up cheap deals.
- The dreaded single supplement is loathed by travellers far and wide. You

can often get cheaper holidays by booking a package rather than travelling independently or booking a hotel through a tour operator but getting the flights yourself.

- Some holidays advertise free child places but you need to be quick off the mark to get these. Book early. But remember that free child place holidays don't always offer the cheapest deal, so compare prices and include all the supplements.
- On charter flights, most tour operators let you pre-book your seats for a small fee. One of the advantages of pre-booking is that sometimes you get added extras, such as a later check-in time, better meals, free drinks and so on. Check with your tour operator when you book your holiday. However, if you cancel your holiday, you won't get your pre-booking fee back.
- Check the price of flights on the airlines' own websites and compare them with the prices on-line travel agents offer. Budget airlines, like Go at www.go-fly.co.uk and Easyjet at www.easyjet.co.uk cut out the agents, so often have great prices.
- Don't always assume that the Internet will be cheapest. Net-based www.ebookers.co.uk and www.travelstore.com have excellent bargains, but take time to call an agent too – just in case.
- Airlines can undercut everybody from time to time by offering special deals. Keep your eyes peeled for these.
- Remember that many prices in brochures are based on midweek flights from London, which don't always have an extra charge. You might have to pay an extra charge for daytime flights, weekend flights or a flight leaving from your local airport. This extra cost can be quite large, so check before you book.

The four top ABTA (Association of British Travel Agents) approved travel agents in the UK are Lunn Poly (0870 333 4400), Going Places (01483 597098), Thomas Cook (0870 566 6222) and Co-Op Travelcare (0870 906 5812).

When booking a holiday with a tour operator, choose one that is bonded – either ABTA or AITO (Association of Independent Tour Operators). If the company goes out of business, you have a degree of protection. Members of ABTA, for instance, have to lodge a bond guaranteeing their solvency. If the tour operator goes bust, holidaymakers will be brought back at no extra cost, while customers yet to go on holiday will have their money refunded.

Package holidays that include flights must be protected by an ATOL (Air Travel Organiser's Licence) which is issued by the Civil Aviation Authority (CAA). A holder of an ATOL is examined each year by the CAA to check that they are fit to hold a licence and are financially sound. Although this is no guarantee that the company won't fail, it means that it's less likely to. There should be an ATOL number in brochures and on invoices.

The best bargains from travel agents are available about two to three weeks before you want to travel.

Never mind the rain in Spain – keep an eye on the weather in Britain. If winter is particularly chilly and grey, there will be a surge in early bookings for summer hols in sunny climates. If the winter is mild or bright, people leave booking until later.

Don't rely on hotel star ratings. It's better to specify the facilities you want – balcony, close to a beach, pool, childcare, etc.

Watch out when all those discounts appear in the travel agents' windows in the early weeks of the new year to try and boost summer bookings. **Ignore the percentages, look at the price**, rather than taking the discounts at face value. Trading Standards Officers have found cases where the prices have actually been increased before Christmas so that the discounts will seem more significant. If you are planning to take advantage of discounts, keep an eye on prices for a few weeks, so you'll know if they have been adjusted. Ask if there is a brochure showing the holiday at its original price. If not, it may not be the bargain it seems. Legally, tour operators can only discount a price that has been held for a period of 28 days in the previous six months. But this is difficult to check as agents will remove old brochures from the shelves. If you think they may be pulling a fast one, get in touch with your local Trading Standards Office without delay.

Another trick to watch out for is **reductions in adult prices**, but with increased child prices and flight supplements.

In previous years, you could always rely on getting terrific bargains if you hung on until the last minute, but tour operators are cutting back on capacity so the high street operators may not have the range of late availability or bargains in peak summer months. If you're stuck with going during school holidays, the safest bet is to book ahead. If you're more flexible about dates, there should still be some great **last-minute offers**.

Shop around. Many of the big tour operators are selling identical holidays. Get the brochures and pore over them. Basic prices and discounts may differ.

Watch out for **hidden extras** such as supplements for departures from regional airports.

Remember **it is illegal** for a holiday company to insist you purchase insurance in order to receive a holiday discount.

Teletext

The best bargains are found a fortnight or less before you want to go. Look at page 210 for Holidays Abroad, and page 218 for Bargains of the Day.

Extra information on holidays listed on Teletext can be found on the web on www.teletext.co.uk/holidays.

For more information than you could possibly need, www.travel.world.co.uk is a huge resource of information on European travel agents, tour operators, airlines, airports car-hire companies and just about anything else you can think of relating to travel.

Many companies will give you a discount if you book your holiday or travel through the Internet.

www.lastminute.com
www.travelleronline.com
www.teletext.co.uk/holidays
www.expedia.co.uk
www.bargainholidays.com

Late offers – read the small print

Bargain hunters beware. If the price is too good to be true, there may be a snag – so make time to read the small print.

• You may not be able to choose the resort or the accommodation you stay in, and the hotel or apartment may not be featured in the tour operator's brochure so you can't see it beforehand. If you add to this the fact you may not even be entitled to the services of a holiday rep, you may find yourself wasting precious holiday time trying to sort out problems yourself.

• Check if transfers to and from your resort are included in the cost. If they are not, you may have to pay an extra charge.

• If you book your holiday at the last minute, there may not be time to send your tickets to your travel agent. Collecting tickets at the airport is not conducive to a relaxed start to the holiday, and you may have to pay an extra administrative charge for 'ticket on departure'.

• Keep an eye on the price of a holiday. You can find yourself paying more than the brochure price. This is called 'fluid pricing'; somewhere, tucked away in the brochure, the operator has probably stated that prices can go up or down at any time. There's no clear right or wrong here. You could try arguing that it's a misleading price indication (stated under the Consumer Protection Act, 1987).

• Most deals come with date and departure restrictions – be sure to check what these are. Cancellation terms are also important.

Brochure-speak

If you speak 'brochure' you're way ahead of the game. A brochure is part of the legal contract you enter with a tour operator, and you should be able to rely on the information that's printed in it. Beware words like 'developing' (it's a building site), 'lively' (thumping disco music and all-night bars), 'just off the main road' (six-lane highway thundering past the hotel). A resort may have a fabulous beach but the industrial complex next door may not be mentioned. 'Only 100 metres away' may be correct but what the brochure doesn't say is that you have to cross a busy road or negotiate a steep hill to get there.

Your travel agent can check with the *Gazetteer*, a publication that travel agents compile and use themselves and which has detailed and honest descriptions of resorts and hotels (but no pictures). Once you've made your choice of holiday, back it up with the *Gazetteer* report. Not all travel agents carry a copy, but you can sometimes find it in public libraries and you can consult it online on www.virgin.net, and on www. travelcareonline.co.uk. Go to their travel sections, pick a destination, and you can read the information on the resorts from the *Gazetteer*.

BOOKING YOUR OWN HOLIDAY

Why book a package holiday? After all, a package is only made up of three things: a flight, the transfer from the airport to your hotel and the hotel itself. In many cases, like a city break, you'll **undercut the package operators** by arranging the package yourself. Check out the separate deals before you opt for someone else's package.

Sort our your own **self-catering holiday**. For example, local French tourist offices have their own list of approved properties. Get them to post or fax the details direct to you by calling the French Tourist Office on 0891 244123, or try the Luxembourg Tourist Office on 020 7434 2800, the Italian State Tourist Board on 020 7408 1254, or the Spanish National Tourist Office on 020 7486 8077. Be aware that calls to these offices, particularly the brochure lines, are charged at premium rates – often over 50p per minute. Or just make life easier and go to the ANTOR website (Association of National Tourist Offices in the United Kingdom), at www.tourist-offices.org.uk. Select from the menu the tourist office you want and you'll be connected straight to their site – most are a bit minimal, and you'll often still have to make that premium-rate call.

Have a read through the **classified ads** in the newspapers, especially the more upmarket ones, for self-catering holidays. Many of the readers will have second homes and they'll often advertise them for holiday rental.

Surf the Net around midweek for last-minute weekend bargains.

Travel agents and operators do not need to give you full details if you are booking a holiday at the last minute (within 14 days of departure).

Remember that **Tuesday to Thursday** are the cheapest days to travel.

While the **Internet** has opened up a whole host of options when it comes to holidays, don't forget good old **Teletext**. It's still a great source for finding last-minute packages and flight-only deals.

If you book your holiday using a **credit card**, you could be able to claim against the credit card company as well as the travel agent or tour operator if things go wrong.

Some really **cheap last-minute holidays** don't specify your accommodation – just saying it will be **allocated on arrival**. This could be a disaster. But you can take advantage of this for deals in countries where accommodation is very cheap, such as India or Sri Lanka. Once you get there you can change accommodation yourself, and the whole deal will almost certainly be cheaper than just buying flights alone, because including accommodation opens up a whole new band of lower flight tariffs.

Don't agree to buy a **tour operator's insurance** – it is not compulsory and you can almost always buy your own independently much more cheaply.

If you have **pre-booked seats**, check with the airline a few days before you fly that the booking still stands. Turn up early to check-in to ensure that you get the seats.

For the **'warts and all' info** on holidays and resorts, go to www.holidays-uncovered.org.uk where real people post their own real opinions on their recent holidays. Fascinating stuff!

HOME SWAPPING

With cheap flights available at the click of a mouse, what's stopping you from going away right now? Accommodation costs, that's what. Unless you have some handy relatives or old school friends to stay with, even the cheapest paid accommodation will soon raise your holiday budget – and your blood pressure.

The solution – home swaps! These eminently practical deals have been going on for years, but the Net has brought them into the mainstream. Just browse to any one of the many, many sites dedicated to bringing home swappers together. You'll be amazed at what is available.

Pros

The standard of comfort far exceeds that of self-catering, because you're in a real home, equipped for daily living, rather than a holiday let.

You can experience a real community in the country you are visiting, rather than being stuck with a bunch of other tourists.

You get your own home looked after – plants watered, pets fed, lawn mowed and your home is less likely to be burgled.

You can find properties to swap with all over the world, and in areas you would probably never think of visiting otherwise. Because the accommodation is so much cheaper, you can think of longer haul, more expensive flights to countries you couldn't normally afford.

The people with whom you swap will probably leave a load of local information on places to visit, restaurants, local shopping and so on. You get an insider's insight which is usually more accurate than a tourist guide, so you save time and get straight to the best local treats.

You may get use of the car thrown in (remember to arrange insurance, and do the same if you are allowing your swap partners to use your car).

Many of the agencies provide information about the family offering the swap. You can find people with similar interests or professions to yours, so you'll be sure that, if you have kids, you'll find age-appropriate toys.

Swapees will often ask friends to drop by (probably to check that you're not wrecking the place), but they will often offer hospitality so you (and your kids) will have a chance to make local friends.

Lastly (and most important) it's a **bargain!** Beyond the expenses involved in joining an agency and advertising, you'll need to communicate with potential swap partners. Then it's just a question of flights, insurance and your living expenses. You could save literally thousands.

Cons

Swapping houses with strangers can be daunting. You'll probably want to do a lot of cleaning – even decorating – before you swap.

There is quite a lot of preparation to do – searching through potential swap partners and finding someone who matches your requirements and dates. Then there's the little matter of whether they want to swap with you! Your email, fax and or phone will be busy as you exchange details.

It can be disappointing if arrangements fall through after you've invested so much time in them. And there's no come-back, of course (although some agencies offer an insurance policy).

If the country you're interested in has different school holidays to yours, finding a match can be difficult.

It is just possible that you'll swap with a psycho, who'll trash your house and crash your car. According to the agencies, this occurs almost never because you're in their house too. It is wise to get a friend to drop round to check up (unobtrusively) on your house and make sure your swapping partners are happy and settled.

Try one of the following:
    Homelink International www.homelink.org.uk
    Intervac www.intervac.com
    The International Home Exchange Network www.homexchange.com
    Digsville.com www.digsville.com – mostly American
    Trading Homes site www.trading-homes.com
    Echangedemaison site www.echangedemaison.com – mostly French
    Latitudes Home Exchange www.home-swap.com – mostly Australian
    Web Home Exchange www.webhomeexchange.com
    Worldxchange www.worldxchange.net
    Homebase Holidays www.homebase-hols.com

How We Beat The System

A warm welcome

Sue Pickard and her family swapped with a German couple for two weeks, staying in a fairytale thatched cottage near the Black Forest. 'We lit the fire in the inglenook on the third night and lost part of the roof in the ensuing inferno! The Gunthers hadn't used it for years but thinking that the weather was quite warm reckoned without leaving us any guidance. Luckily everyone took it very well – they were covered by insurance and we stayed with their neighbours. We're all good friends to this day.'

UNUSUAL HOLIDAY DESTINATIONS

You're going where?

Unlikely or out-of-season destinations can provide great bargains and prompt a few raised eyebrows when you tell your friends where you're going. Make a habit of bucking the trend, think laterally, and keep an eye on world news – these are the techniques the canny traveller uses to sniff out the best deals.

Buy the *Financial Times* and keep track of problems with the economics of different countries. When the bottom dropped out of the Japanese stock market, all Asian currencies suffered, although some hotels promptly started to price their rooms in dollars. Those that stuck to local currency offered the best opportunities for British holidaymakers, Malaysia offers particularly good value.

The weak rand makes **South Africa** a very attractive destination, and buying wine there is a real bargain.

The rate of sterling against the Euro has made **European holidays** cheaper for Brits than in recent years.

Most prices drop **after Christmas and New Year**, particularly to long-haul destinations. Less fashionable resorts can really take a dive at this time of year, particularly in the Far East, and as the Caribbean is gradually supplanted by the Indian Ocean as the glam destination of choice, you can do very well there too. Straight after New Year and before half term are the best times to bargain hunt. Prices in Penang, Thailand and the Caribbean can drop by as much as 50 per cent in the space of a fortnight during this 'down time'. Magic of the Orient (01293 537700) is a specialist Far East operator with unsurpassed experience.

The low season is the perfect **time to start haggling**, and the US and Caribbean are the ideal places to try. Large hotels, or those in a chain, are the most likely to offer discounts, particularly at short notice. Overcome your inhibitions and give it a try – don't be so British. Just ask if they have a better price, or can add another night's stay on a reduced rate. In most cases you'll get at least 10 per cent off, and it could be a great deal more.

Wall Street sneezes. When Americans are encouraged to support their ravaged economy by holidaying at home, it's good news for British bargain seekers in the Caribbean and Mexico.

When US travellers decide not to come to the UK, for whatever reason, **flights to the US** can drop in price by sometimes as much as 50 per cent.

Save on air fares to Australia and New Zealand. Prices fall dramatically every Easter and remain low until the end of June, because this is when temperatures in the southern hemisphere start to drop.

Choose an **unpopular destination**. Civil wars are good news for bargain hunters, as the tourists stay away, even after the trouble has died down, and you can get a fantastic holiday, away from the crowds, for next to nothing.

Volcanoes, earthquakes, civil wars, kidnappings, bombings, reports of shark attacks, oil spills, avalanches, hurricanes, pirates, muggings, riots, gang warfare – all these mean **bargains for the really determined traveller**. Epidemics are probably best avoided. The Foreign Office website www.fco.co.uk has a wealth of information on unrest abroad. There is a list of countries you are advised not to visit – but in many cases it's only an isolated area that is experiencing problems. This has been the case with civil unrest in Fiji, but since the outlying smaller islands are in the low-risk category, you can enjoy the resorts there in relative peace, and at greatly reduced prices. Independent travel organisers are most likely to have taken full advantage of this kind of situation, and can advise you on which airports will be open to international flights.

In areas where unrest may become an issue, as in the aftermath of the terrorist attacks on the US, when many Middle Eastern destinations began to look less attractive, you'll find that tour operators will follow **Foreign Office advice**. If the FO recommend people should not travel there, you're more likely to be able to claim compensation if you cancel. If you just decide that flying any-where is too risky and cancel to areas not considered at risk, you'll be consid-ered to have cancelled for personal reasons.

The former Yugoslavia used to be a popular destination with British holiday makers, and Serbia is now on an offensive (no, not that kind) to rekindle its tourist industry. Scenic lake and mountain holidays were a speciality, and there are cities to visit too, although the damage in Belgrade is likely to remain apparent for some time.

Montenegro, which is seeking independence from Serbia, is also promoting tourism to its coastal resorts and its mountains.

Albania is the recipient of UN investment to rebuild the infrastructure follow-ing the conflict. In a few years, it should be wonderful. Look out for other opportunities like this.

Choose a destination that has recently been very popular. Loads of new hotel bedrooms were built for the Sydney Olympics, so once it was all over there were **plenty of bargains** to be had.

Ski for less

There are more than 1,000 ski resorts in the world. Choose a relatively unknown one and you could schuss your way to a bargain.

Try thinking laterally – skiing in Turkey is about as lateral as you can get, but anywhere that has mountains with snow on could qualify as a skiing area, once the infrastructure is there. Palandöken is a Turkish resort in Eastern Anatolia, but it won't remain undiscovered for long. Kurdish rebels and the occasional earthquake can affect Turkey's popularity, so keep an eye on the news and you may get even more of a bargain.

Some of the cheapest skiing is to be found in **Andorra and Bulgaria**. For the best bargains, look East. **Slovenia, Ukraine and Poland** offer excellent skiing with incredibly low prices – lift passes can be just a couple of dollars for a whole day. Try Crystal (0870 848 7000). **Serbia** also has a number of ski resorts, the best known being Kopaonik. Prior to the war, it was featured in mainstream holiday brochures and the infrastructure of lifts and hotels is still intact. Some resorts in **Bulgaria**, such as Borovets, have English-speaking ski schools.

Skiing in **Greece** is a little known secret, and there are bargains to be had. Lift passes may amount to only about £8 a day. Mt Parnassos is the best-developed resort.

The website www.inghams.co.uk contains some very useful information on low-cost and unusual ski resorts.

BY AIR

Flights have never been cheaper. With consolidators, auction sites and Internet sites jostling for your custom, there are always bargains to be had. And if you understand even a bit about how airlines operate, you'll have all the cards stacked in your favour.

Know your rights – www.rulesoftheair.com lists each airline's contract of carriage and explains the legal terms in simple language. Remember, every time you buy an airline ticket, you are agreeing to that airline's terms.

You can choose from two types of flights: **charter or scheduled**. On a charter flight, your contract is with the tour operator (who chartered the flight) rather than the airline itself. Charter flights are usually cheaper because:

- there is less choice as to when you can travel (that's why they tend to be at rather unsocial hours)
- they carry more passengers (to keep prices down) so there's not much legroom
- in-flight service isn't always as generous as on the scheduled flights
- booking conditions allow the operator to make changes to the flight, even at the last minute.

Don't assume your ticket is correct. If you have booked your own plane ticket, check yourself that all the details are right. There should be a little box marked **'status'** on the ticket; if you have a confirmed reservation, it should say **'OK'** in the box. If not, it means you don't have a confirmed reservation, so call the airline fast. Charter tickets don't usually have a status box because all charter reservations should automatically be confirmed before you get the ticket. Baggage allowance details will also be on the ticket – in a box marked 'allow'.

Breaking your journey for over 72 hours? In many parts of the world you will be required to **reconfirm your return reservation**. This applies to any break in the journey, even a return flight with a holiday in the middle. The holiday is considered a break in the journey.

If the airline asks you to **reconfirm your reservation**, you must do it – otherwise your reservation may automatically be cancelled. You may even have to buy another ticket.

Check-in time is the latest time for getting to the check-in desk, not for joining the end of the queue. If you miss the **check-in deadline** your place on the plane may go to someone on the waiting list and you will have no claim against the airline.

Some airports do not announce flight departures over the public address system. Look for, and keep an eye on, the **flight indicator boards** (usually banks of TV screens nowadays). These will tell you when to go to the gate for boarding – it's your responsibility to get there on time.

Air travel tax is now payable on all flights from UK airports. You usually pay for it when you buy your ticket, but sometimes the cheapest fares don't include it. Remember to check.

The most expensive kind of fare is usually called **'fully flexible'**. You can change your booking without any charge or you can cancel and get your money back. The cheapest fares are the ones with the most restrictions attached (you can't change your reservation, you won't get money back if you cancel and so on).

Airline tickets are **'non-transferable'** – in other words, you can't give your ticket to someone else if you can't use it. This is the case with both scheduled and charter flight tickets.

If you lose your ticket, the airline can either:
- ask you to pay for a new one; you can't claim your money back for the old one until after it has expired (and that can be up to a year) and provided it hasn't been used
- or give you a new ticket free of charge but get you to sign a form saying you'll pay for it if your lost ticket is used by someone else before it expires. They might also charge you an administration fee for issuing a new ticket.

Know your flights. A non-stop flight means exactly that; it doesn't stop anywhere on the way to its final destination. A direct flight, however, means that the plane will stop at least once before reaching its final destination.

When a travel agent sells a seat on behalf of an airline, they charge a fee of several per cent of the fare, included in the price you pay. If you go to a **consolidator**, however, you can get cheaper deals. Consolidators buy up blocks of seats from airlines at a discount; there is no commission. So, buying from a consolidator or a travel agent who has an agreement with one, will cost you the price of the seat plus a variable amount of profit for the seller – but it's still less than the fare from the airline direct or from an agent without an agreement.

A captain has the right to stop a person getting on the plane if they think that the person is drunk. **'Refused boarding'** gets stamped on their ticket, which means that other airlines will probably refuse to carry them as well. There is no chance of a refund if this happens.

If you are delayed for an **'unreasonable time'**, the airline is obliged to compensate you (under the terms of the Warsaw Convention). For long-haul flights, that's usually more than 6 hours. However, it can depend on the reason for the delay. If it was outside the control of the airline, like bad weather, you won't be able to claim much compensation. Whatever the cause, an airline should as least provide you with food and accommodation if necessary.

If you hear a call to say that **your flight is cancelled**, don't hesitate. Make a reservation on the next flight to your destination, either with that airline or with a competitor. There will be a rush to get the passengers on the cancelled flight booked elsewhere.

If you book your flight using a **credit card** you are covered for the cost of the tickets should the airline go bankrupt – as long as the tickets cost more than £100. The credit voucher must be made out directly to the airline or tour operator. Some credit card companies also offer minimal travel cover for lost luggage, around £250.

Buy a return ticket. The cheaper fares often apply to return tickets.

Include a weekend, because most of the lower fares require you to stay a Saturday night.

In most cases, **the earlier you book** the cheaper the ticket.

Travel on **Tuesday, Wednesday or Saturday** – the cheapest days to fly.

Select your airport with care. If there are a number of airports in a city, you may find a cheaper fare to the smaller ones, but the downside is that there is often a longer trip from the airport to the city centre. For example, flying to Venice with Ryanair actually means flying to the airport at Treviso, a charming place in itself, but a 30km (18.5 mile) trip to Venice.

Keep unsociable hours. Early morning and late evening flights often have much lower fares. Avoid peak hours such as 7.30am for flights to Europe from the UK or up to midday for flights from the UK to the USA.

Room to move

Leg room is at a premium on most planes, and with the recent spate of deaths caused by deep vein thrombosis (DVT), it makes sense to move your legs around as much as you can. Unless you can afford business class, on long-haul flights you want to look for the best seat pitch available. For economy flights, American Airways, Air New Zealand, South African Airways and Emirates have the best at around 86cm (34in). Next come Cathay Pacific, Qantas, Singapore Airlines and Thai Airways. British Airways and Virgin Atlantic offer only a stingy 79–81cm (31–2in). If you're tall, vote with your feet!

For anyone over 183cm (6ft) tall, 79cm (31in) is considered to be a minimum seat pitch for comfort on a long-haul flight. The minimum seat width should be 43cm (17in).

If you are over 2m (6ft 7in), Qantas will pre-assign you a seat with more leg room. Ask when you book.

For information on DVT, consult www.travelhealth.co.uk/advice/dvt.htm.

If you have a young child sitting on your lap, with **no seat allocation**, make sure you get a seat in a row that has an extra oxygen mask.

Try to **reserve a seat** before checking in. It's not always possible (usually it's difficult on the scheduled flights) but try asking, especially if you have special needs. Certain seats have more room:
- aisle seats (good for stretching your legs; not good for sleeping because of disturbance from people passing on the aisle or having to let your neighbours out)
- near the emergency exits (most leg room; but can be chilly, seats don't always fully recline and you can't keep hand luggage on the floor). If you're not able-bodied you may not be given these seats
- bulkhead seats (no one can recline back on you but families with babies often get priority for these seats so it can be noisy and you don't get a good view of the movie)
- middle row seats (best view of the main movie screen; good choice for two-children families; often get the chance to stretch right out at the back if the plane isn't full; possibility that one seat will be empty so you can stretch out a bit more)
- window seats (good view and you can rest your head on the side rather than your neighbour; bit more of an obstacle course to get out to the loo).

Seats to avoid:
- near the loos and kitchens (noisy, with people queuing all the time)
- last row of a section (restricted recline)
- front or back row of a non-smoking section (whether you do or you don't smoke...you'll be bothered).

There is no guarantee that you will get a special seat even if you have managed to get one assigned to you when you booked. If someone with special needs books after you, they could well get your seat.

SFU – suitable for upgrade

The holy grail of air travel – a free upgrade. The trouble is, everyone else is hoping for one too. Try some of these tips and you too could be considered SFU.

- Achieve very-frequent-flier status. Joining the ranks of élite-level frequent fliers by sticking with just one airline is still the best path to free upgrades.
- Fly at off-peak times. Don't go when business travellers do: Friday, Sunday afternoons and evenings, and Monday mornings. Try for Saturday, Tuesday or Wednesday. On weekdays, take late-morning, midday or later-night flights.
- Go for certain types of planes. On high-frequency routes where you have a choice of aircraft, choose airplanes with bigger front cabins – say, widebodies with three cabins (economy, business, and first class) rather than narrowbodies with just two (economy and first).
- Choose flights that originate in your local airport. Through flights that originate elsewhere and pick up more passengers in your airport, have often filled the best seats before you even get on.
- Be nice to the check-in agents. There are no two ways about it – the check-in agents are all powerful. And if you fly the same routes frequently, you'll run into the same staff, so establish a relationship – be chatty and ask how they are, a little gift might even be appropriate. If they take a liking to you, perhaps because you've helped them solve a problem, for example by volunteering to give up your assigned seat because another passenger insisted on having it, they may respond by bumping you up a class, if the opportunity presents itself.
- If all else fails, try asking. Someone is going to get that seat – it might as well be *you*.
- Dress smartly for your flight and if anyone has to be chosen for a free upgrade to business class, it may well be you.
- Be pleasant. If you treat staff with courtesy, they are more likely to repay you in kind. If a first-class seat becomes available, they're more likely to 'reward' the passenger who was nice to them. Try complimenting staff on the way they are handling people. A charm offensive can work wonders.
- Frequent flyers often get upgraded. But there's no need to make a big deal about how many miles you've got. The amount will pop up on the screen next to your frequent-flyer number so staff will know if you're one of the élite or not.
- If you fly a lot, it's worth joining an airline club. They are havens of civilisation and peace when you have to wait in an airport. They offer food, drink, newspapers, business facilities and so on.

How to survive an airport

On charter flights to the Med in peak season, you have a one-in-two chance of your flight being delayed. Survival is the name of the game, so try these tips:

- All charter airlines allow you to **pre-book seats** now, most at a small charge. Although you can't choose where you'll be sitting, at least you and your companions will all be together, so no need to be at the airport hours in advance.
- If you're travelling to Heathrow by train, you can **check in** for many major airlines at Paddington, and the same applies to Gatwick and Victoria.
- At Gatwick and Stansted, you can pay around £20 for an Airports Plus package, which gives you **priority check-in**, access to the VIP lounge (but not for under 16s), free currency exchange and a few other perks. Check for details on www.baa.co.uk.
- The website www.expedia.co.uk links to an invaluable airport guide on its US site – with information on what to do if you're stuck there for a while, the best food, shopping, how to conduct business, what to do with kids, and how to travel into the nearest city. Most of the information is about **US airports**, but the major European ones are featured.
- If you're **travelling with toddlers**, whatever else you check in, keep a lightweight buggy with you. Most airlines will accept it as hand luggage.

On the cheap

If you have a friend or a relative working for an airline, they may be able to book you **discounted tickets** on routes which often have empty seats for a substantial saving. Even former employees may be able to do this – and they may get air miles for their trouble. Well worth investigating if you have a large number of tickets to book, for example to attend a wedding, as everyone benefits.

Booking **back-to-backs** will save you money if you don't want to stay a Saturday night at your destination. The idea is that you buy two discount economy tickets that include Saturday night, say one London–Helsinki–London, departing on the day you want to travel out and the other Helsinki–London–Helsinki, departing on the day you want to travel back. You use the outbound part of each one to travel when you want to, and you'll still pay far less than an ordinary return, without the Saturday night stay.

Fly as a courier. You may not be able to take much luggage, and you'll need to be available at short notice. But it's much cheaper – between 50 and 80 per cent reduction in price. Most courier agencies require you to join (pay up for the privilege of getting information on the flights available). A quick Internet search will offer plenty of choice (see page 223 for more information on courier flights).

Book legs of stopover flights on unusual airlines for great prices – for example consider flying from London to New York on Air India.

For a cheaper ticket, try **'backhauling'**. This means instead of going A to B, you go A to C to B, because the cost of a return from C to B plus a return from A to C is cheaper than the direct version. For example going from London to

Amsterdam and then flying to New York is cheaper than from London to New York, and even Birmingham to Amsterdam to Paris is cheaper than Birmingham to Paris direct.

Another way to get a cheap ticket is via a **'hidden city' route**. It doesn't make sense at all, but adding an extra one-way journey (that you don't actually take) on to your ticket can reduce the price. So instead of buying a ticket London–Singapore–London, you buy London–Singapore–London–Chicago, and it can save hundreds of pounds.

Time is precious

Meeting a plane? The BAA website has information on flight arrivals at all the airports it controls, on www.baa.co.uk.

Hand luggage rules. On flights that aren't full, check-in staff are often flexible about how bulky and heavy your luggage is, but on crowded flights they will be strict. If you're travelling in a group, however, they will often accept the average weight for hand luggage among you, so make sure your friends travel light.

If you're in a hurry and on a direct flight, be the last to check in. At the other end your luggage will come off first – no more waiting round the carousel.

If you need to book a flight at short notice, it's hard to get really cheap flights in a short space of time. You might get lucky but you've probably got better things to do (like pack, cancel the milk and so on). So don't waste time shopping around if you need to leave the next day.

Bumped – ouch!

Because a proportion of people sometimes fail to turn up for flights, and because some flights are oversubscribed while others are virtually empty, the operators always overbook. The problems start if everyone does show up. Imagine being bumped from a flight when you're in a hurry! Bumping is a painful fact of life when flying these days, but if you're not in a hurry you can turn it into a competitive sport – you against the airlines – and make a profit, if you're lucky.

If this happens on a scheduled flight, you're entitled to **Denied Boarding Compensation (DBC)**. If you are 'bumped' off a scheduled flight at any airport within the EU the airline must pay you compensation. The rules for payment of DBC are set out in an EC Regulation (EC Council Regulation 295/91). To qualify for DBC you must have:
• a valid ticket
• a confirmed reservation
• checked in by the deadline given to you by the airline.

The airline must give you the choice of:
• a full refund on your ticket, or

- another flight as soon as possible, or
- another flight at a later date of your choice.

The airline must also pay you **compensation in cash**. You can accept vouchers for flights instead of cash if you want to. But if you don't want vouchers you can insist on cash. The minimum amount the airline must give you is set out in the Regulation, and it depends on the length of your flight and on how late you are getting to your final destination. Compensation should be paid in local currency and works out at about £120 (for flights up to 3,500 km (2,170 miles)) and £240 for longer flights, but is set to rise following new rules approved by the European parliament. This could mean on-the-spot compensation of up to £500.

This compensation is currently halved if the airline can get you on another flight within two hours (or four hours for flights over 3,500 km (2,170 miles)) of your original scheduled arrival time.

The airline must also pay for:
- getting a message to your destination
- meals and refreshments (the Regulation says these must be provided 'in relation to the waiting time', so the longer you're delayed, the more you should get)
- hotel accommodation if you are delayed overnight.

Some flights are worse for over-booking than others. For example, the Brussels to London flight on a Friday evening is apalling. Travellers tend to book themselves on to four or five flights and take the first flight they can get so there is a huge no-show problem.

How can I get bumped?

There's **voluntary bumping** (where the airline asks for volunteers) and involuntary bumping (where you've booked a seat, turned up on time and you still don't get a seat).

Book your flights well in advance. You can often get the lowest rate, you are guaranteed the seat of your choice, and you can almost guarantee the opportunity to be bumped if you plan to travel at the busiest times (Christmas, New Year, start of the Easter Holidays, half term ...).

Ideally, **get to the airport early and be the first person in the line.** If you want to get bumped, there's no use in being near the bottom of the volunteer list. If the flight is overbooked by only a few seats, only the earliest birds will get bumped. If you are actually late checking in, then forget it. You've already broken your agreement with the airline (which you made simply by buying the ticket), and you'll have a hard time asserting your rights if you are lucky enough to be bumped.

Make sure you **book an assigned seat** when you book any tickets. If you do not have a seat assignment when you get to the counter, you won't even have a seat to give up, so you will not be eligible to be bumped. Also check with the airline at least a week before your flight to ensure you have a **seat assignment**.

Always **volunteer to be bumped** for any flight unless you absolutely have to be at your destination at a particular time. If the flight isn't full, you won't have lost anything although you will have to board last. Even if your seat is not needed, you may get a discount voucher, just for being nice.

Bumping is more common during the **holidays** and **busy summer months**. Also try to **fly on Fridays** or other days that usually have heavy traffic. Book an **early flight** on a busy travel day so that if you get bumped, you should still reach your destination the same day. Sundays and Fridays are good for this.

Alternatively, volunteer to be **bumped overnight** if there's an early flight the next morning. The airlines often pay more if they bump you overnight and will put you up at an airport hotel for free and give you free meal vouchers. You can sometimes arrive at your destination by the time you would have woken up had you flown the night before.

If you get bumped to a later flight, insist upon an assigned seat and boarding pass. If you're on standby for the next flight, you may end up being involuntarily bumped! Oh the shame of it!

If flights have been cancelled due to bad weather, **offer your seat** to help fellow travellers out – gain their unending gratitude, get the compensation and probably flight vouchers too. Before you offer your seat, however, check what's on offer, to make sure it is worth your time.

Major airlines tend to **overbook** more. The more people they need to give up seats, the more money they will offer.

Travel with **hand luggage only**, so getting your baggage off the flight is not an issue.

Be flexible with the time you can arrive at your destination.

If your destination is a **resort area** you have a better chance of being bumped, as large groups of people may be travelling together and want to stay together.

You can be bumped on a ticket that was purchased with **bonus miles**, but there's a good chance of your getting an upgrade instead of compensation, because they don't want to give money back to you if you didn't pay for the ticket in the first place.

Courier flights

Sounds almost too good to be true. Courier companies buy seats on commercial flights, then use the allotted luggage space to ship packages. The packages go much faster than by cargo freight, and clear customs faster too. They sell the tickets to you at a bargain price and all you have to do is check in their luggage. Once you've flown as a courier, you may never pay regular over-the-counter fares again, and with **reductions of between 50 and 80 per cent** in ticket price, it's a very tempting prospect for footloose travellers.

With the advent of email, there has been less demand for couriers, but there are still opportunities, provided you're flexible about when you leave.

In most cases, you don't even have to pick up the package. Someone from the courier company will generally meet you at the airport and hand it over, together with all the instructions you need. At your destination, you will be met by another courier representative. You give them the manifest and your courier job is over until you return. You generally don't even get to see the luggage.

It's true that the closer to departure date you book, the cheaper the flight, but it's usually possible to book in advance too. The length of stay varies, so make sure it suits you before you book. There are often **restrictions on luggage** on the outward flight, but there may not be on the way home.

Luggage

Wherever possible, try to travel with hand luggage only:
- decant toiletries into small plastic bottles, or buy when you arrive
- roll up socks, underwear and sweaters, and use them to stuff the corners of your bag
- wear the heaviest clothes you are taking for the flight, and wear lots of layers, but bear in mind the climate in your destination
- take the opportunity to buy clothes locally – you'll look less like a tourist straight away.

If your luggage is basic black, it's hard to identify on the carousel. Individualise yours with a bright ribbon or something similar.

Always put your **name and home address inside the case**, but your destination on the outside. Once you've arrived at your destination, tear off the airline-issue claim tag otherwise your bag could end up anywhere when you return. Many business travellers put their **business address** rather than their home address on their luggage. Advertising that you are away from home could encourage burglars.

Avoid cases with **external zip pockets**, unless you're prepared to secure them with a padlock. Too easy for someone to slip in something for you to (inadvertently) smuggle.

If you've got **carry-on luggage**, arrive as early as possible. The overhead lockers fill up fast. A woman's handbag does not always count towards carry-on luggage while a briefcase does.

How We Beat The System

Cabin crew can be very strict when enforcing the 'one piece of hand luggage only' rule. Businessman Douglas Hume once brought boarding to a halt, after arguing with the crew got him nowhere. He stopped at the top of the boarding stairs to struggle into another shirt, suit and tie over the clothes he was already wearing, then folded up his suit bag and stuffed it into his briefcase.

Strange customs

Going through customs is **not a time for humour**. So forget jokes about bombs in your luggage when you go through the security controls. At the very least, you'll get held up and at the very worst you could be arrested.

X-ray machines don't harm laptops, cassette tapes or any other kind of electronically stored data. However, in certain countries, like the former Soviet Union and underdeveloped countries, the motors that drive the conveyor belts are not always properly shielded, which can cause problems. Put your laptop in the centre of the belt to minimise damage or ask to have it manually inspected. If you don't want your laptop to go through the machine, make sure you have the battery charged up so you can boot it up to prove that it's not stuffed full of cocaine.

Metal detectors can wipe the contents of a hard drive. Remove any floppy disks from your pockets before going through.

Avoid problems with immigration when you're travelling. They hate one-way tickets, so in addition to your cheapie one-way ticket, buy a full-fare, fully refundable ticket from a carrier based in the country you will be visiting, then cash it back in for a refund once you're there. You may lose a small deposit, but you'll save yourself a lot of trouble.

Backpackers attract a lot of negative attention, so to take the heat off your entry – buy a cheap suitcase from a charity shop and pack all your stuff including backpack in it. You can throw it away once you're in.

Make a reservation over the phone with a **major hotel chain** before you leave, and put the address down on your immigration form.

Make arrangements to have **plenty of cash** on you when you enter the country. Credit cards are no good – they could have been cancelled for all the immigration officers know. As soon as you're through, pay the money back into your account.

FACT: In-flight meals are never that brilliant. One reason is because in a pressurised air cabin your taste buds function at only two-thirds of their normal efficiency.

Nervous flyer

If you are nervous about flying, try to get a seat at the front of the plane where the ride will be smoother and quieter. However, the rear of the plane is safer. This is where the aircraft manufacturers put the flight recorder because they feel it's the least likely bit of the plane to be destroyed in an accident.

FACT: Statistics show that the larger the plane, the greater the number of survivors after a crash.

Health tips for flying

Everyone is aware of the risks of **deep vein thrombosis**. Particularly on long flights, it's important to reduce the likelihood of your becoming the next tragic statistic:

- Exercise as much as possible on board. Get up and **walk around the plane**, and do some stretches by the doors. This will reduce the swollen-ankle syndrome and many other physical and mental symptoms of jet lag.
- On a long flight, get up every hour and **stretch your cramped muscles**. Try not to sit with crossed legs because this restricts blood circulation.
- While sitting down, **do muscle-pumping exercises:** flex and point the feet, shrug the shoulders, stretch the fingers then make a fist – any movements that will work your muscles are good.

When you use the loo, for goodness sake **stand up before you flush**. The flush works on a vacuum principle and you could end up stuck to the seat with some very nasty side effects for your bowels.

Cabin air is very dry – wear glasses rather than contact lenses. Spritz your face with **spring water** and apply **moisturiser** as soon as you sit down – that applies to blokes too.

Drink at least 250ml (8 fl oz) of water or juice for every hour you are on a flight. Avoid alcohol and caffeine, which can compound dehydration.

With all the **circulating viruses** and the chemical sprays in use, aircraft can be unhealthy places. Wash your hands with soap and hot water before you touch your eyes, nose, mouth or any food. This is a good excuse to visit the loo and get some exercise. Also moisten a hanky with spring water and hold it over your mouth and nose for as much of the flight as you can. It helps combat dehydration, and filters out germs to some extent.

Low cabin pressure causes not only **ear discomfort**, but also nosebleeds and sinus pain, and leads to your whole body swelling slightly, so fly in loose garments and shoes that you can slip on easily.

Up where the air is clear?

Air quality is notoriously poor on board planes. It's kept this way as a method of economising on fuel. The pilots get somewhere in the region of ten times more oxygen than economy passengers. On most jumbo jets, for example, pilots make a practice of switching off one of the air packs, which pressurise the air from outside, and relying on more recycled air unless a passenger complains.

You'll know you're suffering from lack of oxygen if:
- you start to feel sick
- you develop a headache
- you find it difficult to concentrate
- you break out into a cold sweat
- you feel unaccountably tired.

Inform the flight attendant that you're **having trouble breathing**, and ask for the pilot to switch all the air packs on, and the recycling fans off. Tell-tale signs of more oxygen include:
- greater comfort and alertness within about 10–15 minutes
- sometimes a different sound from the air circulation system.

If you do not feel better, you can ask for **bottled oxygen**, which will be supplied free. You can book bottled oxygen in advance when you book your flight, but you usually have to pay for it.

Recycling air also increases the risk of catching any virus that any of the other passengers have. TB is on the increase worldwide, and the infection can be passed on in the air. If someone sitting close to you is coughing badly through the flight, you could discretely ask the flight attendant if you can move, and explain why. They won't want you making a fuss, and you could get yourself upgraded as a result.

On flights where there are both **smoking and non-smoking areas**, airlines do not have to guarantee you a seat in the area of your choice (except for US airlines, which are required to guarantee a non-smoking seat for all passengers who want one). Ask if you can make an advance seating request when you book. If you can't abide the smell of smoke, ask for a seat away from the smoking area, but in front of it, rather than further back the aircraft. The air flows from front to back, so you'll be 'up-wind'. If you're too close to smokers for comfort, ask for a bottle of oxygen. For obvious reasons, no smoking is allowed in the vicinity.

Beat jet lag – before it beats you!

If you are flying east to west, try to avoid taking a nap during the flight. Your day is going to be longer so you need to try and make yourself fall asleep later (and vice versa for eastbound flights).

Try not to sleep if the plane will be **arriving at night**. To help you get over jet lag, you want to sleep at night after landing. However, if your flight lands in the morning, try to get as much sleep as you can on board.

It takes less **alcohol** to make you drunk when you're flying because of the pressurisation of the aircraft. If you overdo it, you could have jet lag plus a hangover.

Ear plugs can help drown out that persistent hum of engines, air con, and too many people in too little space, but don't use a solid plug. Cotton wool is preferable in the reduced pressure of an airplane. **Eyemasks** are also helpful, particularly if you are flying east towards the dawn.

Fasten your **seat-belt** outside your blanket, otherwise the flight attendants may have to wake you up during turbulence if they can't see your belt.

Use your **hand luggage** as a foot rest.

Once you arrive at your destination, spend as much time as possible in **natural light** so your body will adapt more rapidly to the new rhythm of day and night.

BY RAIL

Book your ticket 24 hours in advance and some train companies will give you a **discount and free booking** for your seat. You should be able to book tickets up to three months in advance; you get the best deals this way.

Avoid queuing for tickets or being kept dangling at the end of the line. Buy your rail tickets through the Internet. **The Trainline** (www.thetrainline.com) also lets you compare fares and check out times of trains, and the tickets arrive by post about two days later.

Sunday is not always the most comfortable day to travel on the trains. Your journey may be disrupted by repair work. And there are always loads of people returning home or students with bulging rucksacks on their way back to college.

A train is **officially overcrowded** if people have to stand for journeys of longer than 20 minutes.

To be **officially on time**, a train must arrive at its destination within five minutes of its scheduled time (for short journeys) and within ten minutes (for longer journeys). Mind you, rail companies only measure that from the last destination. So the train could be a lot later along its route. As long as it catches up along the way, it's considered to have arrived on time. Rail companies often cunningly add a bit of extra time in between the last two stops so time can be made up.

Train companies are only obliged to pay you **compensation** for a delayed train if the delay is longer than one hour. To avoid this, it is not unknown for them, after 55 minutes, to move all the passengers off the train and make them walk to a bus that takes them on to the destination. This gets them out of the obligation to pay compensation, *but* they cannot move you against your will. Stay seated for another five minutes and claim the compensation.

You can get a **first-class upgrade** on Sundays for very little extra cost.

A senior citizen BR card allows a third off all journey prices. Check out all the deals that are on offer: student, young person's, family, network and disabled cards often get a reduction of around 25 to 35 per cent on tickets.

Saver tickets often have **time restrictions** on them. Check when you get your tickets.

If you want to take your **bike on the train**, check beforehand. For long-distance and Intercity, you will need to make a reservation (which costs around £3). The fee should cover the whole journey, even if you have to change trains. However, many rail staff are unaware of their own company's policies on this and will try to charge you again or claim that your reservation isn't valid. It is.

If you're **fed up with trains**, you're not alone. These websites are for people like you:

> www.thetrainwhine.co.uk
> www.trainpain.com
> www.saveourrailways.com.

Trains abroad

Use left luggage if you're travelling a lot. You can pack a small bag of essentials and leave your heavy case or rucksack at the station while you get your bearings or have a quick look round.

If you are travelling by a train which is pulled by a steam engine, take eye drops with you in case you get something in your eye.

BY SEA

If you want a floating luxury hotel, then opt for the traditional cruise ships. However, travelling by cargo ship is an unusual, cheaper and different way to travel. Every cargo ship offers a different experience; some are more luxurious than others.

- Freighters don't always leave and arrive exactly on schedule but this doesn't bother many travellers.
- Freighters often spend less time in port than cruise ships and there are fewer activities and amenities. There is usually one lounge where you can meet with other passengers and the officers.
- There may or may not be a swimming pool and sauna, and there are only small areas of deck space for lounging or reading. There is usually no entertainment. Most freighters that carry passengers have cabins for only a few passengers, usually no more than 12, although a few carry more.

- Young children are usually not accepted, and most lines do not take persons over age 79, although some accept passengers older than that. No doctor is required on freighters unless there are more than 12 passengers.
- Passenger state rooms are almost always comfortable and spacious, usually consisting of twin beds and a private bath, and occasionally a suite or an owner's cabin with a separate sitting room is available.
- Dining is informal. Passengers usually eat the same meals as the officers. In port, any shore plans need to be made by yourself or with fellow passengers.
- Port stops may be for a couple of hours or for several days. Check when you book. If they are very short, you'll barely have time to disembark before you have to leave.
- Some lines allow passengers to join for just one segment of the trip instead of the whole voyage. Some allow one-way passage.

Contact the individual shipping companies for information. **The Strand Cruise Centre** has advice on voyages on passenger-carrying cargo ships around the world. They can be found at:

Charing Cross Shopping Concourse
The Strand
London WC2N 4HZ
Tel: 020 7836 6363

Position, position, reposition

Most cruise ships sail in the Caribbean during the winter – but in April many head out for the 'seasonal locations' such as Europe and Alaska and return in October. When the ships change locations, these are known as 'Repositioning Cruises'. These cruises are usually longer than the normal seven-to-ten day cruises of the Caribbean, sometimes from 14 to 21 days instead, and they offer discounts for cruises to their new locations.

BY ROAD

FACT: In 2000 52 Britons died in road accidents in Spain.

FACT: August is the worst month for driving accidents in Europe.

Basic rates for car hire look like good deals but **beware of add-on fees**, which can bump the cost up alarmingly – such as drop-off fees (i.e. where you leave the car when you're finished with it), and refill charges (if you don't return the car with the same amount of fuel it had when you collected it).

Ask for a **car with the least mileage**. It won't have been driven by loads of different people and will probably be newer.

If a rental firm doesn't have a car in the size that you reserved, they have to

upgrade you at no additional cost. If they don't have any larger cars, they have to send you to a competitor and pay the difference. So most rental firms have a greater number of large cars than small ones. If you reserve a small car at a cheap price, you may be lucky and find that they've all been rented out... which means you get a bigger car for no extra price.

Rental firms encourage you to add on **collision insurance** to your hire. This may well be covered by your own personal car insurance. Check with your own insurance firm to see if you're covered.

Greece has one of the highest rate of deaths per 10,000 motor vehicles on the road. Be extra vigilant if you're driving there.

If you're travelling in the **USA**, consider delivering cars across the country for Americans who are moving house. You only pay for the petrol.

Vehicle insurance in **North America** can be different in each state. As a general rule, it has very low third-party limits. You can top this up when you hire your car or arrange it before you leave the UK. Sometimes there are restrictions on your insurance about where you can go – straying into New York City may well invalidate your cover. If you are travelling by ferry or air, keep your eyes peeled when you hit the road. You're liable to meet **fellow Brits** who are having to adjust suddenly to the reality of driving on the wrong side of the road. They can be just as much of a hazard as the other drivers.

Flashing headlights in the UK usually mean **'after you'**. Abroad it's a bit different. It's more likely that the driver means **'get out of my way'**.

If driving in **Cyprus or Turkey**, you will need two warning triangles, while spare light bulbs are compulsory in Spain.

When you're on the road, look our for **trucker's stops**. They often offer the best food at a good price.

HOTELS AND ACCOMMODATION

Hotels in many cities are packed. Rates are up, discounts are fewer, and all the little (and not so little) extra charges – phone surcharges, health-club fees, valet parking – add up to a whacking great shock at bill time. What can you do to whittle down the charges?

Rather than booking direct, try discount agencies on the Internet. For example, www.lastminute.com, www.wotif.com and www.discountcityhotels. At www.frontdesk.co.uk you deal with the website rather than the hotel itself, but on www.laterooms.co.uk you can get in touch with the hotel directly.

Make sure the check-in staff know you're **familiar with the hotel or the chain**. You want to come off as somebody who can give them a lot of business, so mention your last stay or your next, and request a particular room type to show that you know the hotel (you can get room information in advance by phone, on the Internet or from brochures).

Join **frequent-guest programmes**. These are often free, and you don't have to be a frequent guest to benefit. Just for joining you may get benefits such as free use of the gym, faster check-in, and late check-out on request. You also increase your chances of an upgrade.

Don't accept the first rate quoted. Ask if there is a **special weekend rate** or a package that includes breakfast or other extras; if the perks offered don't appeal to you, suggest something else, such as free parking.

See if the hotel will match another's rate. If you arrive with no reservation, try to **negotiate your rate**. Be friendly, polite and a little chatty. If you are travelling on business and you walk into a hotel that costs, say, £150 a night, tell the front-desk clerk that you were just passing by, that you prefer this hotel to the one you are already booked at (make sure you have the name of a likely hotel – you can bet they'll be rivals) because it is more convenient to your morning meeting, but that your company's travel budget is only £120 a night. The hotel may take your offer rather than let the room go empty.

If you are on holiday and you see somewhere you'd rather be staying in, ask to see a room so you can consider the hotel for your next trip. If you like it, enquire about the rate and say that you'd like to switch hotels but you're currently paying less. At off-peak times, a hotel may match what you are paying.

Try for a free upgrade. Making highly specific requests in advance ('a king-size bed in a non-smoking room with a city view, please') increases your chances of an upgrade. At the least, request a room on an upper floor where the better rooms usually are. If some superior top-floor rooms become available and the front desk can hand out free upgrades, you'll be on the list. Tell the desk clerk how much you are looking forward to your stay. If you are planning a romantic weekend, mention that you hope to make it an annual event. And if it's something special you're celebrating – a wedding anniversary, a significant birthday, your first trip alone together since the baby was born – say so, preferably when you are booking and again when you check in.

Consider the **time of day** you check in. The best time for getting a lower rate at city hotels is after dinner. The later it gets, the more eager the hotel is to fill its empty rooms.

Some high-class, older hotels have an 'odd' room. One that they don't let out unless they're desperate – ask if they have a room without a bath, then make them an offer. You might get lucky.

Dispute **excessive phone surcharges**. If you're a business traveller, you're in a good position to tell the manager, 'Look, I've just spent hundreds of pounds at your hotel, and you're trying to charge me two pounds for each phone call. If you were in my shoes, would you think this was fair?' Also, if the call charges are not clearly displayed in your room, you have a good case for arguing them down at check-out time.

If you have a problem that is not solved, complain and ask for some kind of compensation. For example, if faxes, phone messages or emails are not delivered promptly; if facilities, such as the pool or gym are under construction or being renovated; if you are woken by building works; if the iron and ironing board you asked for never arrive; or if the room is not ready within an hour of your arrival – then make sure the manager knows. If you politely state that the standard of service is not what you have come to expect from hotels of that type, and that this will influence your decision to return, you should find that, in most cases, your ruffled feathers are smoothed with a free meal.

If the hotel doesn't give you the type of room you requested (and they confirmed), try asking for a **free night's stay**.

Always write down the **name of the receptionist** who takes your hotel booking. Get a confirmation or reference number too. The member of staff taking your reservation will make sure all the details are correct if they know that their name is attached to the booking.

Always pay the deposit on hotel reservations by **credit card**. If you pay by cash and then cancel the reservation, the hotel can keep it all. However, if you pay by credit card, you may be able to claim some of the amount back. Paying by credit card puts the hotel under a contractual obligation to honour your reservation.

It's a bit of a gamble but, if you're stuck for a hotel room, try phoning around just after 6pm. Most hotels cancel reservations not made with a credit card after 6pm.

Stay on the cheap

Places to stay when your budget doesn't stretch to an hotel:
- Universities and colleges can offer cheap and basic accommodation during the holidays. Many older institutions are ideally placed in the centre of towns, too. Try the website www.venuemasters.co.uk.
- Hostels offer unbeatable prices and contact with savvy travellers who can give you tips for the next leg of your journey. Here are some websites to try:
  Hostelling International www.iyhf.org/iyhf/ehome.html (hostels are featured in the 60-odd member countries, plus a host of information and online booking)
  American Youth Hostels www.hiayh.org
  Canadian Youth Hostels www.hostellingintl.ca/
  YHA Australia www.yha.org.au
  VIP Backpackers Resorts www.backpackers.com.au (a commercial hostelling organisations with hostels in far-flung places)
  Pacific Rim Network www.pacifichostels.net
  Travel-Ys International www.travel-ys.com

- There are monasteries and convents all round the world offering a no-questions-asked bed in exchange for whatever you can afford. Search for 'monastery guesthouses' on the Internet – the Benedictines seem particularly wired. You may have to get up early.
- Old people's homes may have rooms you can rent. Just don't ask why they have suddenly become empty…
- Some Indian and African Sikh temples offer free accommodation.
- If you're the right age you can probably blend in on a university campus. Sleeping in the library is a time-honoured student tradition, you may be able to take a shower and sometimes even eat for free! Be warned, though, that this amounts to trespass and may well be criminal.
- Commit a minor crime, such as jaywalking, and you could sleep in a nice cosy police cell for one night, at least. Choose your country with care!
- Kibbutz are still a possibility – if you don't mind hard work and folk singing.

Safe as houses

If you are worried about security and safety, book a room on the second, third, fourth or fifth floor. Burglars are more likely to target rooms on the lower floors and fire-fighting equipment doesn't always reach as high as the sixth floor.

A good deterrent for would-be thieves: hang the **'Do Not Disturb'** sign on the door and leave the television on when you go out. Call housekeeping to tell them you want your room cleaned when it's convenient for you.

Electronic card keys are used in many western hotels now and give greater security than the traditional metal key. Ideally, your door should have a chain guard, a peephole and a deadbolt.

If an **unannounced delivery** comes to your hotel room, check with the front desk to see if it's genuine.

If the hotel operates a **token system** for getting out of the car park, see if you can get hold of a few extras and keep them, especially if they are the simple metal disks with a groove down the middle. So many places use them, it's handy to keep a few in your car so you can use the car park of some other hotel and get out unchallenged, although please be aware that this practice is illegal.

If you go jogging in a strange city, make sure you carry some ID on you – just in case.

WHEN IT ALL GOES HORRIBLY WRONG

Under the **1992 Package Travel Regulations**, tour operators are responsible for the hotel, transfers and airline contracted as part of the package. If you have a complaint and the tour operator is a member of ABTA or AITO, you can approach them. ABTA has an independent arbitration service while AITO offers an independent dispute settlement service. If the tour operator isn't a member of either association, you can take your case to court under the small claims procedure (look up 'Courts' in the local phone book; ask for a small claims form and information booklet to be sent to you).

Even with bonded operators, if they go out of business, you might not be covered for holidays within the UK, for scheduled flights or car hire or hotel accommodation booked as part of an independent holiday. Check all the details carefully.

If your holiday doesn't match up with what it said in the brochure, you could put in a **claim against the tour operator**. There are ways of doing this successfully:

- take a copy of the brochure with you on holiday so you can compare it with the ghastly reality
- always make your complaint to the holiday rep, fill out a complaint form and keep a copy
- take photos or video for evidence (videos are useful if your complaint is about noise)
- keep a diary of what happens, including the rep's response
- if any other guests are unhappy, get their details
- write to the operator when you return to the UK, concentrating on the areas of complaint; you have 28 days to do this
- don't give in; it may take time and you may have to call on arbitration or ABTA but persevere.

The services of a holiday rep are part of your holiday. If the services they offer are substandard, you are entitled to compensation. If you have a problem while on holiday, approach the rep first. If nothing is done and the situation doesn't improve, follow up the complaint in writing to head office.

Airport delays are every traveller's nightmare, but you may be entitled to compensation.

- Three hours of delay merits a **food voucher** of (currently) £3.
- Passengers delayed for six hours are entitled to a main meal.
- If you miss a business meeting or just a day of your holiday, you may be able to claim **compensation**, but this will depend on what has caused the delay. Airlines are not liable for bad weather delays.
- If you're delayed by 12 hours or more, you may be able to make a claim against your insurance policy. You should get confirmation of the delay in writing from the airline or operator. You will need this confirmation to support your claim. However, most insurance only covers delayed departure. If your arrival is delayed – tough.
- You can usually **go home** to wait – even after you have checked in – but it is still your responsibility to catch your flight, and delays can shorten as well as lengthen.
- The best advice is to buy **travel insurance** and check that you are covered for delays and cancellations.

Forced to stay overnight in an airport due to airline problems? Make sure you are given access to their lounge. Be insistent – they owe you!

A welcome new trend in **airport accommodation:** the Cocoon Hotel on the lower level of Terminal 1 at Charles de Gaulle Airport, Paris. Tiny, window-less, ship-cabin-like rooms are available for rent for day or night use. Many travellers stop here to shower and/or nap after a long flight, or stay over to ensure that they make their early-morning flights. The rate is equivalent to about £25 for one person or £30 for two. Call 00 331 48 62 06 16 to reserve.

If your car breaks down on the way to the airport, and you miss your flight, make sure you get a repairer's report to prove that the vehicle suffered from mechanical breakdown. Your **travel insurance** should pay at least some of the extra costs incurred in getting you to your booked destination.

Still staring hopelessly at the luggage carousel when everyone else has left? Report the missing item before you pass through customs, then contact the rel-evant airline authority as soon as you get to your resort, and get a **Property Irregularity Report**. If the airline finds your luggage, they should contact you to make arrangements to deliver your luggage to your accommodation. If they do not contact you, either ask your holiday representative for help or contact the airline authority at the airport you arrived at.

If your luggage is missing for at least 12 hours, you can claim a limited amount for essential items if you're not in your country of residence. The **'first needs'** payment is about £50. On the next two days without luggage, you are entitled to another £25. If your luggage is missing for longer than 72 hours, you can claim more. Keep receipts for the essential items you buy, so you can make a claim when you get back from your holiday.

Under the **Warsaw Convention of 1929**, airlines are obliged to pay out for lost luggage according to its weight, but the amount is pitiful – about £15 per kilo.

Most airlines only pay out the **value of your luggage at the time you lost it**, rather than what it will cost to replace all your clothes with new ones. If you bought new items especially for the trip, keep the receipts – but not in your suitcase.

If your suitcase is **damaged in transit**, you should report the damage immedi-ately to the relevant airline authority and obtain a Property Irregularity Report. If you don't have this report, you don't stand a chance of making an insurance claim.

If you **lose your passport** while abroad, report the loss to the relevant con-sulate (in the country you are in) immediately. They will arrange a new or tem-porary replacement passport for you. Your insurance policy will cover your expenses for replacing your passport, up to £250.

If you lose your passport or put it through the washing machine shortly before you go, you can get a **speedy replacement** if you contact Globe House, 89 Eccleston Square, SW1 (0870 521 0410) and choose one of the options on the message. Then you can get an appointment to get an emergency replacement. You've got to be prepared to pay, though. It costs around £28 to replace and an additional £12 for a fast-track, three-day service.

Take a **photocopy of your passport** and any relevant visas with you, and keep them in a different place to your passport.

If a holiday company promised you a sea view and you end up looking over the car park, you are entitled to **claim compensation**. Similarly if you have booked at a hotel and when you arrive it is full, then they owe you either compensation or to cover expenses such as any costs incurred finding other accommodation.

Bear in mind that **accepting compensation** in the resort may reduce your chances of pursuing your case when you return. If you do accept compensation while on holiday a tour operator is sure to ask you to sign a form saying the issue you've complained about has been resolved.

You return from holiday and send off your film to be developed. A letter arrives from the photoprocessing company saying they've lost your photos but they'll give you your money back and a free film. This is not acceptable. You are entitled to **compensation for the value of the film** and for the disappointment and upset that the loss (or damage in some cases) has caused. The amount you get will depend on the importance of the photos; a wedding would score more highly than an away-day in Blackpool, for instance (no offence, Blackpool). If the company claim that they are covered in the small print of their contract, check that the terms are fair and reasonable (as stated by the Unfair Contract Terms Act, 1977).

Our man in Havana (or wherever)

FACT: Between April 1999 and April 2000, consular staff issued 10,074 emergency British passports.

FACT: There are 586 Britons in US prisons.

FACT: There are 302 Britons in Spanish prisons, 184 of them on drugs charges.

If your passport is nicked, your travellers' cheques lifted, or you get mugged, you may find yourself at the consular office. When you step through that door, you are officially on British territory – and there are moments when that will be just what you need. The Foreign Office can be a big help before you go abroad, too. Their website www.fco.gov.uk is a mine of information on:
• local unrest
• safety and security
• motoring conditions
• driving laws
• local travel and restrictions on movement

- terrorism
- local laws and customs, including the best currency to take and appropriate clothing
- visa and local registration requirements
- health, including inoculations required, tap-water quality and medical facilities
- natural disasters
- the address of the consular office
- the safety of the local airline.

The most exciting bit is the list of countries you are advised not to visit, www.fco.gov.uk/travel/countryadvice.asp, but you can select a country from a menu, and the information is all there, with links to other sites. Even if you have no intention of travelling, this site is very addictive – did you know there is no decompression equipment on the Solomon Islands, and that swearing causes much more offence there than in most other countries? The information is also available on Ceefax page 470 onwards. The travel advice unit can be contacted by telephone (020 7238 4503) or fax (020 7238 4545).

The British Consul can:
- issue emergency passports
- contact relatives and friends and ask them to help you with money or tickets
- advise on how to transfer funds
- at most Posts, in an emergency, advance money against a sterling cheque for up to £100 supported by a banker's card valid for the appropriate amount
- as a last resort, and providing that strict criteria are met, make a repayable loan in exceptional circumstances for repatriation to the UK or other country of nationality
- help you get in touch with local lawyers, interpreters and doctors
- arrange for next of kin to be informed of an accident or a death and advise on procedures
- contact and visit you if you are under arrest or in prison
- give details of organisations experienced in tracing missing persons
- in certain circumstances, make representations on your behalf to the local authorities.

Most British Consulates have an answerphone for out-of-hours callers. You can get an emergency contact number from that. Hotels, tour operators and the police usually have the number of the nearest British Consular Office.

Consuls cannot:
- intervene in court proceedings
- get you out of prison
- give legal advice or instigate court proceedings on your behalf
- get better treatment for you in hospital or prison than is provided for local nationals
- investigate a crime
- pay your hotel, legal, medical or any other bills

- pay for your travel tickets, except in very special circumstances
- obtain accommodation, work or a work permit for you
- undertake work more properly done by travel representatives, airlines, banks or motoring organisations.

Check that any **prescription medication** you need when you are abroad is legal in the country you're going to. The best way is to phone the consulate of the country in question and ask them before you leave. Sometimes a doctor's letter may be required to confirm that you really need it and are taking it legitimately.

Don't cross **land borders** with people you don't know and never carry a parcel or any luggage through customs for anyone else. Don't drive a vehicle across a border for anyone, and be very careful about lending anyone your car.

If you're going abroad to pursue a hobby such as bird-watching, botany, or train-, plane- or ship-spotting, be very careful about **using binoculars and taking photographs**, particularly near military sites. You could be mistaken for a spy.

Take enough money to pay for a flight home if your ticket becomes invalid for some reason.

Victims of crime, make sure you are issued with a police report. You'll need it if you want to make an insurance or compensation claim.

INSURANCE

Holiday Facts:

- In 1999–2000, 425 UK residents died of non-natural causes while overseas. Road accidents, drowning and suicide were the most common causes of death.
- In the same period, 190 UK residents travelling abroad were robbed, 120 assaulted, 117 raped, 35 murdered, 29 abducted, and four were the victims of terrorist action.
- Out of 50 million trips abroad by British residents in 1999–2000, there were 45,000 incidents that required consular assistance.
- Incidents requiring consular involvement in Southeast Asia have increased by several hundred per cent in recent years.
- Between April 1999 and April 2000, 17 Britons died in accidents from balconies, 13 of them in Spain.
- One in five British travellers goes abroad without any kind of insurance cover.

Check that the **insurance deal** offered by your tour operator or travel agent is competitive – you might be able to find a cheaper deal elsewhere. The Government banned travel companies from insisting that people buy travel insurance from them to qualify for a discount holiday in 1998. You don't need to buy it as part of your holiday package. Shop around. You might even be **insured automatically** if you pay for the holiday with a credit card but do check this out thoroughly. In such cases, you probably won't be covered for cancellations. It's also worth looking to see if you are covered by your **house insurance**, but excess payments and loss of no-claims bonus may still make it cheaper to buy specific holiday insurance.

If you've paid for your flight with **air miles**, check whether your policy covers you for a refund of their full value if you have to cancel.

Travel insurance isn't a **legal requirement** but having it does mean that you're covered against most problems (lost/damaged luggage, accidents, medical expenses, legal bills, cancellation, money, personal belongings and so on). Make sure you know what is and isn't included and find out what you need to do if you have to make a claim.

The most important type of holiday cover is **medical**. An accident or emergency operation could result in a bill for many, many thousands of pounds, and if you need to be air-lifted, or flown home in a private aircraft with medical attention, you can say goodbye to your savings, your pension and maybe your home. Many travel policies now offer emergency medical and repatriation cover of up to £5m. Don't leave home without it.

Don't rely solely on a **Form E111** for medical insurance. A simple broken leg on a ski holiday in France could still result in you being out of pocket by over £1,000, and it doesn't cover third-party liability at all.

If you're booking a really expensive holiday, you should take out **extra cover**. Most policies will cover you for around £3,000 to £5,000 per holiday.

A Green Card is an internationally recognised document that shows you have minimum legal insurance cover abroad. If you are driving in Spain, get a bail bond from your insurers before you leave; this acts as a surety, preventing you being banged up. It's no longer a legal requirement but the Spanish Tourist Board recommends it.

If you make more than three trips a year, it might be worth getting an **annual travel insurance policy**. Check that it covers medical insurance, personal belongings, delay, baggage loss and check any exclusions.

Are you covered for what you need? One woman took out annual insurance only to find that she was covered for travel anywhere in the world…apart from the UK. It's just as easy to lose baggage, be delayed or have your purse pinched in this country as it is abroad. So you need insurance cover for holidays and travel here as well.

When you are travelling, keep a **copy of the insurance policy** and any phone numbers that you need. Advice on what to do if there is a problem is usually included with your insurance documents, so make sure you take them along with you as well. And if anything does happen, **keep copies of everything** – police reports, receipts and so on. When you get home, you should contact your insurer at once. Payment should come within three weeks.

Holiday Which? has taken a look at travel insurers recently, and some of the best were reported as Atlas (020 7609 5000), Bradford & Bingley Building Society (01707 275371), Churchill (0800 026 4050, www.churchill.co.uk), Direct Travel (0800 318228, www.directtravel.co.uk), Options (0870 848 0870, www.optionsinsurance.co.uk) and Worldcover Direct (0800 365121).

Insurance

One independent tour operator made money by booking holidays for himself under different names. As a tour operator he cancelled them and then for each holiday claimed as a holidaymaker on the insurance. He got caught.

LOST AND FOUND

FACT: For the first time, missing luggage has overtaken flight delays as the major cause for complaint among travellers, according to the Air Transport Users' Council.

FACT: The most you're likely to get back from your insurer for lost luggage is around 25 per cent of its worth. Many insurers will give you far less.

Airlines are liable for **delayed or damaged luggage** (Warsaw Convention, 1929). You must put your claim in writing within seven days if your luggage is damaged and within 21 days if it has been delayed. Try to sort out the problem when it happens rather than wait too long.

At check-in, make sure that your **luggage receipts have the correct flight number** and destination so that you both end up in the same place.

Most insurers will not cover **'valuables'** placed in check-in luggage. They say airline passengers should keep these items in their carry-on bags.

All policies cap the amount paid on any single item to about £250 or £300.

A Vuitton case stuffed full of designer clothes? Very posh! By law, airlines must pay £15 per kg (2.2 lb) of lost or damaged baggage. That's not much (£289 for a standard baggage allowance of 20 kg (44 lb) – and that includes the value of the case as well). If you are asked to estimate the value of the contents, err on the high side. The International Civil Aviation Organisation has approved the Montreal Convention which allows higher limits for compensation (it's not based on weight and recommends an absolute limit of £850) but this will only operate in countries which have ratified the agreement.

If you are travelling on a **code-share flight** (i.e. you buy a ticket from one airline but travel on the plane of another) the airline whose name is printed on your ticket is responsible for your compensation.

You don't always need the receipts for every item lost to make a successful claim. Photographs, user's manuals, guarantees, bank and credit-card statements help to support your inventory.

If your bag is lost for good you might have to wait up to two months before the airline accepts that it really is lost, and before they will begin to look at your claim for compensation. If they have given you cash to buy emergency supplies they may deduct the sum from the final compensation due to you.

The airline should contact you when your bag turns up, but it's worth checking on their progress in tracing it. When they find it they should deliver it to you at their expense.

The things that turn up at lost property offices around the world ... anything from stuffed alligators to false teeth! But now you don't have to worry about leaving your teeth or your crock behind – www.ilostandfound.com is an Internet site that aims to bring people and their lost possessions together.

Weird and wonderful travel laws

London Hackney cabs must carry a bale of hay and a sack of oats.

Chewing gum on subways in Singapore may result in fines and/or a stretch in jail.

It's worth travelling in Scotland; if you are caught short and knock on someone's door, they are obliged by law to let you use their commode.

Also in Scotland, it is illegal to be drunk in possession of a cow.

In Denmark, before starting your car, you are required to check that there are no children underneath it.

Oklahoma will not tolerate anyone taking a bite out of another person's hamburger.

In Indiana, hotel sheets must be exactly 99 inches long and 81 inches wide.

Be warned: in North Carolina couples staying overnight in a hotel must have a room with double beds that are at least two feet apart. Making love in the space between the beds is strictly forbidden.

USEFUL ADDRESSES

Access to the Skies
c/o RADAR
12 City Forum
250 City Road
London EC1V 8AF
Tel: 020 7250 3222
www.radar.org.uk
A guide for people with reduced mobility

Air Travel Organiser's Licence (ATOL)
3rd Floor
CAA House
45–59 Kingsway
London WC2B 6TE
Tel: 020 7453 6427
www.atol.org.uk

Air Transport Users' Council
CAA House
45–59 Kingsway
London WC2B 6TE
Tel: 020 7240 6061
www.auc.org.uk

Association of British Insurers
51 Gresham Street
London EC2V 7HQ
Tel: 020 7600 3333
email: phil.ward@abi.org.uk
www.abi.org.uk

**Association of British Travel Agents
  (ABTA)**
68–71 Newman Street
London W1P 4AH
Tel: 020 7637 2444
www.abta.com

**Association of Independent Tour
  Operators (AITO)**
133a St Margaret's Road
Twickenham
Middlesex TW1 1RG
Tel: 020 8744 9280
www.aito.co.uk

**British Airways Medical Services for
  Travellers Abroad (BAMSTA)**
51 Gower Street
London WC1E 6HJ
Tel: 020 7436 2625
Advice line: 01276 685040
www.british-airways.com/
  travelqa/fyi/health/health.shtml

British Red Cross
9 Grosvenor Crescent
London SW1X 7EJ
Tel: 020 7235 5454

Department of Health
International Branch
Room 512
Richmond House
79 Whitehall
London SW1A 2NS
Tel: 020 7210 5318
www.doh.gov.uk

Department of Health
Public Enquiries Office
Richmond House
79 Whitehall
London SW1A 2NS
Tel: 020 7210 4850
www.doh.gov.uk

Department of Social Security
Overseas Branch
Tyneview Park
Whitley Road
Benton
Newcastle-upon-Tyne NE98 1BA
Tel: 0191 218 7777

Disabled Living Foundation
380–384 Harrow Road
London W9 2HU
Tel: 020 7289 6111
www.dlf org.uk
Produces a practical guide to air travel for
  elderly and disabled people

Gap Activity Projects
44 Queens Road
Reading
Berkshire RG1 4BB
Tel: 0118 9594914
www.gap.org.uk

HM Customs & Excise
New King's Beam House
22 Upper Ground
London SE1 9PJ
Tel: 020 7620 1313
www.hmce.gov.uk

Holiday Care Service
2nd floor
Imperial Buildings
Victoria Road
Horley RH6 7PZ
Tel: 01293 774535
Has information about travel within the UK
   and overseas for elderly and disabled
   people

Hospital for Tropical Diseases
(Travel Clinic)
4 St Pancras Way
London NW1 0PE
Tel: 020 7388 9600
Healthline: 0839 337733

Institute of Travel & Tourism
113 Victoria Street
St Albans
Herts AL1 3TJ
Tel: 01727 854395
www.itt.co.uk

Liverpool School of Tropical Medicine
Liverpool L3
Tel: 0151 708 9393
Advice line: 0906 7088807
www.liv.ac.uk/lstm/travelmed.html

Malaria Information Line
Tel: 0891 600350

National Passport Hotline
Tel: 0990 210 410

Office of the Rail Regulator (ORR)
1 Waterhouse Square
138–142 Holborn
London EC1N 2TQ
Tel: 020 7282 2000

Organisation for Timeshare in Europe
  (OTE)
15–19 Great Titchfield Street
London W1P 7SB
Tel: 020 7291 0901
www.ote-info.com

Social Security Agency
Overseas Benefits Unit
Block 2, Castle Buildings
Stormont
Belfast BT4 3SP
Tel: 028 9052 0520

Solo's Holidays
54–58 High Street
Edgeware
Middlesex HA8 7ED
Tel: 020 8951 2800

Strand Travel
Charing Cross Shopping Concourse
The Strand
London WC2N 4HZ
Tel: 020 7836 6363
www.strandtravel.co.uk
For information on travelling by cargo ships

Timeshare Consumers Association
Hodsock
Worksop
Notts S81 0TF
Tel: 01909 591100
www.timeshare.org.uk

Tripscope
The Courtyard
Evelyn Road
London W4 5JL
Tel: 020 8994 9294
Advice and information on travel
   arrangements and journey planning

Voluntary Service Overseas
317 Putney Bridge Road
London SW15 2PN
Tel: 020 8780 2266
www.vso.org.uk

Youth Hostel Association
Trevelyan House
8 St Stephens Hill
St Albans
Herts AL1 2DY
Tel: 01727 855215

 # Work

'I like work; it fascinates me, I can sit and look at it for hours.' *Jerome K Jerome*

I work, therefore I am. It's a sobering thought that you'll probably spend over two-thirds of your adult life – and probably your healthiest, most productive years – engaged in some kind of paid work. But if you're not on the treadmill with everyone else, you're made to feel like a skiver, a loser or, worst of all, unambitious. There may not be any real option to getting yourself gainfully employed but, with a little privileged knowledge on how to work the system as you work, you might even find you enjoy it!

BENEFITS

Life on benefit is probably tougher than ever – unless you've acquired multiple identities from somewhere, and are claiming under several names in which case you're committing fraud! No one is unemployed anymore, they're all Job Seekers. To qualify for JSA (Job Seekers' Allowance) you have to be seen to be actively seeking work. If you don't jump through the hoops with a sufficient show of enthusiasm, you can have your JSA suspended until you shape up. So play the game.

'New Deal' or 'No Dole'

In 1998, the Labour Government introduced the 'New Deal' – a number of schemes for different groups of people who are out of work and claiming benefit. Depending on your standpoint, either the New Deal offers claimants an opportunity to escape from poverty and exclusion into prosperity and full participation in New Labour's radiant vision of society, or else it's yet another ploy to reduce the number of unemployed. The New Deal is mainly aimed at young people, between 18 and 24, who have been unemployed and claiming JSA for more than six months. However, the following are also marked for attention:

- older claimants who have been unemployed for more than two years
- people with disabilities
- lone parents
- former regular members of the armed services
- those who have become unemployed as a result of large scale redundancies
- young people who have recently left local authority care.

Claimants in the 18–24 age bracket are presented with a number of options, with the threat of **withdrawal of benefit** hovering in the background.

First of all, they go through a preliminary process, known as **'The Gateway'** for one to four months, during which a 'personal adviser' will try to talk them into taking up one of four options (rather than signing on):

- a 'proper' job
- a subsidised job, lasting six months or more, with one day a week's training. The employer will receive a subsidy from the Government of up to £75 per week, while the worker gets whatever the employer decides to pay.
- full-time vocational education or training. Although this can last up to a year, it could be very limited, with the emphasis again on eventual long-term employability.
- work with an Environmental Task Force, such as reclaiming waste land. This will be similar to the work that the Probation Service currently enforces under Community Service Orders! The payment is either a wage or an allowance equivalent to JSA.
- work in the voluntary sector, working with charities or community organisations, again for 'benefit plus'. The emphasis here, as well as in the environmental option, will be on improving long term 'employability' and instilling 'skills and work habits appropriate to the workplace'.

If the ex-claimant decides not to take up a place in one of the New Deal options, the Employment Service will simply press a job on them. If they refuse that, they can lose their benefit first for two weeks, then for four weeks, then indefinitely.

How to be (and stay), a Job Seeker

To be a Job Seeker (and qualify for JSA) you have to be able to prove (if necessary) that you are **available for work** and **actively seeking work**.

If you leave your job, avoid being classed as **voluntarily unemployed**, which you will be if you:

- resign
- walk out
- are sacked for misconduct.

You won't be considered as **voluntarily unemployed** if you:

- are made redundant
- reach the end of a contract
- have to stop work on medical grounds
- are unfairly dismissed.

The worst-case scenario is that you'll face a sanction of up to 26 weeks without any benefit at all. If there is any dispute of the facts, your case will be referred to an Adjudication Officer who decides if it's fair and, if so, how long the sanction applies for. They will write to your employers for their side of the story. During this period you will be on no benefit, or reduced benefit in cases of hardship.

If you leave work on medical grounds – make sure your GP will back you up.

If your GP is signing you off work completely, you should claim Incapacity Benefit and/or Income Support on an A1 form (claim both if you haven't paid enough National Insurance contributions).

To stay 'on the sick' you will have to pass the 'All Work' test. This is a medical test introduced under the regulation concerning Incapacity Benefit. Once incapable of work for over six months, benefit is payable to people who pass this test. Contact a local advice centre or claimants' group before you claim, for information and help.

If you want to claim JSA, but you left your job because of ill health, you must make it clear that your ability to do other types of work is not affected (i.e. you're still 'available for work').

You won't get any money for the **first three days** of your claim. But even if it's less than 12 weeks since your last claim they shouldn't impose a further waiting period.

You have to say you are **available to start full-time work** (at least 40 hours a week) immediately, unless you're a carer or do voluntary work, in which case you have a massive 48 hours' notice to ditch all your commitments and responsibilities. If you're in part-time work or study, you have 24 hours' notice. If you can't make yourself available for work, you'll plunge back down to being on income support.

You can still be counted as **available for work** (and therefore eligible for JSA) even if:
- you are on an employment-related course of no more than two weeks in one year
- you have a short period of illness – between three days and a maximum of two weeks, and then only twice in any year. Don't push it though.
- you're not available for three days in any week because a close friend/ relative is seriously ill; there is a funeral of a close friend or relative; there is a domestic emergency affecting a close friend/relative or if someone you have caring responsibility for dies
- you're abroad for at least three days to attend a job interview and you let them know at least one week in advance
- you're unavailable for up to eight weeks because you have to take a child abroad for medical treatment
- you're unavailable for up to eight weeks because you are part of a couple with children and your partner is abroad, away from home, ill or looking after a sick relative.

You are now supposed to give **advance warning** if you are going away from home, even if this is only for a day. Obviously there's no need for them to know unless you're away on your signing day. But never use 'being away from home' as an excuse for being late signing on, not attending interviews, receiving letters, etc. If you do go away, you are supposed to continue to actively seek work and be available for work immediately!

You can be treated as **not available for work** if you:

- refuse without good reason to apply for or take a suitable job and the vacancy still exists
- deliberately spoil your application or interview for a job
- fail to take up a reasonable offer of local short-term work
- place unacceptable restrictions on availability in terms of hours, days and wages
- fail to attend an interview with a Client Adviser
- fail or refuse to complete forms about availability for work.

Under the JSA you have to agree to sign a contract, the **Job Seekers' Agreement**. Don't agree to something that you're not prepared to do – it will only cause you problems later on.

Fortnightly signing can be used as a test of your **'availability for/actively seeking work' status**. The logic is, if you don't turn up to sign on (and ostensibly have a look at the Job Centre boards), you must be doing something that makes you unavailable. If you're persistently late or miss appointments, you may have your JSA suspended.

Have your **signing card and proof of 'job seeking'** with you when you sign on. You can't sign on without it. Try not to be late unless you've got a good reason or have told them in advance, but don't say you're away. They usually provide booklets laid out like a diary for you to fill in with proof of your endeavours, but you can use your own sheet of paper instead.

Two job-seeking steps a week is the minimum legal requirement, and lots of things can count as job seeking. You can:

- apply for jobs in writing, personally or by phone
- get information on jobs from adverts, recruiting agencies and employers
- register with employment agencies and businesses
- draw up a CV
- get a reference from a previous employer
- visit the job centre and look at the boards
- research potential employers and possible occupations.

Looking in the papers two days a week and **visiting the Job Centre** once a week should meet the requirement for job seeking, so make sure you list these for your Job Seekers' Agreement.

If they're hassling you to do more, suggest you could contact family and friends and ask if they can find you work, or agree to apply for an advertised vacancy by phone. This is a good one, because you can't be expected to do it every week – only when there is actually a vacancy.

Keep a note of any **job-seeking activities**, not just applications you send off. Phone calls and visits count too – not just written applications. But if you want to avoid aggravation, send at least one application off a week, preferably two, and keep photocopies.

Take a couple of **photocopies of likely employers** from *Yellow Pages*, and keep that in case you have to prove what you've been doing. Make some squiggles in red pen to add authenticity. Do be warned, though, that it is fraudulent to keep false records of your activities.

Putting all the **evidence of job seeking in a little folder** makes a killer impression – and it's easier to find if you're in a hurry to get to the Job Centre.

Could try harder! If the signing clerk still thinks you haven't been trying hard enough, you could be referred to an Employment Service (ES) Adviser for an interview. If you fail to impress with your zeal, your benefit can be suspended immediately and you won't get your giro. Your case will be referred to an Adjudication Officer for a final decision. Appeal against it as a matter of principle, but just turn up to sign on as usual the next fortnight and, provided you have sufficient evidence of job-seeking, you will receive payment as usual.

No shows. If you don't turn up to sign on or to an Employment Service Interview your benefit will be cut off unless you visit the Job Centre within five working days to explain why – and it had better be good. You could claim a misunderstanding due to language difficulties, wrong information by ES staff, a medical or dental appointment, a job interview, a lightning strike – but you'll need proof.

If you still don't look keen enough, you might be forced to carry out a particular job-seeking activity by means of a **'Job Seekers' direction'**, or offered a **'Notified Vacancy'**. Signing clerks can offer notified vacancies, but they don't have the right to issue a direction.

Keep control. Even if you have to apply for a notified vacancy or by a direction, you'll be the one at the interview – not the Adviser. You can make sure you don't get taken on without being too obvious about it.

Job Centre staff may ask to see your CV. Don't panic. It doesn't have to be the same one you send out to potential employers, does it? If you don't produce one, they may send you on a course to learn how to do one, so it's better to come up with your own. But do remember that if you produce a *false* CV you may well be committing fraud.

You can place **restrictions on the type of work you will consider** for the first 13 weeks, after that you'll have to consider anything. But if you can come up with physical or mental reasons for not doing certain jobs, or develop sincere, religious or conscientious objections to doing certain jobs, you should be all right.

When sending you for interviews, the Job Centre staff must take account of your skills, qualifications and experience, the type and number of vacancies within daily travelling distance and any jobs you've been turned down for. If you look as if you've been making a real effort but have got nowhere, they have to accept that you're unlikely to land a job – through no fault of your own!

It's barely worth the bother of applying for a **Business Start Up Allowance**. You need to produce a realistic business plan and to have some financial backing, and they only give you £500 anyway.

On Income Support

If you end up on Income Support, despite your best efforts, you automatically qualify for other benefits:
- free school meals
- free prescriptions
- free dental care
- vouchers for spectacles
- free milk and vitamins for expectant mothers and children under five, free vitamins for nursing mothers
- maximum Housing Benefit
- maximum Council Tax Benefit.

Checks and balances

These pesky computers are everywhere nowadays – and sometimes they work! This means that information about you can be winging its way from one office to another.
- Be aware that the Benefits Agency can carry out checks to make sure that the information you've given on the claim form or during an interview is correct. They can compare what you've said or written on the claim form with records held by another government agency. This means that the Benefits Agency could ask the Inland Revenue if its records show that you are paying tax, in order to check whether you are working. Local authorities, who administer Housing Benefit and Council Tax Benefit, can also carry out checks on benefit claims. **Checks on a benefit claim can be made at any time while you are claiming benefit, not just when a claim is first made.**
- You may be asked to provide evidence to back up any statement on a benefit claim form, for example, evidence of income and capital. You will also have to provide a national insurance number or, if you don't have one, apply for one, or provide information which will allow your number to be identified.
- If you are receiving a benefit because you were unemployed and started working but did not tell the Benefits Agency, you may be committing fraud. And you may have to repay any overpayment of benefit.

Altogether, it's probably easier and more fun to give in and get a job – but how?

FACT: That annoying work ethic even troubles the newly very, very rich. Camelot says that 51 per cent of all winners of more than £50,000 have returned to work.

FINDING A JOB

Every profession will have its trade press. This is a good place to look for jobs. You can get details of these and other publications from the BRAD (British Rate and Data) directory, available from your local library. The national newspapers are a good source of new jobs. Different days in different papers will specialise in certain careers:

Daily Express
   Tuesday: Education
   Thursday: General employment

Daily Mail
   Thursday: General employment

Daily Mirror
   Thursday: General employment

Daily Telegraph
   Thursday, repeated on Sunday: General employment
   www.jobs.telegraph.co.uk runs a particularly good Job Alert service that will email jobs that fit your specification straight to you.

Financial Times
   Monday: Accountancy
   Wednesday: Finance, banking
   Thursday: Accountancy

The Guardian
   Monday: Media
   Tuesday: Education
   Wednesday: Public sector
   Thursday: IT
   Friday: General employment

Independent
   Monday: Media and sales
   Tuesday: IT
   Wednesday: Legal and finance
   Thursday: Education and graduate appointments

The Times
   Tuesday: Legal
   Wednesday: Marketing and secretarial
   Thursday: Executive appointments
   Friday: Education

Good job hunting

FACT: Some 50 per cent of executives moving to new positions say they are disappointed with their new job and about 30 per cent wish they had never left their old jobs.

If you're working already, there are two distinct approaches to looking for a new job. One is to conceal it from everyone at work at all costs, the other is to make it perfectly obvious (usually by dressing smartly and asking to take a long lunch hour), in the hope that your current boss will suddenly realise what a gem you really are and offer you a big fat pay rise.

Just remember, even if you're trying to be discreet, taking a day off sick to go for an interview with another company is using your employer's time inappropriately and could be grounds for dismissal.

In fact, there is every reason to be discreet when looking for a new job. The truth is, you may not get one and you'll have to stay put for some time. If you want to keep it low key, stick to these rules:
- Don't tell anyone you're looking for a new job.
- Don't start moaning about the company to your work mates.
- Give out your mobile phone number, rather than your office line. Simply turn your mobile off if it would be inconvenient to take the call – but check messages regularly.
- Make any phone calls in private offices or in the washroom. Whispered conversations in an open-plan area always arouse suspicion.
- Restrict phone calls to your lunch break.
- Discourage prospective employers from calling you at work – arrange to call them back at a suitable time.
- Don't use the company email, and don't use the web at work to surf job sites.
- Make sure application forms are sent to your home address.
- Use a recruitment agency to reduce the number of speculative calls you have to make.
- Don't sever links permanently with your current employer – even when you've got the reference you wanted. Make them part of your network, for possible future use.

RECRUITMENT AGENCIES

FACT: In the UK, over a million workers are placed in temporary work every day through recruitment agencies.

Recruitment is big business. Industry earnings went up by almost 10 per cent between 1999 and 2000 to a staggering 18 billion pounds. There are hundreds of them out there – some better than others – but with all the specialised agencies around, you are pretty much certain to find one that caters for your type of work.

Many agencies have an **Internet presence** and some are entirely web-based, but there is a lot to be said for a face-to-face encounter, particularly for more high-powered employment.

Regard your **interview with the agency** as seriously as you would a job interview. For a start it's good practice for the real thing, and the agency want to know what you're capable of before they send you out.

Be up front with the agency about any **shortcomings in your CV or experience**. They may know of positions where your personality and willingness to learn are more important.

Make sure you're **absolutely clear about what you want**. Recruitment agencies aren't mind readers, and if they keep sending you on interviews for jobs you don't fancy, and keep turning down, they may not continue to make such an effort.

Some agencies will help you **brush up your CV** and interview skills. Let them help – they'll respond well to your enthusiasm.

All agencies charge for their services, of course, but the **1973 Employment Act** means that they don't charge you, even if their fee is expressed as a percentage of your salary. It's the employer that pays.

You can sign up with more than one agency, but each agency may be less inclined to make as much effort for you if you do.

Make sure the agency knows if you want them to be **discreet**. If you're currently employed, you won't want them calling you at work, so give them your mobile number or arrange to call in regularly,

There are many, many agencies out there. *Yellow Pages* and the Internet will yield more than you could ever need, but here are some leads:

> www.great-british-pages.co.uk/Business/Employment/Agencies provides a long list of employment agencies
> www.fish4jobs.co.uk
> www.monster.co.uk
> www.workthing.co.uk
> www.career-world.co.uk
> www.jobsite.co.uk

PASSED YOUR SELL-BY DATE?

FACT: Ageism costs the country £31 billion, according to a report by The Employers Forum on Age.

FACT: The number of people aged between 50 and 64 who are not in work increased by 125,000 between 1998 and 2000.

That's how it can feel for 'mature employees'. But as the nation ages, 'Grey Panthers' are increasingly returning to work post-retirement. Sometimes, to be honest, this is because they simply can't afford to live on their pensions; sometimes it's because they know they have a lot to offer. Whatever the reason, a new breed of employment agency has grown up to deal specifically with their needs, the Government is offering incentives to the over-50s and the more enlightened employers are coming to see what a fine thing it can be to employ someone who isn't going to roll into work with a hangover or take maternity leave just when they've been trained. You may need a bit of training in IT, but you can spell!

For specialised recruitment, try one of the following:

> The Bridge Project (020 7247 7819, www.bridgeproject.co.uk)
> Forties People (020 7329 4044)
> Part Time Careers (020 7437 3103)
> Thirty Plus Recruitment (020 7323 4155)
> Wrinklies Direct (0870 600 1921), www.wrinklies.org

The **New Deal 50+** is available to anyone over 50 who has been claiming benefit for at least six months. Taking a full-time job will bring an extra £60 per week tax free, and a part-time job will earn you an extra £40. Information is available from your local Job Centre or at www.newdeal.gov.uk/english/fiftyplus.

THE JOBS YOU NEVER HEAR ABOUT

FACT: Between 50 and 75 per cent of jobs are never advertised.

FACT: The chance of any individual getting a particular advertised vacancy is below 7 per cent.

It's a sad fact that the majority of vacancies are filled by people who have built up a network of contacts and are known, directly or indirectly, by someone in the company, or who approach companies directly. It's a jungle out there, and only the fittest survive. So take the initiative. Rather than looking at the jobs that are available already, why not contact the firms you're interested in direct? Getting to the job you want before the competition even hears about it can be a winning strategy. There are two main channels into the unadvertised jobs market:

- networking, and
- speculative applications.

Networking

The aim here is to develop a network of personal and business contacts who can help you to find job vacancies that have not yet been advertised, or who can refer you to someone else who can. Everyone knows this is what networking is all about, but the one thing you don't do is ask your network contacts for a job directly. It's all done by stealth, through the exchange of advice and information. Done properly, it isn't about using. It should offer mutual benefit. Here's how:

- First, draw up a **network list**, starting with anyone you can think of who might be able to help you in your job search.
- Leave your desk. Contacts won't come to you, so seek them out yourself. Try training courses, exhibitions or conferences.
- Get your own **business cards** – never resort to the back of an envelope.
- At functions where you expect to meet others in your field, **work the room**. Set yourself the goal of coming away with, say, six business cards.
- Force yourself to **mingle** at conferences and exhibitions – it's expected, so approach groups of people and introduce yourself.
- Ask for **help or information**. You're almost sure to get it. The sort of thing you can legitimately ask for is advice about your CV and career options, information about possible opportunities, and referrals to other people who could help.
- Follow up contacts within a few days. First make a call then follow up every couple of weeks with a call or an email.
- If you've promised to do something, do it promptly. You want to make sure your new contacts see you as reliable.
- Don't just ring when you want something. **Offer information or ideas** and you'll probably get some back.
- Although your best contacts may be at the management level, where the decision makers are, valuable information and further contacts – and jobs – can come from **contacts at all levels**.
- Grab **every networking opportunity**. Attend exhibitions, conferences or trade fairs relevant to your target field. This gives you the chance to meet/renew contacts.
- Join a **trade association or professional institute**. Most hold regular local meetings that are terrific for making new contacts, and provide a way of keeping up-to-date with what is happening in your sector.

Speculative applications

Before putting pen to paper, consider exactly what company you are targeting and why. You can approach companies directly at any time, but you are more likely to get a positive response if you can **present yourself as a solution** to a new challenge or problem faced by that company or organisation. So read the papers and trade press, and listen to gossip to find out if anything is going on that could create new job opportunities.

An obviously generic letter stands a less than 0.1 per cent chance of getting a good response, but **a timely, carefully targeted, well researched letter, followed by a phone call** is likely to produce an interview or meeting in about 3 or 4 per cent of cases. Don't assume that sending out lots of letters will bring more results. The important thing is targeting. You can often find out who to apply to from the company's website or by phoning up. Receptionists are usually more forthcoming with information than personal assistants.

Getting through on the phone can be no easy matter. Make sure you know the first name of the person you need to speak to. **If you say you're calling from**

abroad, you're more likely to get through. (Makes you sound high-powered too.) Just hope that they don't do 1471 call back to check on you. Never say that you're calling about a job – say you're calling about your recent correspondence.

If you get a brush off, ask if you can call back in a few weeks to check on the situation. Your persistence may be rewarded.

How We Beat The System

Tim had an average degree in computer science but a fascination for telecommunications. He targeted a few companies that were at the cutting edge of the telecoms technology then started his investigations. He not only looked at the companies' own websites, but at financial sites that gave share tips on the basis of City gossip as well as checking up on planning applications for the companies' offices. Once he was on the scent of a take-over, he swung into action and sent in his speculative application, making sure his ability to speak German was near the top of the page. Within a week he'd been invited for an interview and now works at the company's Swiss subsidiary. His boss still congratulates himself on finding the perfect man for the job!

CVS

A successful CV is one that gets you the interview, and that's the bottom line. Employers will form their initial opinion of a CV in around six seconds and decide whether or not to call the applicant to an interview in under 30 seconds. If you want it to reach the in-tray, it's got to **stand out from the crowd**; if it's too much effort to plough through it will just get binned. A good CV is **clear and concise** and should contain:

- a summary of your qualifications and skills
- a summary (not an essay) of relevant work experience and achievements
- other work experience, listed chronologically, with a title and a date
- any university or post-graduate qualifications
- a list of professional affiliations
- any computer or other relevant skills (for example, speaking a foreign language)
- other information such as a clean driving licence, interests and hobbies.

Don't go over two pages, and one is better. It's got to be punchy and to the point.

Leave wide margins and plenty of space so the interviewer can jot down notes – it also looks **clear, efficient and uncluttered** – just like you, right? Emphasise important points with bullet points or bold type. Use a computer and get a laser-printed copy for a sharp, professional look. Try using heavier paper with a **subtly different colour**, such as off-white or cream, to make it stand out from the rest. Don't go wild though. Day-glo lime isn't exactly sending out the right professional message. **Choose your typeface** to match the job sector. Technology job applications look best in a sans-serif face, like Arial, Verdana or Century. For more traditional areas, stick to faces like Times. Wacky fonts, like Comic, should be reserved for design and advertising. Courier can work for journalists.

Focus on the last three to four years. Heading this section **'recent experience'** implies there's more (even if there isn't). **Summarise your qualifications** and list your top selling points in five or six sentences. This is not yet common practice, but employers say it is an ideal way to get noticed.

Put relevant **abilities and achievements** first.

Use your CV to show off your best bits. Regard it as **edited highlights**. No need to confess failings or account for your every move.

A gappy CV is not necessarily a problem. You have two choices – be up-front about it or divert attention from it. Just don't try outright lying – so embarrassing if you're found out!

You don't have to **structure your CV** in reverse chronological format. You could group similar kinds of work experience together, and this also helps to disguise any gaps.

Explain longer breaks caused by travelling, studying or child-rearing, but always identify (or make up) skills you have acquired in the process. Focus on your core transferable skills – make where you've gained them of secondary importance.

Show **'year to year' dates** on your CV rather than go into detail with months. Once you get an employer interested in you, you can explain any reasons for short breaks in your career history.

Hide **shameful facts** that have to be included on the far right of the CV. Employers tend to speed-read applications, and words on the right-hand side of the page get overlooked more.

If you've had lots of **short-term jobs** but with a similar role, group them together so it looks like a good block of experience, rather than listing every job individually.

Experience can count more than good A-levels or a top degree. A survey among blue-chip employers revealed that students with the relevant work experience got an extra £1,000 on their starting salary, compared with £600 for a first-class degree.

Make a feature of **skills** gained outside paid work – in a voluntary or social capacity. The organisational skills you use as chair of the PTA or running a reading group are just as valid as any gained in paid employment – and voluntary work shows you are a self starter.

Target **voluntary work experience** so that it runs parallel with the sector you want to work in. Working in a charity shop could help if you want to get a job in retail, for instance, providing admin support to a community organisation offers skills that could transfer to an office job.

Be selective. Avoid the temptation to put every single job in that you've ever had (who wants to know when you got your first paper round?). It's irrelevant and, at worst, could make you look like you can't hold down a job.

Don't rubbish previous employers or reveal confidential information, such as sales figures – this goes for the interview as well. What kind of an employee will you look like?

It's generally better not to mention **family** on your CV. Obviously you wouldn't lie about having a partner and kids if asked during the interview, but actually including them makes them seem like too high a priority. Sad, but true.

Don't lie on your CV – there are agencies that check them out (see below). If you get caught out you certainly won't get the job, and could lose your credibility.

Check and double check your CV for errors. Mistakes, bad grammar, typos…they'll all count against you. Your CV is meant to represent you professionally; don't let it let you down. One mistake could undermine all your effort and experience.

Target your CV and covering letter rather than having a standard one you churn out every time – employers want specifics on how you can do the job for them.

Every CV should have an **accompanying letter**. This needs to be brief and straightforward but you should explain why you think your particular skills and experience would be of interest to the company. Don't tell them why you want the job; tell them why they want you.

Find out who you should address the letter to and **use their name**, making sure you spell it correctly. Sign yourself 'Yours sincerely' and then your full name.

Be quick off the mark sending in your application. Responses to job ads tend to come in slowly at first and if yours is one of the first it is likely to be read with greater attention.

Give yourself two chances: fax your CV as well as post it. If you email it make sure you include any attachments, and send it in an easily opened format – rich text format for example.

Keep copies of your CV for future use.

If you have to complete an **application form** for a job, take care to fill it in correctly. It's sometimes a way of putting off time-wasters. Every box is there for a reason, so use all of them.

Brush up your CV

FACT: Recruiters suggest that at least 70 per cent of CVs contain lies – ranging from 'improving' A-level results to creating an entirely fictitious work history.

FACT: Employers are currently able to check degree results for anyone graduating in the UK since 1995 – so don't be tempted to bump that 3rd up to a 2:1 – unless you're class of '94 or earlier.

Don't be tempted to improve on your past. With recruitment costs increasing all the time, many companies run a **credit check**, a **check on the electoral roll** and **verify work history and qualifications**. Even a fairly low-level banking job might entail a drugs test, declaration of investments and directorships of companies, and you'd certainly have to own up about any court judgments. In fact, a county court judgment wouldn't necessarily mean that you wouldn't be offered the theoretical bank position, although being sacked for embezzlement wouldn't look too good. As usual, honesty would be the best policy. To be discovered trying to cover up your past looks much worse than being up-front about it.

Although it may seem an invasion of privacy, employers are now legally obliged to exercise a duty of care when they hire. If someone they take on ends up harming another employee, the employer could be sued.

If you know your CV is weak, but you have an attractive personality and give a good interview, go to a recruitment consultant. They can send you to an interview that your CV might not get you to.

INTERVIEWS

FACT: Many interviewers form their impression of you in the first 30 seconds, and will have decided on the outcome of the interview after the first four minutes.

Well done! You've got over the first hurdle. Now remember, preparation is the key to a good interview. At any interview you are selling a product – *you*. So do the appropriate market research in order to present yourself in the best possible light.

A job with MI5

Start with a little spying. If you have time before your interview, go and loiter near the company, preferably in a café where you can watch the staff coming out at lunchtime. Look at how they dress and, if you can, go to the same restaurant or sandwich shop so you can earwig their conversations. You needn't go as far as to don a trenchcoat and dark glasses, but look inconspicuous. When you go for your interview, you can be sure that the clothes you choose (a smarter version of what the staff wear normally) will make you look as though you'll fit right in.

Plan to arrive **15 minutes before your appointment**, and leave any excess baggage with the receptionist. Go to the loo and make a last minute check on your appearance. Be **pleasant and polite** to everyone you meet, especially the doorman, the receptionist and the office manager. If you get the job, these are people who you'll depend on.

The rine in Spine...

Worried your accent will let you down? Don't be – provided you speak clearly and can express yourself well, dropped aitches needn't be a headache (no need for aspirates then). Some accents do carry a meta-meaning, however. Yorkshire is thought to be hard-working and trustworthy, while Scottish implies integrity and financial acumen. London sounds savvy and streetwise, Manchester is straightforward and honest.

If you've got a new outfit, make sure you wear it at least once before the interview so you'll feel comfortable.

Take examples of previous work, a copy of your CV, a notepad and pen, and the letter asking you to attend the interview. And that should be about it. You don't need to turn up with a bulging briefcase, it will only weigh you down. And please, no shopping bags!

When the interviewers ask **'What are your strengths and weaknesses?'**, for goodness sake don't really tell them. The correct ratio is three strengths to one weakness, and only mention weaknesses that could be considered positive, like: 'I'm too much of stickler for detail, and I sometimes don't know when to stop checking my work'. This can sound a bit corny, so try admitting to a real failing that could easily be improved. Something like, 'Sometimes I lack confidence in my own abilities...' sounds about right. It indicates insight and self-knowledge, but the subtext is that you're not too pushy. For goodness sake, never say you're poor with figures or have trouble relating to people. There's such a thing as being too honest.

Strengths that sell include commitment, ambition, being a team player and getting on well with co-workers. Make sure you can back up your claims with examples.

Don't commit yourself to **salaries or conditions** while you're in an interview. You need to check through the contract at home, not in the highly charged atmosphere of an interview situation. And **don't mention money** until they make an offer.

Have something to eat before you go in. There's nothing worse than your stomach making sounds like Victorian plumbing throughout a crucial interview.

Don't be lulled into a **false sense of security** if the interview takes place in informal surroundings. You're not there for a cosy chat, but to sell yourself. Even if you're offered a cup of tea or coffee, **politely refuse**. It's one less thing to worry about. Don't smoke, even if they say that you can.

Keep your hands in your lap; don't wave them around. Too much eye contact and you look cocky; too little and you look shifty. If you're not sure, look at the interviewer's ear; they won't notice the difference. And remember to smile! Try **mirroring the interviewer's position** while you're sitting down during the interview – it's a sign of harmony. Lots of interviewers are wise to this, though, so don't make it too obvious. **Don't invade the interviewer's space.** Sit only when invited and never put your briefcase or files on their desk.

Try not to say 'I' too much – it makes you sound like a lone wolf, rather than a corporate type.

If you've got as far as the interview, your background and qualifications are almost certainly appropriate for the job, so rather than plugging away at how well qualified you are professionally, try another tack. What can make you stand out from the competition is your **'soft skills'** – communication, team-building skills, willingness to learn, motivation, the ability to keep up with change, positive attitude – these are the touchy-feely qualities that you can emphasise.

When you leave the interview, find out **what will happen next**. Will you be phoned or written to? Make sure you follow up your interview with a short letter. Thank the interviewer for their time and say how much you enjoyed the interview. If you haven't heard from them by the time of the deadline for a decision (which you should have been told during the interview), it's okay to phone up and ask.

A little knowledge

If you don't know the first thing about the company that you've applied to, there's no way of faking it. You'll just have to do the research. And it pays dividends – showing off even a little knowledge of the company and its operations shows the interviewer that you are serious, interested and prepared to put yourself out to get the job.

Collect information from:
- your local library
- college and university careers resources (even if you don't go there, they'll often let you browse if you ask nicely)
- Companies House provides information (for a small fee) by post or fax on over one million companies registered in England and Wales
- newspapers and trade journals
- company websites, for the official company profile and info on their activities, and investment websites for the kind of info the company may not want to give you

- factsheets published by the company, either for prospective employees or for investors.

Collect information on:
- the areas of activity the company is involved in
- name and location of the parent company
- market share, annual turnover, profitability and performance
- number of employees, number and location of sites/outlets
- recent activities such as mergers, acquisitions, announcements, new appointments
- product launches, new designs/ranges
- plans for expansion
- main competitors.

Travel to interview scheme

If you have been unemployed and receiving benefit (directly or indirectly) or signing on for National Insurance credits for 13 weeks or more, you can get help travelling to interview, but not if you are claiming incapacity benefit. A 'New Deal for Lone Parents' participant will be eligible to apply for help without waiting 13 weeks, provided the job meets required conditions:

• The interview must be beyond normal travel distance (as defined by the Job Centre) from your home and payment can include overnight expenses.

• The interview must be for a job in the United Kingdom, that is more than 30 hours a week and is expected to last more than one year.

• You can only apply for a pre-arranged interview and the application must be submitted before the interview takes place. Payment will cover costs of the cheapest available method of transport and, under some circumstances, overnight accommodation costs may be considered. Payment can be made for second or subsequent interviews.

You're in!

Congratulations – you have a job. Now what? Well, a contract would be nice. Make sure it specifies:
- the parties (you and your employer)
- when it begins and ends
- your rights and when you become entitled to them
- your job title
- job requirements
- who you report to
- the hours of work
- the place of work
- salary or wages: how much and when
- holiday pay and entitlement
- conditions of termination.

PERKS OR FRAUD?

Passing your personal mail off as office mail, taking envelopes for personal use, stocking up on post-it notes? Sounds familiar? Over one-third of managers consider this kind of 'shrinkage' to be so much a part of everyday working life that they factor it into their costings. Where do you (or your boss) draw the line? Fraud is a sackable offence, but most employers would consider it a matter of degree. Personal taxi receipts, making personal calls and emails and taking extended lunch breaks – all of these constitute fraud at some level. But provided you get your work done on time and aren't blatant about what you're doing, you'll probably get away with it.

Creative timesheets

FACT: Some 50 per cent of managers say they don't have time to build relationships outside work. A mere 25 per cent of men, yet 33 per cent of women, in managerial positions say work is harming their sex life.

FACT: Work has become – well, harder work. Two-thirds of employees say they 'always' or 'regularly' work longer than their basic working hours.

Bumping up your timesheet is illegal – basically, it's stealing. But many people don't charge properly for the time they work, especially freelances and temps. Make sure you keep an accurate record of travelling time in the course of work, thinking time, meeting time, and expenses incurred in carrying out your job. It'll probably come to more than you would have got by cheating on hours.

'They say hard work never hurt anybody, but I figure why take the chance?'
Ronald Reagan

Tips for slackers

Or 'how to make it look as if you're doing more than you are':
- Always leave a jacket on the back of your chair when you're away from your desk but change the jacket from time to time.
- Look busy and always move around briskly. Get up, sit back down, go to the filing cabinet and back again, sort things into piles – never get caught staring into space.
- Come in early some days, leave late on others, but either way make sure your boss sees that you're there when they arrive and when they leave. Try to exchange a few words – it's a nice trick to ask if they've seen your immediate superior around (but only if you know he or she isn't in the office).
- On a stay-late day, make sure you're the last person to leave, then arrange your desk to make it look as if you're in early the following day. Leave the

computer on and with work in progress, change the jacket on your chair and leave a pen with the lid off beside a half-written note.

- If you're going to take a long lunch-break, go early so that you can still get back slightly before everyone else.
- Try to get hold of a project that involves spreading out lots of papers. Make a mess of trying to do it at your own desk, then 'reluctantly' conclude you'll have to go the conference room. Once there, spread out your papers (in case someone checks on you), then relax.
- Travel light – don't carry a briefcase with you on your coming-in-late or going-home-early days, so people will just assume that you have just popped out for a moment.
- Change the clock on your computer so that the emails you send show a later or earlier time.
- On your early days, send lots of emails first thing so everyone can see how hard you're working. On late days, send them just before you go home.
- Pretend to be on the phone when someone you don't want to speak to is near by.
- Offer to get sandwiches for people, and fit in some shopping while you're out – ooh those queues!
- Similarly, offer to go to the post office or the mail room.
- Make sure you know how to fix the photocopier – you'll always be getting called away from your desk, and can spend quite a bit of time scratching your head and adjusting things that are working anyway.
- Never clear your desk completely. Have pens with the lids off, post-it notes, and open pads so it looks like work in progress.
- Make sure you've got a bookmark for a website that is connected with your work, so you can change to it quickly when anyone approaches while you're booking your holiday.
- Get sent on training courses for computer programmes. It helps make you seem keen and can waste days.
- Offer to make decent coffee, to replace that disgusting freeze-dried stuff, then turn it into your main occupation. Buy the beans, grind the beans, make the coffee, check on the coffee, clean the pot out, go and get more filters, make sure the sugar hasn't gone yucky…the possibilities are endless.
- Always go to meetings at other people's place of work, preferably just after lunch. That way you can leave the office just before lunch, because you have to eat first, and you don't have to come back until the next day. You could always come in late, though, if you know your boss is going to be around, and claim that you have to catch up because the meeting was so long.
- Look after the plants in the office. This can waste a lot of time, but also gives you access to offices you wouldn't normally go into. Keep your eyes open!
- Volunteer to run the company newsletter – you can bet no one else wants to. It's the perfect opportunity to spend ages away from your desk, apparently gathering information.

Unlucky in love

Lawyers, estate agents, accountants, and execs in advertising and PR are most prone to relationship disasters. This seems to be because the long hours involved prevent them from forming satisfactory relationships. Worse than that, lawyers and workers in the legal profession are twice as likely to get divorced compared with the national average. At the other end of the scale, some 80 per cent of civil servants and employees in the less glamorous, manufacturing industries said they had made room for a relationship in their life.

Some 20 per cent of advertising execs and estate agents and 13 per cent of time-starved lawyers form a relationship with one of their colleagues, but accountants seem to have no office romances at all. Wonder why?

RUNNING YOUR OWN SMALL BUSINESS

'There's no better cure for flu than being self-employed.'
Crispin Bearman, self-employed builder

Running your own business can be fantastically rewarding – but you have to be able to cope with uncertainties and working all hours if necessary. If you're the one reaping the rewards, you're more likely to put everything you've got into work. If you're contemplating taking the leap, draw up a business plan. Every high street bank has got a small business adviser so talk to them all until you find one who is prepared to help you. Local authorities are a good source of information when it comes to finding out what grants are available for starting up a small business.

- You will also be surprised at the number of contacts you have who could be useful to you when you start up your own business. Talk to friends and family who might be prepared to give you advice or lend you money to start up.
- Don't be afraid of approaching people you don't really know but are involved in the kind of work you want to do; pick their brains for advice, help or potential partnerships.
- Talk to people who are already working in the industry and get a job yourself to gain knowledge and skills that will help you run your own business; any mistakes you make will cost them, not you.
- If you decide to set up on your own, you are not allowed by law to use your former employer's database to gain clients. Most contracts prohibit people from approaching clientele for one to five years after employment has ended. However, if customers approach *you* once you have left your former employment then you can take them on.
- Start to read the business section of your local and national newspaper. Keep an eye out for trends, businesses and people who are connected in some way with your potential area of business.

- If your new business will need an actual location, look closely at how viable a spot could be. It's the all important location, location and location that will play a major part in whether you succeed or not. A cheap rental could end up costing you if customers can't find you.
- If you are contemplating working from home, check the deeds of your property or lease to make sure that you can work from home. You should consider getting extra householder's insurance to cover any extra equipment. Having a business run from home can raise tax issues. If you work from a spare room, keep a camp bed in there as 'proof' that it is also used as an extra bedroom.

Trading places

If you're self-employed, you could consider trading in the following ways:

- from your home – this has the advantage of low costs. Check the tenancy agreement, mortgage agreement or title deeds of the property to make sure use is not restricted. Depending on the kind of work, you may also need to get planning permission for change of use.
- from premises you rent or buy. Before you hand over any money, make sure the property has been approved for business use. You may also need planning permission for change of use.
- from a market stall. Your local authority will have details of where and when these are available and how much local markets charge. You can do some of your own research here by seeing which locations in which markets are the most successful.
- at craft, specialist or antique fairs. Again local authorities will have the information you need.

When you run your own business you can be a:

- Sole trader – when you operate under your own name or 'trading as ...'. If the name of your business does not immediately identify you as the owner, you must display your name on letterheads, invoices, receipts and where you conduct your business. You are personally liable for all debts and have no limited liability. Tax is payable on profits and income in the form of income tax.
- Partnership – legal rules are the same for a partnership as they are for a sole trader; the only difference is that there can be any number of partners in a partnership. You are liable for the debts of the other partners if they do a runner, so do have a proper agreement drawn up, setting out details of how partners are to be paid, whether decisions are made jointly or separately and what should happen if a partner decides to leave. Income tax is paid on profits and income.
- Limited company – directors of a company are not personally liable for that company's debts (apart from National Insurance contributions). The name of the company has to be registered with Companies House (there are restrictions on the use of certain words but Companies House can tell you what is allowed and what isn't). Limited companies are legally required to

submit their annual reports and accounts to Companies House. Corporation tax is paid on income and profits.

Your presence on the web

Get ahead by getting yourself a **good web address**. With more web addresses being registered all the time there may soon be as many as 100 million. Try to find something original and memorable that really sums up your business, go to register it, and you're likely to find that it's registered already. Incidentally, around 70 per cent of British businesses that have adopted e-commerce admit that they did so partly as a way of looking more modern, but only a third said that it had improved their profits.

- Cyber squatting is a trick that can sometimes pay off handsomely – Bank of America had to pay $3 million dollars to secure loans.com from a far-seeing punter.
- If .com, .co.uk, .net and .info are taken already, try the country names: Tuvalu, with .tv, Moldova with .md, and Puerto Rico for .pr.
- Different name traders offer different rates – nominet.uk is the keeper of all net names in the UK, but there are many different providers.
- The world's biggest domain name broker is US Network Solutions, the second largest is NY-based Register.com – all make their own various charges.
- Namezero.com will provide a webname for free, but in return you have to carry the advertisers they choose. If it's credibility you're after, for goodness sake register your own domain name, and don't have your ISP as your domain name. Would you trust a business that wasn't prepared to shell out a hundred quid or less to register their own name?

Name brokers:

www.networksolutions.com
www.icann.org
www.nic.uk
www.register.com
www.totalnic.com
www.namezero.com
www.thelist.internet.com/countrycode/44.

Questions to put to your Internet Service Provider

Make sure you're getting the best service by asking:
- Is there a single one-off set up fee?
- Is there a monthly, quarterly or annual fee?
- How long does domain name registration last before it must be renewed?
- Are call charges included in the fees?
- If not, what is the charge per minute, off peak and at peak times?
- Do you offer technical support, and is there a fee, either directly or through premium rates for the call?

- What is the maximum modem speed?
- Do you support ISDN, ADSL or other broadband services?
- Can you get the email and web addresses you want, and how many are included in the fee?
- Is there a minimum period for the contract?
- Is there a charge for cancellation, if you choose to move your business elsewhere?

Boxing smart

Don't put the boxes that your brand new computers came in outside the door for the bin men to take. It's an advert for burglars that there is new kit inside. Also, remove software from the boxes and store it separately from the instruction manuals – it makes it far less attractive to thieves.

HOW GREEN IS MY OFFICE?

Big business may be polluting the planet, but you don't have to. Buck the trend, and see how green you can make your office.

- Don't use those awful polystyrene cups at your drinks vending machine. Encourage staff to bring their own ceramic cups from home (although someone will have to wash up, and it may be you) or make sure your cups can be recycled.
- You can recycle batteries, CD-ROMs, printer cartridges. Even computers can be reused for education projects. Try contacting Computers for Charity (01288 361177), www.computersforcharity.org.uk.
- See if your office paper can be recycled, and look into buying recycled paper for your own office needs (including recycled loo paper).
- Cut down on paper use – what's email for?
- Buy electronic products that have lower emissions and that have a stand-by mode for down times. They won't be the cheapest, but the long-term savings and health considerations make it worthwhile.
- Don't use throwaway pens – choose refillables.
- Allow as much daylight in as possible, by removing blinds and furniture that blocks windows, then you can swap to long-life, low-energy light bulbs.
- Get some plants. Office equipment can give off nasty emissions, but plants will go some way to improving air quality again.

TIME OFF WORK

There are 365 in the year. Take off 104 for weekends, leaving you with 261. Take an average 25 days holiday, and you're down to 236. The usual nine or ten days of public holiday take you to 226. If you take, say, eight days of sick leave – you don't want to make anyone suspicious – you've got 218. Depending on your contract, you may be eligible for a few days off for long service, compensation for overtime in lieu of payment, and you can always pull compassionate leave (see below) and/or dependent care leave (see below) – say another five days altogether, and you're down to 213. Paternity leave can bring it comfortably under 200. Maternity leave will take up 90 to 200 days, leaving you a minimum for 13 days work in a year. It's exhausting just thinking about it!

Taking time off for a funeral?

Most employers would be reluctant to appear as unsympathetic as to refuse an employee leave to attend a funeral, particularly of a close relative. The usual procedure is to give time off as compassionate leave, rather than insist that holiday is used. But there is actually no legal obligation for the employer to do this – it's entirely discretionary, although the subject may be mentioned in your contract or in company regulations.

The only circumstance that is covered by law is when the deceased is a dependent of the employee – defined as a spouse, child or parent or someone who could be considered to depend on the employee. In this case, you are entitled to take off a reasonable length of time during working hours.

Basically, you shouldn't push your luck when bumping off grannies and aunties. And make sure you keep a careful count of them – it may be that someone else in your company is counting them off too.

Taking a sickie

> **FACT:** Out of every three days off work taken because of sickness, one of them is not genuine.
>
> **FACT:** Absenteeism costs industry well over £10 billion a year.
>
> **FACT:** The most common reasons given for absenteeism is now stress, which has overtaken colds and headaches, the previous favourites.

You may be at death's door – or you may just be a little the worse for wear. Just be aware of the pitfalls of calling in sick.

Don't call in sick then turn up the next day with sunburn.

Diarrhoea and vomiting are old favourites – no one in their right mind would want you around with those.

Taking just **one day off** is more often assumed to be skiving than taking two or three. So don't rush in from your sickbed too early.

If you're going to call in with a **sore throat**, don't have your cup of tea until you've made that call. The croakier you sound, the better.

Stress is one of those really hard-to-define conditions, so no one can disprove it

– but if you claim stress too often, it may create a bad impression of your ability to do the job.

A bad back is another difficult condition to diagnose, but is probably best kept for manual labourers.

Makes you sick!

The time-honoured method of phoning in sick just doesn't fool anyone anymore, it seems. Over 60 per cent of bosses say their suspicions are raised by an employee taking a sickie on a Monday or Friday, but only 30 per cent of employees confess to having faked illness to get over a hangover or a late night.

Hold your nose

Staff who phone in sick with a headache, backache or stress are suspected by managers of skiving or looking after their children, according to a study Maximising Attendance by the Industrial Society. Only people with a cold or the flu are totally believed by their manager – not least because the evidence is clear over the phone. This is despite the fact that back problems, repetitive strain injury and stress are now the main causes of illness at work.

A poll of employers shows that there is a gap between what employees say when they call in sick, and what their bosses think is really going on.

What you say when you call in sick	What your boss really thinks
Cold/flu	Cold/flu
Tummy upset/food poisoning	Stress/ personal problems (if on a Monday, probably a hangover)
Headache/migraine	Hangover
Backache	Bored with job
Stress/personal problems	Childcare problems
Period pains/cystitis	Yuck!

Hooray for Brussels!

You never thought you'd have reason to say that, did you? But your right to time off to look after a sick child or other dependent (wife, husband, parent or someone living in the same household who is not an employee, tenant or lodger) is now protected by Brussels.

- There is no qualifying period of work before you can take dependent care leave.
- If you are dismissed because of taking dependent care leave, you will be deemed to have been unfairly dismissed.
- It covers not only your own children, but any others for whom you have assumed responsibility, even temporarily.
- It could extend to leaving work to pick up a sick child from school, or accompanying a dependent to an important medical appointment.
- The legislation does not specify the word 'emergency', but it does state that the time off must be 'in order to take action which is necessary'.
- It does not extend to staying in for the washing-machine repair man, and it does not give you any right to payment for the time off (although this may be covered in your work contract).

From here to maternity

Well, motherhood is a job in itself, but some working mothers are more equal than others. Some women do not have any statutory maternity rights. They are:
- share fisherwomen
- women who are normally employed abroad (unless they have a work connection with the UK)
- self-employed women
- police women, who are entitled to statutory maternity pay but not to the other rights for pregnant women workers.

Time off for **ante-natal care** – if you're working and pregnant (unless you come into one of the categories mentioned above) you qualify, regardless of how long you've worked for your present employer, and of how many hours per week your work. Sadly, shopping for maternity bras and having pedicures do not count as ante-natal care.

You can have **time off for appointments** for ante-natal care if your doctor, midwife or health visitor advises that it is needed. The employer should pay your usual wage for the time off, as long as it is a reasonable amount of time. If you take too much you may be treated as if you were off sick, and will only get paid if your contract of employment allows.

After the first ante-natal appointment, you will have to show your employer, if requested, a **medical certificate** stating that you are pregnant, and an appointment card for the ante-natal care.

What if your employer refuses to allow time off for an ante-natal care appointment or refuses to pay? You can **complain to an employment tribunal** but it has to be within three months of the appointment. The tribunal may tell the employer to pay the wages they withheld.

You have the **right to return** to your old job after 18 weeks of ordinary maternity leave. After those 18 weeks are up, you don't need to give your employer notice that you are returning to work. You can just turn up for work on the pre-arranged day.

What if you're not allowed to return to work? This is one your employer will not want to get into, because you can claim your dismissal is automatically unfair for a reason to do with the pregnancy or maternity leave. You could also claim sex discrimination, and both of these claims can be made regardless of how long you have worked for your employer or how many hours per week you work.

If you are sick when you are due back to work at the end of your 18 weeks maternity leave, you must get a medical certificate to send to your employer. You will then go on to **sick leave**, but you're protected against unfair dismissal for an additional four weeks after the 18 weeks maternity leave if you are sick for that long.

If you are **dismissed because of pregnancy**, you can claim unfair dismissal. It does not matter how long you have worked for your employer or whether you work full- or part-time. If you are **unfairly treated** in connection with your pregnancy or maternity, for example, if you are passed over for promotion, you can make a claim to an employment tribunal.

Like to qualify for a **fabulous 40 weeks off work?** If you've worked for the same employer for at least one year by the beginning of the 11th week before your baby is due (that means that roughly, you will have been employed for one year and three months on the date the baby is due), you're entitled to 29 weeks additional leave. This additional leave is on top of the 18 weeks leave that all pregnant workers are entitled to, but it is subject to your being entitled to a maximum of 40 weeks maternity leave altogether.

FLEXIBLE WORK PRACTICES

FACT: A large-scale survey found that some 70 per cent of businesses provide flexible or non-standard working time arrangements for at least some of their employees.

No harm in asking if you can work a flexible schedule. This can be as varied as your needs and those of your office – maybe starting and finishing early on four days a week and taking a half day on the fifth. It's hard to see how this could be of benefit to your boss, but offering to accept emails and urgent calls during your 'time off' will make you seem more willing.
- Make your proposal in writing.
- Try to prove that your employer will benefit!
- Choose a good time to ask (not during a crisis).
- Make sure your desk is cleared before you take off.
- Emphasise that you will always be contactable, and can come in for an emergency.

- Make sure you look as if you're still interested in advancing your work, and are not winding down. Let your boss know that you're taking courses to further your career – even if you have to do them in your own time.
- Make doubly sure you keep your phone switched on – you can bet your boss will try it out the first time you're away.

VOLUNTEERING

Use your skills for the good of humanity – and bump up your CV in the process.

- Become a **Red Cross** befriender, giving presentations on drug abuse to kids at youth groups, or acting as a telephone befriender. Volunteers can also be taught to give beauty therapy. The Red Cross (020 7201 5164) trains you, gives you equipment and oils, and pays travel expenses.
- The **Samaritans** (08705 627282) look for volunteers with good listening skills. The training is stringent and you have to commit to a three-hour shift every week and an all-night session every month.
- Volunteer someone else, simply by the click of a mouse. At www.thehungersite.com, you click on 'donate food' and the site sponsors undertake to give food to the starving. You don't pay anything, and the glow of satisfaction is terrific.
- Try **Community Service Volunteers** (020 7278 6601) if you think you could offer support to local schools, or want to get involved in a mentoring scheme that matches you to a student from an inner city school – all done by email.
- National Association of Volunteer Bureaux (0121 633 4555) provides information on local volunteer schemes.
- National Centre for Volunteering (020 7520 8900) runs a befriending scheme that involves offering career advice to teenagers whose parents may not have the experience of work to give the guidance.

SALARIES

FACT: The average woman will earn almost £250,000 less than the average man in her lifetime (*Financial Times*).

FACT: Women are less likely to ask for a rise than men.

FACT: Women spend less time networking after office hours than men.

Are these facts in someway related?

We all believe we're worth a good salary. If you're in an industry or an area suffering from a skills shortage, then you may have a very good case for requesting a pay rise.

- Take an honest look at your performance and start tackling problems gradually, well in advance. Suddenly turning up for work on time a couple of days before you ask for a pay rise is just creeping.

- Make an appointment with your boss and treat it like an interview. Go in there armed with what you want to say to convince him or her that you are worth more money. Don't expect to get an answer straight away. You need to give your boss time to think about it or get authority from someone higher up.
- And what happens if you don't get what you ask for? Histrionics and ultimatums rarely do the trick. If the answer is no, ask for a list of objectives you would need to achieve in order to get the pay rise and pin your boss down to the timescale involved.
- When you're asking for a pay rise, play on your strengths rather than anything negative (such as whingeing that you're not getting as much as your colleagues or you want to replace your clapped out old banger and can't do it on your current salary).
- Sound confident. You need to be business-like, and negotiating a pay rise is part of business. Have a figure in mind when you start and agree with yourself what you will settle for.
- Timing is everything. If the company is going through a lean patch, now might not be the best time to ask for more money. If your boss is a bad tempered so-and-so, plan your appointment for his or her best time of day.

PROMOTIONS

Decided it's time you were promoted? Reckon you could do your boss's job as well as he or she can. You're not alone. Some 60 per cent of employees think they could do as well or better than their boss. It's time you got to work persuading everyone else in your organisation – especially if you want to make them think it was their idea!

- Don't rely on flirtation (or worse) to move you up the ladder. At worst, you could end up getting sacked, at best everyone will say you only got ahead because of your sex appeal. No one will ever remember Monica Lewinsky for her hard work and talent.
- Watch how your boss organises the working day, the projects and the time management. It all adds up to their **management style**. Try to think of ways it could be done better, more effectively, then show some initiative and make a proposal (not to your boss, but someone further up and with some clout). Try to avoid looking as if you're sneaking.
- Sign up for office official dinners or management initiative courses, or organise the Christmas party. **Get yourself noticed** higher up in the company so you have contacts on that level that you've made yourself.
- Keep a note of all the contacts you make, even if they don't seem very promising at the time.
- Don't thrash your boss at tennis or squash, or *The Times* crossword. It may seem like fun at the time, but think ahead.
- Brush up on small talk, for when you have to meet spouses, people from the accounts department, or bigwigs you've nothing in common with.

- Imitate the behaviour of staff at your boss's level or the level above that. If they come in early, you come in early. If they have a tidy desk, you have a tidy desk.
- Don't, of course, imitate their bad habits. Just, as they say at Alcoholics Anonymous, 'act as if'.
- Get more qualifications. Find out what your boss has and go for it (or even one better). In-house courses are great, but if there aren't any, check out www.city-and-guilds.co.uk, www.uk-courses.co.uk, or if you live in London www.floodlight.co.uk.
- As well as 'act as if' , try 'look as if'. Dress for the job you want, not the job you have, and you'll find you're taken more seriously. Ridiculous though it is, appearances count if you're looking for promotion. There are plenty of books available on style and presentation. One of the best is Mary Spillane's *Branding Yourself* published by Pan, and you can contact her company at www.imageworksuk.com.
- Get your boss to place more responsibility on you, and angle to be seen as the boss's deputy when he or she is away. From there it should be a small step to getting that title officially. Once everyone is used to this situation, you're well on your way.
- Once you're ready to make your move, you've got to get rid of the boss. Start pointing out suitable jobs – if your boss doesn't apply, you may now be so qualified that you can apply instead!

LOSING YOUR JOB

Nothing makes you appreciate your job like suddenly finding out you're going to lose it. The important thing is don't panic! It can happen to anyone. If you've been in continuous employment for more than two years you can ask for a written statement giving the reasons for your dismissal. Your employer cannot refuse to do this and has to comply within 14 days of your request.

An employer does not have to give you a **reference**, but if they do, it can't be malicious otherwise you could get them for defamation of character.

Even if you have a **contract**, there are some basic duties to employees that all employers should adhere to and which can be enforced:
- you should not be treated unreasonably, humiliated or picked on and perse-cuted
- you must be paid for work you have done according to the terms of your contract
- if more than five people are employed, the employer has to issue a safety policy
- you can't be discriminated against on sexual or racial grounds.

Fire drill

Things to do if you think you're about to get fired.

Get rid of **personal emails and personal files** stored on your hard drive, your web-surfing history and your 'favourites' listing. Copy all your **email contacts** from your desktop. Make copies of any **projects** you might be able to use in your portfolio, as well as any documents and reference material that will be useful to you in the future. But do take heed that this practice may be a breach of your employment contract.

Throw away any **personal paperwork**. Make sure you don't leave anything that could cause problems for you after you've gone.

Send our your **CV** quick, and get your network going – it's always easier to gain new employment if you already have a job. Try to get a replacement job while you're still at the current one so your potential new employer won't be suspicious that you don't quote your current boss as a reference.

If you think the situation can be salvaged (or you want to buy some time to find a new job) ask to have a talk with your boss about your performance. Say you're aware that you haven't been doing a very good job (think up some personal reason, if you can) but that you want to turn over a new leaf and you want some time to prove yourself. **Alternatively**, come clean and say that you're looking for a new job, and that you'd like to give two months' notice. Your boss might welcome the chance to avoid the unpleasantness of sacking you.

Don't get into that **revenge** thing. Sticking double-sided sellotape inside your boss's mouse roller isn't big and it isn't clever. It won't even make you feel better – will it?

Sweet revenge

Some ex-workers have got themselves into serious trouble getting revenge on their bosses. Here are a few not to emulate:

• An office worker in the US carefully unsealed packets of photocopy paper and photocopied the image of a pen on to them all, then slipped them back into the packets. When the paper was used, and every copy bore the image of a pen, the boss concluded that a biro must have slipped into the mechanism of the copier. The technician was duly called out and the copier was stripped down completely before the truth was discovered.

• A worker sacked by his female boss got revenge by posting her details, along with her email address on a website for marrieds looking for some hanky-panky on the side. Her mailbox was awash with graphic offers for weeks, but investigation revealed the culprit and he was eventually sued for defamation of character.

Organise a pink slip party

No, not that kind of slip. Yet another brilliant idea from the US, where pink slips are redundancy notes. Recruitment agencies subsidise these bashes in fashionable clubs, and scour the guest list for new recruits. Apart from the awful humiliation of drinking cheap alcohol and dancing to loud music, all you have to do is wear a coloured dot to distinguish employers from job seekers. It's kind of like a job centre with music, or a singles bar for the unemployed.

Sackable behaviour

Fair dismissals are when:
- the employee has been unable to do the job and/or conducted themselves poorly
- in some cases of gross misconduct (dishonesty, consciously breaking a contract term or obtaining unauthorised information) the employee can be sacked on the spot (summary dismissal).

Good mousekeeping

Be careful about using your office email for personal messages, and not just smutty ones. Bosses are entitled to check staff messages, although lawyers maintain that this constitutes a violation of human rights, and the Data Protection Commission suggests that workers should be informed first. Staff at one City bank were dismissed on the spot for circulating pornography on the internal email system, and as bosses exercise their right to check emails, more instant dismissals are sure to follow.

Grounds for instant dismissal

Yes, that's right – instant. No notice or notice money. It seems drastic, but it is still valid in cases of 'gross misconduct':
- improper use of emails for illegal or non-work related purposes known to be contrary to management rules
- pilots and other air-crew members who drink before flights in defiance of regulations
- wilful disobedience
- offensive language to a superior, except as a one-off.

Wrongful or unfair?

Wrongful dismissals (proper notice not given) are dealt with in civil courts:
- there has to have been a breach of contract
- you have six years from the breach to claim
- the loser is liable to pay the winner's costs
- it's within the Legal Aid system (now known as Public Funding).

Unfair dismissals (being sacked unreasonably) are a matter for industrial tribunals:
- there need not have been a breach of contract
- you must apply within three months
- you must have worked for two years full time or five years part time (unless your claim is to do with race or sex discrimination)

- there is a minimum and a maximum award
- your employer can be ordered to reinstate you
- it's not within the Legal Aid system (now known as Public Funding)
- if you are a member of a union, they can help you with representation.

Tribunals

Now don't go getting yourself permanently scarred by a mad axeman – the compensation is pitiful. But if someone hurts your feelings at work – well, it seems the sky's the limit.

The figures are huge, the sums astronomical. Is it worth your while to be **wrongfully dismissed**? Try these cases:
- a nurse was awarded £100,000 for psychological trauma induced by having to wear latex gloves that caused severe eczema on her hands
- a policewoman who became pregnant was therefore unable to have scans that would have determined how serious the injuries were that had been sustained at work and that had prevented her from working for a whole year. It was decided that she was the victim of sex discrimination, and she received £250,000 in damages
- psychological scarring as a result of being told she was 'confident for a woman' won a police officer a payout worth £500,000.

If you take your company to a tribunal over a matter arising from your contract, and the contract is ambiguous, the tribunal will construe any ambiguity against your employer.

INJURIES AT WORK

If you have an accident at work:
- report it immediately and put it in the firm's accident book
- if there were witnesses, take down their names and get their statements
- if you were injured as a result of faulty equipment, take photographs
- don't accept financial compensation until you've had legal and medical advice – your injury may prove to be more serious than you think
- get legal advice
- find out if there have been similar incidents and get statements in writing
- keep a record of any expenses incurred as a result of the injury. Calculate the loss of earnings to you.

Weird and wonderful employment laws

In Altoona, Pennsylvania, it is illegal for a babysitter to clean out the employer's fridge.

In Washington, a babysitter can be jailed for substituting another child than the one they were left with.

In St Louis, Missouri, it is illegal for a milkman to run whilst making deliveries.

In Michigan, it is illegal to put a skunk under your boss's desk. Damn!

USEFUL ADDRESSES

British Red Cross
9 Grosvenor Crescent
London SW1X 7EJ
Tel: 020 7201 5164
www.redcross.org.uk

City & Guilds
1 Giltspur Street
London EC1A 9DD
Tel: 020 7294 2468
www.city-and-guilds.co.uk

Commission for Racial Equality
Elliot House
10–12 Allington Street
London SW1E 5EH
Tel: 020 7828 7022
www.cre.gov.uk

Companies House
Crown Way
Cardiff CF4 3UZ
Tel: 029 2038 0801
www.companieshouse.gov.uk

Computers for Charity
26 Hollabury Road
Bude
Cornwall EX23 8JA
Tel: 01288 361177
www.computersforcharity.org.uk

Department for Education and Skills
Sanctuary Buildings
London SW1P 3BT
Tel: 020 7925 5000
www.dfee.gov.uk

Department of Trade & Industry
Companies Investigation Department
Ashdown House
123 Victoria Street
London SW1E 6RB
Tel: 020 7215 5000
www.dti.gov.uk

Equal Opportunities Commission
Overseas House
Quay Street
Manchester M3 3HN
Tel: 0161 833 9244
www.eoc.org.uk

**National Association of Volunteer Bureaux
 (NAVB)**
New Oxford House
16 Waterloo Street
Birmingham B2 5UG
Tel: 0121 633 4555
www.navb.org

National Consumer Council
20 Grosvenor Gardens
London SW1 0DH
Tel: 020 7730 3469
www.ncc.org.uk

The Samaritans
10 The Grove
Slough
Berkshire SL1 1QP
Tel: 08705 627282
www.samaritans.org

TEC National Council
Westminster Tower
3 Albert Embankment
London SE1 7SX
Tel: 020 7735 0010
www.tec.co.uk

Index

Index compiled by
Indexing Specialists